Bangalore Girls

Bangalore Girls

Witnessing the Rise of Nationalism in a Progressive City

Supriya Baily

ROWMAN & LITTLEFIELD
Lanham • Boulder • New York • London

Published by Rowman & Littlefield
An imprint of The Rowman & Littlefield Publishing Group, Inc.
4501 Forbes Boulevard, Suite 200, Lanham, Maryland 20706
www.rowman.com

86-90 Paul Street, London EC2A 4NE

British Library Cataloguing in Publication Information Available

Library of Congress Cataloging-in-Publication Data Available

ISBN 781538198018 (cloth) | ISBN 781538198025 (epub)

♾™ The paper used in this publication meets the minimum requirements of American
National Standard for Information Sciences—Permanence of Paper for Printed Library
Materials, ANSI/NISO Z39.48-1992.

For Amina—a most uncommon friendship
&
For Mrinaal and Nishaad—with all my love
&
For the women who came to be who they are
in the gardens, halls, classrooms, sports fields,
and dormitories of Baldwin Girls High School

Contents

Acknowledgments   ix

Introduction: Setting the Stage   1

PART I: GROWING UP IN A PROGRESSIVE CITY   19

Chapter 1: The Making of a Metropolis   21

Chapter 2: Mopeds, Cafés, and Bookstores: Coming of Age on a
    Public Stage   33

Chapter 3: School, Home, and God: Girls in Private Spaces   47

Chapter 4: The Gathering Storm: The Rise of the Bhartiya Janata
    Party   63

**PART II: FAULT LINES IN A FRACTURED SOCIETY:
    FROM PAST TO PRESENT**   79

Chapter 5: Women's Safety and Security   83

Chapter 6: The Battle for Education   97

Chapter 7: Chipping Away at Belonging and Secularism   111

Chapter 8: The Backlash
    Against Intellectualism   125

Chapter 9: Politicians and Patriotism   141

Conclusion: Seeking a Critical Hope   155

Epilogue   167

Contents

Notes	169
Index	197
About the Author	201

Acknowledgments

To acknowledge people is to give them their due, and this project would never have come to fruition without the support, encouragement, belief, and critique of a host of people—I am indebted to their willingness to share my vision to help make this book better.

I could not have completed this work without the support of friends, mentors, and colleagues who read drafts, asked questions, and gave me so much encouragement that this was in fact a worthy project. Drs. Beverly Shaklee, Dawn Hathaway, Shelly Reid, and Elizabeth (Lizzie) Worden were constant cheerleaders—thank you!

Lizzie was also instrumental in connecting me with Nigel Quinney, who took ideas and made them tighter. He asked tough questions, edited with a fine-toothed comb, and then helped clarify things on paper that often only made sense in my head. Thank you for your help in getting this to a place that allowed me to see the potential.

I have to thank my Norwegian sisters—each of them had a part to play in different ways. From Halla Holmarsdottir and our decade(!) of friendship to Heidi Biseth, Greta Björk Gudmundsdottir, and Lihong Huang—thank you for making me a part of the Jenteklubb. And to Sissil Heggernes, who brought the idea of critical hope to my attention on a memorable day in Oslo, nursing what turned out to be a broken ankle—thank you!

One is not often lucky to have a friend who is also a cartographer. For Alan McDowell, I am eternally grateful that you gave me the gift of your time and talent to create the maps of India and the city of Bangalore. I never knew I would need your help this way and I am grateful!

The team at Rowman & Littlefield and Michael Kerns especially, thank you! Your enthusiasm and confidence in this book came at a crucial time. Thank you for championing it and finding it a home.

Tami Carsillo was invaluable in her research support and her diligence and determination to find thirty-year-old newspaper articles was tenacious.

Her own work is inspiring and I am grateful to have had a small part in her journey to become a researcher.

My parents moved my brother and me to Bangalore in the mid-1980s, changing the course of my life. I appreciate all they have done for me and know that my life would not have been the same if we had never moved there when we did. I love you three very much. Moving to the wilds of Koramangala—a part of Bangalore that was a paradise for teenagers—brings forth a whole host of friends who feature in some of my most memorable moments as a teenager. We hung out at the complex, cafés, and corners, going to parties and picnics, and listening to music and dancing. Suffice it to say that life was pretty idyllic.

Jerry Lorengo—thank you for putting up with me and always standing by me. In nearly thirty years, you have always believed in me—even when I might not have believed in myself. And how lucky we are to have Nishaad and Mrinaal. No Adventure Saturday, dinner out, board game, death march on holidays, and movie night would be complete without the two of you. You boys are my heart and soul.

And finally—to every girl who walked through BGHS with me and graduated in 1989, thank you for all the memories. From tuck shops, to reading my cheesy stories of romance and tragedy, from sports and swim meets and morning chapel services, to train rides and adventures in Ranchi and Pune. Thank you for trusting me with the stories, memories, worries, and hopes and being willing to pick up almost right where we left off. Listening, learning, and laughing with each of you reminds me of how lucky I was to have known you all. This book is the result of schoolgirl bonds that I have treasured for four decades. Thank you.

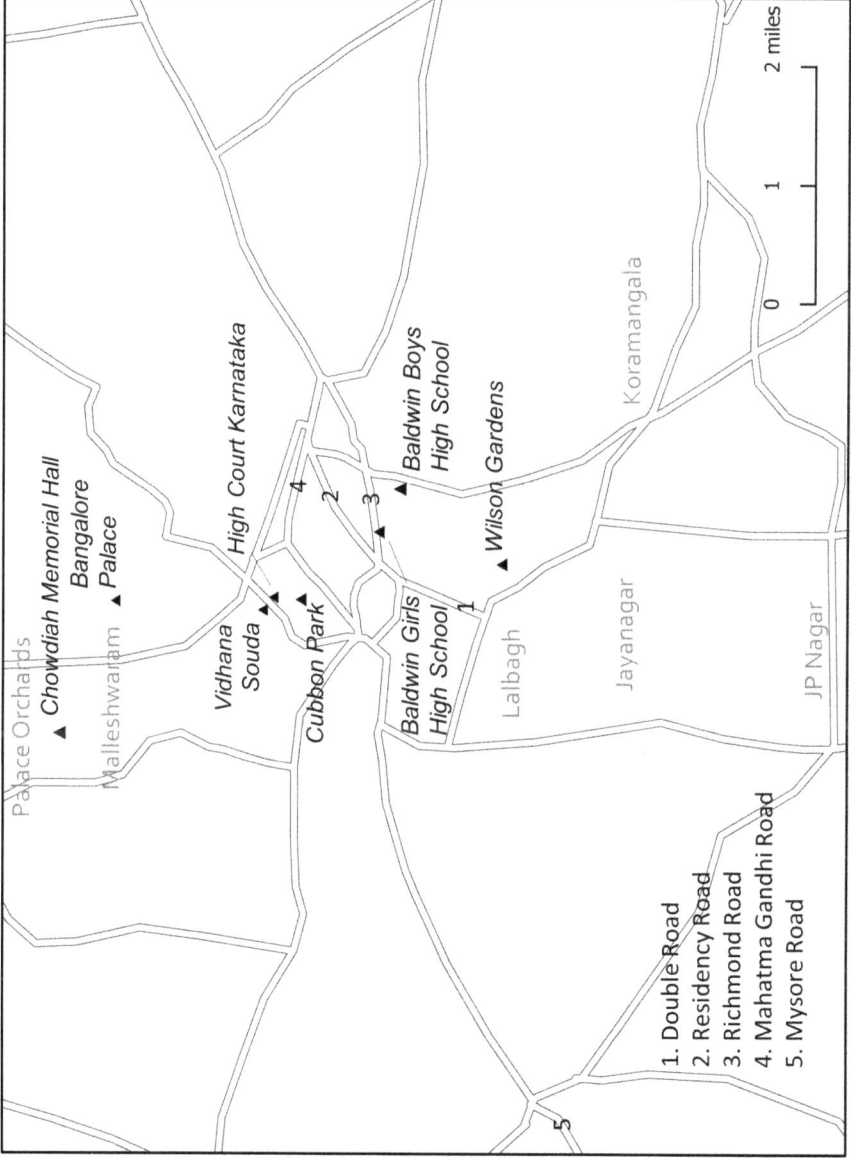

Map 1. Bangalore City Limits and Key Landmarks
(Courtesy Alan McDowell)

Palace Orchards

Chowdiah Memorial Hall

Bangalore Palace

Malleshwaram

High Court Karnataka

Vidhana Souda

Cubbon Park

Baldwin Boys High School

Wilson Gardens

Baldwin Girls High School

Lalbagh

Jayanagar

Koramangala

JP Nagar

1. Double Road
2. Residency Road
3. Richmond Road
4. Mahatma Gandhi Road
5. Mysore Road

0   1   2 miles

Map 2. Map of India
(Courtesy Alan McDowell)

Introduction

Setting the Stage

"Ayodhya is in flames! The whole country has erupted in a massive mess."

At the tail end of my teens, as a prolific diary keeper, I documented school friendships, crushes, and the challenges of growing up in my hometown of Bangalore, India. When the Babri Masjid mosque was demolished by Hindu fundamentalists in an act of unfathomable savagery, I took to my diary to share my fears to try to make sense of the hatred and anger that, to me, seemed to be the antithesis to the secular, open, and progressive teen life I had been used to. I wrote, "Why this? Is it worth it? . . . Religion is wrong, because it has nothing to do with god, but to do with rites and rituals, and blind beliefs, and stupid superstitions, and if people are going to be fanatical, let them shred each other to bits and *then* let secularism revive." I go on to say India's "name in the international community is lost. We can never be called secular, tolerant again! Hypocrisy!"

Adolescent hyperbole aside, each generation of adolescents seems to experience at least one moment that transforms how they see the world. Everyone in the society, younger and older, may well be affected by the same moment, but for adolescents the impact tends to be particularly powerful, reshaping their worldview in a profound and enduring way. In adulthood, they might remember a spectacular human accomplishment, such as landing on the Moon or the explorations of *Curiosity*, the Mars Rover. Others might look back at events that broke historic barriers, such as the elections of Barack Obama and Kamala Harris in the United States. There are also pivotal, sometimes traumatic moments where, as adults, people will forever ask, "Where were you when *that* happened?" For most of the world, 9/11 is such a moment. These moments stay with young people, uniting them with others who experienced this same history. For young people growing up in India in the 1980s and 1990s, the assassinations of prime ministers Indira Gandhi in 1984 and Rajiv

Gandhi in 1991 left indelible impressions. So, too, did the 1992 destruction of the Babri Masjid mosque in the city of Ayodhya by Hindu extremists and the riots that subsequently erupted across India.

For me, Ayodhya was a crystallizing moment, where the safety and security I felt shifted. I had cherished Muslim friends, I went to a school where we sang Christian hymns, and I had attended gatherings with students around the country to create bonds across communal, caste, religious, linguistic, and ethnic boundaries. The foundation of my identity was no longer on firm footing, but life went on, as it does, until 2019, when the Supreme Court of India ruled that the land on which the mosque stood could be handed over to a trust, which would then build a temple. This decision brought back the trauma of 1992, but also heralded a slew of questions: What did people think about this? Was this the high=water moment for a nationalist movement that has centered its power on religious supremacy? And then I wanted to know, how did the girls I grew up with see all this? How did women, who were beneficiaries of a solid middle-class education, who were Hindu, Muslim, Christian, Sikh, and Jain process the events of the past thirty years, where a marginal political party, the Bharatiya Janata Party, the BJP, was calling the shots? What did this tell us about gender, nationalism, and religious fundamentalism? And what could others learn about the steady rise and ambition of authoritarian movements through the eyes of women who had watched Bangalore shift and change over the past thirty years?

So I returned to my hometown, the southern Indian city of Bangalore,[1] to try to understand what was happening. I thought that finding a cohort of women who could trust me with their feelings about these issues and would be willing to talk to me would be of interest to a wider audience of people. Finding my old classmates was easy. With a graduating class of just 120, we were all still connected through webs of social connections, and nearly thirty-five women reached out to me and agreed to be interviewed. All of us graduated from Baldwin Girls High School (known to its pupils just as "Baldwins" or by the abbreviation BGHS)[2] and came from a wide range of backgrounds. While the "Ayodhya riots" had crashed through our adolescent concerns about exams, fashion, and friends, growing up in Bangalore, a city with a youthful and vibrant energy, was quite different from most cities in India. Tradition and modernity were incorporated into the lives of a relatively well-educated, forward-thinking population. While well aware that the country's moment of independence in 1947 began with deep trauma and religious animosities, Ayodhya was a new generation's moment that mirrored their grandparents' painful experiences during India's Partition. But in Bangalore, while the Ayodhya riots were painful, they did not fully pierce the bubble of secularism that middle-class families had come to expect. Now, thirty years later, for me and many of my classmates from Bangalore, it feels like the progressivism that was attacked in 1992 has fully capitulated to right-wing ideologies. The city we knew in the years since 1992 seems vastly different today.

Politics in India have been tilting right since the Ayodhya riots, and the fringe political party, the BJP, that was involved in spurring that unrest is now the country's dominant political force. As the tide of nationalism and religious extremism has risen, so have patriarchy and misogyny. While the whole country is challenged by these forces, in Bangalore the changes have been particularly dramatic, maybe in part due to the fact that Bangaloreans were never defined by the communalism of other Indian cities and always had an outward focus. While it is still a global presence, continually attracting new people, the freedom and security it once offered have sharply declined. This change has been felt acutely by women in the city in particular.

This book examines the intersecting forces of rising nationalism, religious extremism, and misogyny through the eyes of those girls with whom I went to school and who are now well into their adulthood. In the following chapters, we hear their stories about growing up in Bangalore and how the city has changed under the impact of powerful political, ideological, and social forces. The women I spoke with have much to tell us about India's recent rightward trajectory and its effects on the lives of "ordinary" women. They also offer food for thought for other countries that are experiencing a turn to the right, including Brazil, France, the Netherlands, and, of course, the United States of America.

These women draw attention to how, over the past thirty years, nationalism and religious extremism have affected issues such as education, democracy, religion, personal security, and freedom. These issues have affected all of India, but the women's outlook is also distinctively shaped by their memorable adolescence in progressive Bangalore.

The stories shared in this book are powerful, vulnerable, angry, and honest. The candid nature of these raw recollections reflects, in part, our shared history as former classmates. We spent many years together at Baldwins, and while only some have remained in close touch, none of us had forgotten each other. Logging onto Zoom, meeting in cafés in Bangalore, or picking up the phone to have many of these conversations, I often felt as though no time had passed since we graduated.

I think their stories, our stories, are compelling for a number of reasons. As a scholar who has been looking at gender and power for more than two decades, the rise of extremist movements has been worrying. I spent my formative years in late twentieth-century Bangalore, where attacks on girls and women were uncommon, and the increased frequency of violence against women in India has been jarring. Other news over recent years—from the murder of a journalist outside her home in 2017 to the 2021 arrest of a young woman for her interest in supporting farmers protesting the government's agricultural policies—have revealed the extent to which progressivism has been overwhelmed by violence and repression. The 2019 Supreme Court decision to permit the contested land where the Babri Masjid mosque stood to be transferred to a trust that will build a Hindu temple on the site,[3] along with the acquittal in 2020 of all thirty-two people who in 1992 had been "accused of conspiring to destroy the structure and stoking religious enmity,"[4] has only deepened concern at the unholy marriage between the Indian state and religious extremism. How did India, and Bangalore in particular, come to travel this dispiriting journey?

AYODHYA AND ITS AFTERMATH

To understand the present, we need a quick overview of the events of 1992. The Babri Masjid mosque was built in 1528 by Babur, who is considered the first Mughal ruler of India. The Mughal dynasty was Muslim, and Babur constructed the mosque on land that had been considered the birthplace of the Hindu god Ram. Despite its existence being challenged at various points over the next four centuries, the mosque remained in place, representing a different facet of India's history. This balance held until the 1980s, when a political party, the Vishwa Hindu Parishad (VHP), made "reclaiming" the land part of its political mandate.[5] By 1992, the BJP had taken over this issue and made it the party's raison d'être. Through much of 1992, the BJP organized a national procession, or *yatra*, to build popular support for the demolition of the mosque and the construction of a new temple. In December 1992, a crowd of BJP supporters and their leaders arrived in Ayodhya, creating a media crescendo, drawing public attention to the mission of rebuilding the temple.

Over the years, many people have labeled the events of December 6, 1992, as a "demolition."[6] Yet this description sanitizes the reality on the ground. Thousands of Hindu extremists, or *kar sevaks*, overran the Babri Masjid mosque, shouting, "We will build the temple in this very spot," and "Whoever plays Babur's game will die a dog's death."[7] Journalists describe a "mania" that started to overtake the crowd, which was armed with iron rods and pickaxes.[8] The *kar sevaks* destroyed much of the mosque, bringing down three of its four domes, while the few police officers on the scene stood idly by. According to Dilip Awasthi, a reporter for the newspaper *India Today*:

> The forest of gleaming *trishuls* [tridents], raised high in militant victory. And, the twin plumes that snaked to the skies: the dust from the demolished structure, and the smoke from nearby Muslim houses torched in the orgasmic

fever. Religion was their opium and it returned Ayodhya to the medieval ages. Ultimately, it might have seemed like the pebble that started an avalanche, the lone man who broke through the security cordon, followed by ten others, and then hundreds and finally, thousands.[9]

The violence spread nationally, with Hindus and Muslims clashing across the country. Police were often suspected of being in league with Hindu groups.[10] In Bombay, the police were reported to be responsible for most of the violence against Muslims.[11] Homemade weapons deployed by the rioters included inner tubes filled with acid that were stretched across roads and used as slingshots. The army was deployed to states such as Gujarat, where twenty-four people were burned alive in the town of Surat.[12] In Karnataka, the state in which Bangalore is situated, things were less bloody. Only six districts out of thirty-one in the state were affected by the riots, with reports of sixty people dying. Yet, nationally, by the end of 1992, over one thousand people had lost their lives in twenty-five days of violence.[13]

The political aftershocks reverberated soon after. The idea that India was a secular bastion was destroyed.[14] The prime minister, P. V. Narasimha Rao, of the Congress Party, which was founded on secular rather than religious principles, was vulnerable to criticism from both the left and the right.[15] On the right, some were angry that the ruling Congress Party accused the VHP and the BJP of a national betrayal, blaming them for the riots. On the left, the confidence of the Muslim minority was badly dented, with newspaper opinion pages reporting that the "lethargic and indifferent approach of Mr. Rao . . . denigrated the nation."[16] The National Front-Left Front (NF-LF) Party met with the Indian president, Shankar Dayal Sharma, also a member of the Congress Party, to tell him that the attack on the mosque was the "gravest onslaught" on secularism in the country.[17] By December 10, 1992, five political parties were banned by the central government, though oddly enough the BJP was not among them. Despite this, it seemed clear to most people that the BJP was the sole instigator of the violence. As the union minister at the time Madhavrao Scindia commented, "What is most shocking is that the desecration at Ayodhya was fully planned, manipulated, and connived at by the BJP-VHP . . . working for narrow political ends."[18]

Over time, the horror of December 6 faded. People moved on, as they are wont to do, but in some ways, the stage was set for the continued rise of these right-wing forces. The BJP was able to use the legacy of Ayodhya to build a more cohesive movement. Over the rest of the 1990s, the BJP fanned the flames of religious extremism in many of India's northern states. Furthermore, market reforms and the establishment of a quota system for jobs and education for non-upper-class Hindus created a sense of disaffection among Hindus, driving them to join radical parties such as the VHP and BJP.[19] In the mid-1990s, the BJP was able to form short-term coalition national governments under its then-leader Atal Bihari Vajpayee, but those forays into power did not last long, and the BJP remained an opposition party for the next twenty-plus years.

While the fits and starts of Hindu political power at the central level waxed and waned, certain political leaders were finding more success at the state level. One such leader was Narendra Modi, who got his political start in Gujarat, where he was elected as the chief minister (an office equivalent to that of state governor in the United States) in 2001. He served in that role until 2014, when he was elevated to prime minister after the BJP broadened its agenda and appeal and won enough votes to enable it to form a coalition government under his leadership.

Modi has been a controversial leader from his days in the executive office of Gujarat. Gujarat has always had a history of interreligious violence. Two of the eight cities in India that have seen the bloodiest Hindu-Muslim confrontations are in Gujarat.[20] It was under Modi's watch that one of the most violent Hindu-Muslim clashes occurred. In 2002, fifty-eight people, primarily Hindus, were killed on a train in eastern Gujarat that was carrying passengers participating in a religious pilgrimage. While the reasons for the burning of the train have been contested,[21] much of the blame, without hard evidence, was placed on a Muslim mob. Over the next three months, retaliatory violence against Muslims took the form of murders, rapes, arson, and looting.[22] In his role as chief minister, and reinforcing his claim that the BJP was the champion of the rights of India's Hindus,[23] Modi showed limited interest in bringing those guilty of violence to justice. In 2014, with Modi's "bona fides within Hindu nationalist circles" well established, the BJP-led government "focused largely on issues of development, anticorruption, and good governance."[24] But as will be discussed in chapter 4, since it came to power, the BJP has by no means abandoned its pro-Hindu agenda, employing authoritarian tactics to intimidate opponents and to promote the idea that India is a fundamentally Hindu state.

The rise of nationalism and religious extremism is not unique to India, of course. Across the globe, the past three decades have seen an assortment of right-wing, extremist groups take control of local, provincial, and national governments. Other, even more extreme groups—such as Q-Anon in the United States and the National Rally (formerly National Front) in France— are building formidable levels of support. In India, extremists have targeted thinkers, journalists, and scholars—and women. In a global assessment of women's views of their safety in their own countries, Thomson Reuters found that Indian women in 2018 under the BJP were perceived to be, by their own perceptions, the most insecure in the world.[25] For the women growing up in

Bangalore in the 1980s and early 1990s, the contrast between their lives then and now is markedly different.

GROWING UP IN BANGALORE

Every city has an epoch—a period marked by distinctive characteristics, a time when what was past is present and what is future is not hidden. Residents remember these epochs in a variety of ways, but they are often pivotal fulcrums, transitory movements from town to city or from city to metropolis.[26] Bangalore experienced one of these epochs between the mid-1980s and the mid-1990s, a ten-year period during which city planners and policymakers cemented the foundation of Bangalore as a thriving middle-class city but just prior to the city's arrival on the global stage.

When people reminisce today about their youth in Bangalore in the late 1980s and the early 1990s, they mention many of the same places.[27] Ice creams at Corner House and Lakeview (which, sadly, did not have a lake view), movies at Rex and Plaza, and strolling along "Brigades" and MG Road. Neighborhoods were known for their bakeries and parks, local theaters thrived, and everyone prized the imposing government building Vidhan Soudha and the architecturally innovative violin-shaped Chowdiah Memorial Hall. We would recall attending the *arangetrams* (a dancer's first public performance) for classmates who learned the ancient art of the *Bharatnatyam* dance on one day and spend the next day at the local disco (Knock Out). We would wear sarees and go to a family wedding and eat our meals on banana leaves in the morning and then put on our jeans and head over to a pub (Black Cadillac) to see our friends in the evenings. There were a plethora of bookstores in the city. Everyone knew the Premier Book Shop, a hole-in-the-wall store, with books piled up in no apparent order and an owner who could find you anything you were looking for and always gave you a discount.[28] The more upwardly mobile could spend lazy afternoons and sociable evenings at vast and grassy membership clubs. These clubs were vestiges of the colonial era, where we played snooker, badminton, table tennis, housie (bingo), and cards. Many teenagers would make their way to Casa Piccola on Residency Road, where long afternoons would be spent with a milkshake or a cappuccino, talking to friends, figuring out how to change the world.[29] Bangalore was a small city with big aspirations and a cosmopolitan outlook, and young people could easily step between the traditional and the modern without missing a beat.

These commonalities, which are explored in chapters 2 and 3, highlight the ways in which Bangalore was still a small town. People recollect hitchhiking without fear for their safety in a city where, if you waited anywhere long enough, you would invariably see someone you knew. This was a city that was not as bound by tradition as other small cities such as Madras, nor as overwhelmingly hectic and vast as Delhi and Bombay. The pace of life in Bangalore was slower than in those megacities but the city was confident of its intellectual and global heft. This was a city that was built around innovation and technology, with a long history of housing new industries, even before it became known the world over as the "Silicon Valley of India." Chapter 1 traces a brief history of the city and explains that even during the time of the British Raj, the state, Karnataka, and its capital, Bangalore, were designed to bring aspirational people together. A wide variety of white-collar jobs supported a population that was more forward thinking than the residents of many other Indian cities.[30]

It was in this environment that a generation of young women found intellectual and social freedom. A large middle-class population fueled a culture in which young women often found that their fathers were their strongest champions, encouraging them to be independent. The girls went to schools where they would get what was widely regarded as a "good education." Such an education included high-quality curricular and extracurricular opportunities and was a stepping stone to being a well-rounded person, a woman who could aspire to a career of her choice but could also be seen as a poised and articulate adult. In a society built on arranged marriages, families also knew that middle-class brides-to-be would require a solid education to be competitive in the marriage market, so there were personal, familial, and cultural reasons why enrollment in these schools thrived.[31] Middle-class aspirations led families of a variety of religious and linguistic backgrounds to send their daughters to missionary-founded all-girl schools that were commonly called "convent schools," even though they were seldom run by nuns. Established during the colonial era by Christian churches of all denominations, it was in these schools that girls like me built enduring friendships.

"LOYALTY AND SERVICE": THE BALDWINS EXPERIENCE

Schools established by Christian religious orders are common in most Indian cities, whether large or small.[32] English is usually the medium of instruction in these often single-sex schools, which have educated generations of children of middle-class or aspiring middle-class families. Brother and sister schools are often associated together (for instance, Baldwin Boys was located about a ten-minute walk from Baldwin Girls), and students can spend their entire school career at such institutions, progressing from prekindergarten to tenth grade, when, around the age of sixteen, they take the national board exams in a wide range of subjects. After graduating, a student might spend two years in a junior college, taking "preuniversity courses" in four core subjects of their choice.[33]

In Bangalore in the 1980s and 1990s, there were about a dozen such schools. Four of the most popular girls schools have been located in the heart of the city for more than a century, drawing their students from an assortment of families, spanning not just generations but also languages, religions, and castes, living in neighborhoods in all quadrants of the city. The fees were not exorbitant at the time, but families might have had to cough up a substantive donation to gain admission, and that might have been challenging for some who were not in the middle or upper classes. Yet for many students in these schools, classmates often discovered that the strongest ties binding them together were frequently not their religion, caste, or neighborhood but their middle-class status.

These institutions, it should be noted, had played important roles in maintaining power structures during the colonial era, educating a small slice of the population to work with the British, while neglecting the vast majority of Indian children.[34] In the postindependence era, they were ladders to success for Indians who could afford to attend them. For young women, these schools did two conflicting things at the same time. The first was to educate them as young women to seek out their own futures and to aim as high as they wanted to go professionally. The second was to teach them to be well-behaved, decorous young women.[35] For instance, we would be encouraged to debate, take computer classes, and read a wide variety of literature, but we were also expected to talk, dress, and comport ourselves as one might expect a lady to do.

I spent my formative years in Bangalore. I arrived at age nine in 1982, having spent my earlier years in the United States. I started in the fourth standard (grade) at Baldwins Girls High School and ended up spending one year in the primary school and six years in the high school, graduating from tenth standard in 1989, along with nearly 120 other young women. Baldwins, while a Christian school with strong Methodist traditions, was a progressive institution that sought to help girls become "poised, concerned, highly principled, adventurous, enquiring and self-confident."[36] It was not the most expensive or prestigious of the city's convent schools, but it boasted some unique characteristics. It was one of the first schools in Bangalore to run a special education program. It was home to the first all-girls school band in South India, was the only girls school with a twenty-five-meter swimming pool in Bangalore, and introduced computer science classes as early as 1985. BGHS was both a day school and a boarding school. The "boarders" stayed in the hostel on campus, while the "day scholars" would commute between home and school every day. In the Class of 1989, about 20 of the 120 girls were boarders.

The school and its grounds occupied almost ten acres when I was there. The primary school was a warren of stone buildings at one end of the campus. The high school students were housed in an elegant, two-story building with large verandahs on the other end of the campus. The older girls wore pinafores of royal blue, with white shirts, a tie, a belt, and a little lapel pin that was one of seven colors, marking which "house" you belonged to. Long before the Harry Potter books opened Americans' eyes to the system of school houses, life in many convent schools was shaped by that system. While most schools had three or four houses, BGHS had seven, named for seven former principals: Benthien (green), Delima (pink), Fisher (purple), Laura Gill (orange), Stephen (red), Watson (light blue), and Weston (yellow). These houses were one way to define your allegiances on campus. The other way was through your class "section," which was the home room that you were assigned to for your grade at the start of your time at BGHS. Each section usually had just over sixty students. In 1989, there were just two sections at BGHS, section A and section B. Today, reflecting the population explosion in India in the past two decades, some schools have numerous sections, running all the way to the Ls or Ms. Once you were assigned to a section, you and your classmates would usually remain in that section until graduation.

The teachers, in the eyes of their teenage students, often seemed as old as the school itself, which had celebrated its centenary in 1980. The teachers followed the curricula set by the Indian School Certificate Examination (ICSE), one of three national boards of education and commonly believed to be both the hardest and most prestigious of the three. Unlike the other two boards, which were controlled by either the national or the state governments, the ICSE board was an independent body. Teachers taught the same subject from year to year, and students would often have the same teacher for a subject from grades 5 through 10. Some teachers struck a chord with all of the girls; others were strict and less well liked; and a few had as many detractors as loyal followers. Wild backstories were woven about the teachers, especially the ones who lived on campus. These single women, we students imagined, were either mourning lost loves or hiding from families. The school had an active extracurricular program, with music, sports, art, band, and literary activities. The campus community was tightly knit, with friendships, rivalries, a few sworn vendettas, and an overall camaraderie that spoke to the school motto of "Loyalty and Service."

THE GIRLS OF BGHS

I still travel back to Bangalore several times a year, but things have changed there in the past decade. It feels different—less easygoing, more fearful—and the local news includes grim stories about rising violence, especially against women and girls. Over the past fifteen years, I have conducted research on education and gender in the region,[37] and in spending time with friends and family in India, the city has felt different. I was curious to understand more.

The murder of a journalist in 2017, which is explored in subsequent chapters, was gut-wrenching. Stories of right-wing gangs destroying stationery stores on Valentine's Day seemed at odds with what I remembered growing up.[38] Knowing the variety of religions among my classmates, the rise of Hindu extremism and its intolerance of other religions was jarring. I decided in 2020 that I wanted to better understand how these changes were viewed, not from my vantage point as a researcher, scholar, and academic but through the eyes of women who came of age in Bangalore thirty years ago and have continued to live there or, if they have moved elsewhere in India, retain deep connections to the city.

I spent much of 2020 reconnecting with these women. I had stayed in touch over the years with about a dozen of my classmates, and I first reached out to them. But then I decided to try to contact all the women who made up the BGHS Class of 1989. Nearly 50 of the 120 women I contacted responded and were open to my questions, and I spoke with just about thirty-five. I had prepared about fifteen formal questions, but as we reconnected, some after six months, others after thirty years, it was often not surprising to any of them that I was doing this. Not just an avid journal keeper, I was known for writing overly tragic stories that were a smorgasbord of genres, from mystery, to romance, to tragedy. It was a nostalgic way to begin to speak about current events, drawing from our shared history and memories of each other.

While the women were all my former classmates, I have needed to consider how I protect them in the pages of this book. Their words have deep resonance as we consider the role of these complex issues, not just in India but in other parts of the world. I was not interested in putting them in a vulnerable or dangerous position as they met and spoke with me. I do not use their real names in this book. Pseudonyms and composite identities offer them protection in the sensitive and insecure political environment of today's India. This reality was grimly illustrated when, in late 2020, just as my conversations were drawing to a close, a twenty-one-year-old activist, Disha Ravi, was arrested in Bangalore for exercising her right to support a nonviolent protest by farmers against policies being undertaken by the Modi government.[39] Most of the women in this book went to the same preuniversity and university that Disha Ravi attended. Her arrest reminds us that while India might still be a democracy, many people are not confident that they can speak freely.

My graduating class spanned the religious fabric of India; we are Hindu, Muslim, Christian, Jain, and Sikh. Some of us have married, some divorced, and some widowed; some have children, others do not. Those of us who are employed work in a wide variety of professions—journalism, media and communications, medicine, teaching, as well as partnering with family members and spouses in running a variety of businesses. Those who do not work outside the home play active roles in our communities. In short, although we are drawn from roughly the same socioeconomic strata of society, we are a diverse group.

The group that I was closest to includes Ahana, Faye, Darika, and Ela, all of whom were day scholars, like me. These are four people with whom I spent almost every day at BGHS and with whom I have remained in touch since we graduated. We have spent time in one another's homes. We know older sisters and younger brothers, and back in the 1980s and 1990s we would chat with the "uncles" and "aunties," which is how we addressed one another's parents. During our school days, we have been to camps and spent time with extended families outside of the city together, and we tended to get into trouble at school together too. Harini and Zara came later to join this core group. All of us were well known in school, in part thanks to our active involvement in extracurricular activities. A few of us would always score high on annual exams, while the rest of us were somewhere in the middle of the pack.

Boarders include Kiara, Meher, Nisha, Inara, and Juhi. These were girls who called the school their second home; their parents were either in other parts of rural India or were overseas. They were their own tight-knit band and had a different vantage point from which to view both the school and the city. Many would make their home in Bangalore as adults, having come to feel disconnected to the towns where their parents lived. The openness of the city was one of the main reasons they stayed on.

Queenie and Ginny are today on opposite ends of the political spectrum. Remembering them in school, I am not surprised that they diverged as they got older. They came from different middle-class income brackets, belonged to different religions, and lived in different types of neighborhoods. They appear frequently in this book, in part because they represent different ends of the spectrum of opinion, and in part because they were willing to speak bluntly.

Chaya, Rachna, Vedhika, and Chanchal were women I cared for deeply as friends in BGHS, but we very quickly lost touch after graduating. Reconnecting with them after thirty years was both touching and fascinating. Their careers had gone in four diverse directions. All of them took an active interest in politics and offered thoughtful assessments of the ways in which Bangalore has changed and is continuing to change.

While it would be helpful to provide detailed accounts of each woman's personal and professional life, the current political environment in India makes that a risky proposition. I have given each of them a pseudonym and have deliberately avoided providing details that would allow them to be identified by any of their classmates. The bonds of BGHS are strong enough that even a description of how they came to school each day or what they typically ate for lunch could easily give someone enough clues to start to unpeel the onion of anonymity and confidentiality. What I will say is that each one of them could easily reminiscence about school, recall the city, and relate their favorite memories while also critically analyzing the changes that have occurred in the past thirty years, the political and ideological forces that have driven those changes, and the direction in which the country seems to be heading.

WHAT LIES AHEAD

Trying to organize this book for people who don't know the girls, the school, or the city has been an interesting challenge. The book is divided into two parts, the first of which sets the stage, providing a multidimensional view of Bangalore, its citizens, and its culture as well as the energy in the 1980s and 1990s as seen through the eyes of the women I went to school with—women who were teenagers at the time. The second half offers key insights into issues that are central to the rise of an authoritarian regime and the ways in which the women saw the city responding to those shifts.

In part I, chapter 1 provides a brief history of the city, from its feudal origins and Mughal rule to the British colonial period, to the development of a democratic and secular society after independence, and finally to the emergence of a high-tech metropolis with a global reputation. In different ways, each of these stages in the city's evolution have shaped the environment within which the women in this book have lived.

Chapters 2 and 3 show readers how the girls spent their time in both public and private spaces. First, we venture into Bangalore's neighborhoods, cafés, and bookstores in the late 1980s and 1990s, as the women recall their teenage selves, their pastimes, and the cosmopolitan nature of the city. It was a time when the economic power of the city's well-educated middle class was growing, in the process influencing how families raised their children, particularly their daughters, who enjoyed the kind of freedom relatively unknown to middle-class girls in other parts of India. Following this foray into the public sphere, our "Bangalore girls" recollect how they steered their way through their adolescence, allowing us to enter their personal spaces of family relationships, teenage crushes, and school friendships. Those friendships tended to encompass girls of different religious, linguistic, and ethnic backgrounds. Studying in a Methodist school, but coming from Hindu, Muslim, Christian, Jain, and Parsi families, the women discuss their perceptions of these varied religions in their lives. The picture painted in chapters 2 and 3 of Bangalore toward the end of the last century, with its easygoing attitudes and the free-dom experienced by young women, stands in stark contrast to what unfolds in the remaining chapters. Chapter 4 offers an overview of the birth and expansion of the BJP and presents, in their own words, the women's recollections of the fear and uncertainty generated—even in middle-class Bangalore—by the Ayodhya riots and the subsequent violence and political changes occurring around them.

Part II moves from the past to the present to explore how the Class of 1989 has experienced the social, political, cultural, and other changes wrought by the rise of Hindu nationalism and how they view the current situation in Bangalore and in India generally. These are conflicting and contradictory narratives. The women know they have had more professional opportunities than their mothers and grandmothers did, but they now have far less personal safety. They miss the secularism of their youth, but they have a grudging respect for the political skills of Narendra Modi, who they feel is unapologetically proud to be Indian. They remain nostalgic for the open welcome Bangalore used to offer newcomers but also resent the newer immigrants to Bangalore, especially from the north, who then compete for limited resources.

In chapter 5 I look at women's concerns about their safety. While people throughout the world were appalled by the grotesque rape of a young woman on a bus in New Delhi in 2012, little has changed since then in terms of women's security in India; indeed, the situation has grown worse. My class-mates talk candidly of their fears for themselves and their daughters when they venture into public spaces and of their sense of loss of the personal freedom they knew when they were younger. They speak of the restrictions as a result of greater disrespect for women, the lack of male engagement in women's issues, and an increase in a "blame the victim" mindset embedded in expectations of womanhood outlined by Hindu extremists.

Chapter 6 reveals the influence of Hindu extremism on education and the numerous ways in which political pressures and religious ideologies have impacted the educational system. The women raise concerns about the ways in which textbooks and curricula are shifting what students are taught and how they are taught. They describe the problems posed by a dearth of places for their children at good schools, with the rapidly growing population out-stripping the city's supply of high-quality education. They worry that schools have become centers for indoctrination in Hindu nationalism and for the marginalization of non-Hindu students.

One of the most striking aspects of the conversations was the extent to which the women embrace secularism as a core value of their national identity. But as chapter 7 reveals, they are now witnessing the breakdown of India's secular values and systems, while trying to make sense of what it means to be an Indian and a Bangalorean. They still embrace inclusivity as an ideal, critiquing practices such as not renting apartments to Muslims, but they are also candid about their worries about the influx of northerners into the city and the impact that population surge has had on their physical and economic security.

Their sense of insecurity is accentuated by the intimidation and repression of writers and thinkers. Chapter 8 begins with the 2017 murder of an influential journalist outside her home in Bangalore and the reverberations that event had on the women. Gauri Lankesh is widely believed to have been murdered by right-wing extremists, and her death was taken as a warning that no one would be safe if they criticized the BJP and its affiliates. The women explain how the escalation of violence against thinkers, scholars, and higher education institutions has suppressed public criticism of the BJP's agenda and created fear among those who are not aligned with the nationalist movements that they will be targeted as prominent figures have been.

Chapter 9 delves into the recent political machinations of the BJP, from the ways in which patriotism is "performed" to their views on recent laws around citizenship. My former classmates point to the official insistence on public displays of patriotism and the anger voiced against those who are viewed as insufficiently "Indian." The government's efforts to tie citizenship to religion is another political move that the women discuss. In this chapter, I also explore their attitudes toward Modi, who won a resounding victory in 2019, in part due to winning a larger share of women's votes.

Weaving together the strands of these women and the city in which they came of age, the book concludes by reflecting on some key issues raised in the preceding pages. The women share their hopes for the future, wondering how they should balance their competing allegiances and conflicting emotions. Their reflections in turn inspire concerns that are not limited to Bangalore or even just to India. Globalization, internationalization, and cosmopolitanism have been blamed for the rise of jingoistic and ethnocentric leadership—does that mean that other cities like Bangalore, cities that have been melting pots of migrants and different cultures, will experience an upsurge in intolerant nationalism? How does misogyny that is deeply enmeshed in nationalism and religious extremism impact the gains made in terms of asserting and expanding women's rights and freedoms? Do women—such as the "Bangalore girls" highlighted here—who speak openly and frankly about the negative aspects of populist and authoritarian movements make themselves targets for violence and intimidation? These are worrying questions for women not just in formerly progressive parts of India but in cities across the world; in that sense, we are all Bangalore girls.

THE PAST AND THE FUTURE

It is easy to look back on the heady days of one's adolescence and recreate a past that is brighter than it actually was. And the past can seem even more enchanting when we put on our rose-colored spectacles in the company of others—as, for instance, during a conversation between former classmates. Yet according to Robyn Fivush, a scholar who specializes in autobiographical memory, the ways "we reminisce about our personal past with others" and "internalize others' perspectives and experiences into our own understanding" allow us to make and create meanings "within and across narrated experiences."[40] In other words, when we remember in more systematic and collective ways, it can be possible to see deeper meanings in what might otherwise seem to be random events.

To have frank conversations, trust must be pooled, and to understand the context deeply, certain inside knowledge of the events, places, and ideas must be shared where "reminiscing with others is a critical part of the process of forming our memories across time in ways that create coherence and durability."[41] The common bond between myself and the women I spoke with, as well as our mutual familiarity with our stories, provides a narrative framework that balances the importance of nostalgia and reminiscence with that of meaning making and nuance. This should allow an author to use the power of nostalgia and reminiscence to understand the ways in which the past is linked to the present in an effort to better understand the future.

By prodding my classmates' memories, I wanted to see if connections could be made between how they saw the demolition of the Babri Masjid and what that says about the city and the country thirty years later. What progress do they see? What concerns do they have? How are women's day-to-day lives connected to the rise of nationalist and extremist movements? What lessons do the stories they tell about their city offer to people living in other cities around the world where progressivism is under attack and misogyny is on the rise? How does the story of Bangalore in recent decades echo or foreshadow the trajectory of such movements elsewhere?

Journalist Thomas Friedman, who coined the phrase "the world is flat" in his book of the same name, talks about how the changes in Bangalore caught him by surprise in 2005:

> Alas, I encountered the flattening of the world quite by accident. It was in late February of last year [2004], and I was visiting the Indian high-tech capital, Bangalore, working on a documentary for the Discovery Times channel about outsourcing. In short order, I interviewed Indian entrepreneurs who wanted to prepare my taxes from Bangalore, read my X-rays from Bangalore, trace my lost luggage from Bangalore and write my new software from Bangalore. The

longer I was there, the more upset I became—upset at the realization that while I had been off covering the 9/11 wars, globalization had entered a whole new phase, and I had missed it.[42]

Bangalore is a very different city today than it was when I graduated from Baldwins. It is considered to be a remarkably vibrant city and often makes the lists of the world's most influential cities.[43] The culture of good food and theater, the well-educated population, and the cosmopolitan nature of the city continue to make the city a go-to destination for businesses[44] and tourists, and the number and variety of schools from which families can choose (if they can afford the fees) for their children have grown exponentially.[45] Yet beneath this veneer of cosmopolitan dynamism, the undercurrent of the city has changed. The political landscape has shifted dramatically since the Ayodhya riots, and the citizens of Bangalore, women especially, must now navigate a much more repressive, censorious, and dangerous city.

PART I

Growing Up in a Progressive City

Chapter 1

The Making of a Metropolis

The story of Bangalore is one that encompasses how a settlement in the south of India became a burgeoning city that is now synchronous with technology, innovation, and globalization. To understand the stories shared by the women in this book, it is important to understand the story of Bangalore and the city's growth from a small mud fort in 1537 to the thriving megacity that it is today.[1] The city's evolving political life and economic fortunes as well as its architecture, culture, and people offer a snapshot of how the city evolved and created deep connections for the women both toward the city and also toward others who grew up and lived in Bangalore. The chapter is not meant to be an exhaustive history but illuminates certain key moments central to the development of the city and highlights aspects of the city that have been influential landmarks and moments in the lives of the women who share their insights in the subsequent chapters. This is also my family's history. For over five generations, my family has called Bangalore home. Both my paternal and maternal sides of the family have served the city as leaders and civil servants, engaged in city planning, development, and infrastructure. I am not unaware of the privilege of growing up in a family who had ancestors who played prominent roles in the story of Bangalore, but it also provides a view of the city that is more intimate and personal than what is shared in a history book. Growing up, I would hear my parents and grandparents speak of the evolution of the city, often discussing influential figures who had led the city and directed the work of government employees in service of the city. While family members would emigrate, or leave to study or work in Canada, Australia, or the United States, Bangalore still was home for all of us, in great part due to the long history of service to the city.

Bangalore, or Bengaluru, as it is officially known today, is the capital of the south Indian state of Karnataka. Located on an elevated region of the south called the Deccan Plateau, Karnataka is one of India's five southern states. Bangalore sits at a height of just over three thousand feet (nine hundred meters), and this elevation gives the city its national reputation for "crazy good" weather.[2] With its balmy climate, fertile land, and abundant water supply thanks to the rivers and streams that cross the undulating landscape, Bangalore's natural gifts set the city up to thrive.[3]

In thinking about the evolution of the city, four distinct periods frame the city's growth: the early history prior to the British colonization of India; the colonial period, during which the British maintained control over the city; the postindependence period, when city planners laid the foundation for Bangalore's role as an industrial center; and finally, the rapid economic and geographic growth of the city into "the Silicon Valley of India" in the new millennium. Each of these eras is explored in subsequent sections to assist readers with facets of the city's story that retain their importance in the current context.

THE PRECOLONIAL PERIOD: 1200–1799

Earliest records show that Bangalore was a small village in the twelfth century. For much of the next two hundred years, the region was ruled by a series of dynasties, including the Cholas and the Hoysalas,[4] who were known for their architectural accomplishments.[5] Temple complexes in parts of what is now Karnataka showcase the artistry and architecture of these times. The temples in the capital cities of Bélur and Halébid are now popular tourist destinations, frequently sites for school trips for students from Bangalore as well as for a steady stream of international visitors.[6] The dynasties presided over a generally peaceful land, dominated by agriculture but visited by traders bringing news from places as far away as Persia, China, and the Malay Peninsula.[7] Historians document a more visible role for royal women during these times as compared to female members of the nobility in other parts of India.[8] During this period, the local vernacular of Kannada[9] became increasingly widely used (centuries later, it would become the official language of the state government). It was in this region, bounded by the cities of Bélur and Halébid as well as the emerging royal kingdom of Mysore, that a new city would be formed.

The first formal boundaries of Bangalore were established in 1537. The city's founder was Kempe Gowda I, a feudal ruler under the dynastic control of the Vijayanagara empire, who ordered the construction of a mud fort. Four watchtowers created a perimeter around the city. Evidence of those four watchtowers can still be found in today's city center,[10] but Bangalore has expanded far beyond the area they guarded. Instead these historic markers illustrate today's city center. In 1638, the Marathas, a Hindu dynasty from the north, conquered Bangalore and ruled it for almost fifty years. Power then shifted to a local dynasty, after which the city was captured by its first

Muslim ruler, Haider Ali, who governed until his son, Tipu Sultan, ascended the throne in 1782.[11]

This history is set against the larger tapestry of feudal and regional rulers across the subcontinent and the expansion of the Mughal dynasty in the northern part of India. Hinduism and Jainism were joined by Buddhism, and then with the 1498 arrival of the Portuguese were joined by Christianity, which created a patchwork of religions in the South Asian peninsula. The rise of the Mughal empire introduced Islam to the region and a distinctive style of architecture, most famously represented by the Taj Mahal in Agra, which was built in 1653 by Mughal emperor Shah Jahan. While the north dealt with the battles of the Mughals, who fought not just the local people but also waged wars between fathers and sons,[12] the Deccan Plateau would begin to witness the arrival of European powers at the coasts, leading to the emergence of more militant Hindu rulers, among whom were the Marathas.[13] Yet for reasons difficult to explain, the city-state of Mysore, while "vulnerable to the expansionist ambitions" of the Mughals and the Marathas, had somehow been ignored by both. During the mid-1700s, the region continued to be disregarded despite the relative weakness of Mysore's feudal leaders, the Wodeyars. This allowed for local conflicts and allowed Haidar Ali and his son Tipu to seize control away from the Wodeyars.[14] In the late eighteenth century, as the British moved from trading partners to colonizers, using force to expand their control, Tipu Sultan, also known as the "Tiger of Mysore," sought to hold off the British. Fighting the British off and on between 1782 and 1799, Tipu Sultan lost power and ceded much of the control of his empire to the British in 1799. The British returned the region to the stewardship of the Wodeyar dynasty while maintaining their hold on the cities of Mysore and Bangalore.

This early history has of late become a political battleground, a conflict that will later feature prominently in this book. Haider Ali and Tipu Sultan were the first Muslim rulers of what is now the state of Karnataka, and until relatively recently they were widely considered admirable leaders, depicted in plays and songs, and even in children's stories, as brave and resourceful kings. The "Tiger of Mysore" was a key element in the social studies curriculum in the state through the 1990s. Tipu's resistance to the British was taught as a model for the subsequent battles for Indian independence. However, Tipu's accomplishments have in recent years been questioned by Hindu nationalists, who have sought to elevate narratives in which Hindus, not Muslims, take center stage. For instance, recent news articles report that a candidate for election from the BJP party said that Tipu was "a terrorist."[15]

Responding to such attacks on the historical record of Tipu Sultan, in 2016 a scholar at a university in Bangalore shared this opinion in the national newspaper *The Hindu*:[16]

Focusing solely, as right-wing discussions do, on Tipu's religious views, threatens to eclipse his versatile personality. His letters to the Nizam and the Marathas show that he viewed the British as a new kind of political enemy whose rule would hurt the region's future in drastic ways, qualifying him perhaps as an early freedom fighter. His keenness in the upgradation of his military equipment has impressed engineers, scientists and others who value advances in technology. And those who admire the institution of the modern state have appreciated that Tipu fine-tuned his revenue collection networks and tried to create a centralised bureaucracy. The over 2,000 books in Tipu's personal library, which were sent to Oxford and Cambridge Universities in England and to the College of Fort William and Royal Asiatic Society in Calcutta after his death, show the rich range of his intellectual interests: astronomy, law, mathematics, among others.[17]

As this article suggests, Tipu's rule helped set the stage for the eventual emergence of a progressive and educated population in the city. But in today's Bangalore, not everyone wants to celebrate Tipu's influence. As in many parts of the world, history, the teaching history, and the social studies curriculum more broadly have become contested spaces, battlegrounds on which nationalist movements are wresting control from more liberal forces.

COLONIAL POWERS AND PRESSURES: 1800–1946

The era of the British Raj began when the British captured Bangalore from Tipu Sultan, after their victory in the 1799 Fourth Anglo-Mysore War. As mentioned earlier, the British colonizers did not manage the city themselves but returned the control of the city administratively to the maharaja of Mysore, part of the Wodeyar clan, who was considered a "nominally sovereign entity of the British Raj."[18] The maharaja, or king, would usually name a diwan, or the city's chief administrator. These individuals worked in partnership between the king and the colonizing powers in order to ensure the growth and development of the city. While the British established an encampment, or "cantonment," in Bangalore in 1809, the structure of relatively shared governance in the city was unusual but maybe illustrative of why Bangalore is so different from other cities in India.

Today, the central part of the city is still called the "Cantonment." Even though the city has expanded dramatically, the city center remains the hub of much social, economic, and political life. The parks, broad streets, and private clubs that now cater to the middle-class Indian were first developed in a process of urban development that lasted from 1800 until India attained independence in 1947.

The colonial legacy is particularly evident in the city center's architecture, not least its churches. The British built churches that still stand today in key locations. For instance, the imposing St. Mark's Cathedral was built in 1808 and subsequently rebuilt after one of its shoddily constructed towers toppled in 1902 and its nave was destroyed by fire in 1923.[19] Today, the buttery yellow church is the heart of the Catholic community in Bangalore. My cousin, the late Nikhil Moorchung, and his son, Siddharth Moorchung, authored a series of historical anecdotes for the *Bangalore Mirror*, tracing the evolution of the history of these landmarks. They describe the cathedral as "beautiful colonial style architecture . . . modeled on the lines of St. Paul's Cathedral in London . . . with intricate woodwork and elaborate carvings"; it also boasts the best-maintained bells in India.[20] Other churches include the Holy Trinity Church built in 1852 on the largest promenade in the city; the East Parade Church, constructed in 1865, which is run by Wesleyans; and the Scottish St. Andrew's Church, built in 1866.

Nikhil and Siddharth Moorchung also trace the history of other colonial buildings that are still part of the current fabric of Bangalore life. For instance, Mayo Hall, named for Viceroy and Governor-General Lord Mayo, housed municipal offices. Its classical construction became the style that was popular and mimicked by other city buildings. Cubbon Park, where today city residents, young families, and courting couples seeking privacy often spend their leisure time, was thought to be designed as a barrier to separate the Indian masses from their British overlords. Within the park is the Seshadri Iyer Memorial Hall, which houses the State Central Library. Constructed during the colonial era, the establishment of the library was the inspiration of the diwan of the time, Diwan Visveswaraya.[21] As such, the library illustrates the influence that educated locals had on the colonizers in the city.

The colonial architectural influence is evident in residential construction as well, as Bangalore is also known for its bungalows. Much like Cubbon Park, the homes were an effort to distinguish between the British and Indian residents of the city. The bungalows shared a variety of features, including "the high compound wall, tall imposing gates, the long driveway to the porch." The larger the home, the greater the status of its resident within the British hierarchy.[22]

The development of carefully planned infrastructure is a key element of Bangalore's story. Local leaders were committed to the development of the city for its residents. Tracing the history of engineering advances made in Bangalore during the latter stages of the colonial era, scholars have found that city leaders, with the support of the diwans and with investments from the Wodeyar family, sought to build water and electricity systems able to support the inflows of people coming to settle in the city. By the late nineteenth century there were municipal entities that managed water, electricity, and sewage systems, and even "employed workers to light kerosene lamps in theatres, clubs and public buildings frequented by the colonial establishment and the city's elite."[23]

At the end of nineteenth century, "an outbreak of bubonic plague forced the rapid expansion of the city as people moved away from the old city quarters, prompting a rush to service new extensions [neighborhoods] such as Basavangudi and Malleshwaram."[24] Shivanasamudra Hydropower Station, established in 1905, would light the first electric lamps in the city. The diwans played a major role in making such improvements:

> Histories of infrastructure development in Bangalore include heroic, visionary administrators, such as the Diwan of Mysore, the chief public administrator of the State, who held responsibility for both drinking water and electricity provision. Among the 13 Diwans appointed in Mysore . . . three had a direct imprint in the spatial configuration of the city. K Seshadri Iyer, Diwan from 1883 until 1901, experimented with initiatives to bring about modern infrastructures in Bangalore. M Visvesvaraya (Sir MV), Diwan from 1912 until 1918, brought an engineering-based vision to the city that was instrumental in the development of extensions and networked infrastructure. Mirza Ismail, Diwan from 1926 until 1941, promoted infrastructure as support for industrial development.[25]

It is important to point out that Bangalore's diwans were both Hindu and Muslim. Diwan Mirza Ismail, for instance, was a Muslim, whereas Diwans Iyer and Visvesvaraya were Hindu. These choices for leadership helped foster visibility and a sense of belonging among people of both religions. The nascent city, at the time, benefited greatly from the investments of the kings and the British but also the work of the diwan who spearheaded the various projects that supported both modernity and innovation in the emerging city.

Investments in infrastructure and schooling, as well as growth in industries such as textiles, armaments, and engineering,[26] inspired a steady stream of families to Bangalore. While these movements led to relatively peaceful interactions between groups, there is evidence that the British would exacerbate caste and religious differences to create tensions between groups as a way to divert attention away from the British themselves.[27] As the city grew, the outlying areas were incorporated, expanding neighborhoods and creating new boundaries for Bangalore. Early forms of gentrification created more segregated neighborhoods, setting up a process of geographic differentiation between classes, castes, and religions that intensified in the postindependence period.

POSTINDEPENDENCE ADMINISTRATION: 1947–2000

The birth of India was advertised as a moment of triumph, marketed globally as the result of the power of nonviolence resistance. Yet with a famine under-way; increasing violence between Hindus, Muslims, and Sikhs; and growing political unrest, the British left India. After the celebration of independence, one last gift from the British was a newly drawn map, splitting the region into two countries. One would come to be Muslim-majority East and West Pakistan, and the other the Hindu-majority India.[28] The 1947 Partition was devasting, especially for those who lived in the northern states. "It was one of the largest and most rapid population exchanges in human history,"[29] dis-placing 16.7 million people between 1947 and 1951. An additional one to two million people lost their lives during the chaos. According to historian William Dalrymple:

> Across the Indian subcontinent, communities that had coexisted for almost a millennium attacked each other in a terrifying outbreak of sectarian violence, with Hindus and Sikhs on one side and Muslims on the other—a mutual geno-cide as unexpected as it was unprecedented. In Punjab and Bengal—provinces abutting India's borders with West and East Pakistan, respectively—the carnage was especially intense, with massacres, arson, forced conversions, mass abduc-tions, and savage sexual violence. Some seventy-five thousand women were raped, and many of them were then disfigured or dismembered.[30]

While historians disagree about the impact of India's Partition in the southern part of the country,[31] it seems that Bangalore escaped the worst of the vio-lence. Instead, upon India's independence from the British, two municipali-ties were joined together to create the capital of the new state of Mysore. The state itself was then renamed Karnataka in 1956 by drawing a boundary that encompassed regions where Kannada was the dominant language; Kannada became the new state's official language. The city of Bangalore itself was drawn into fifty wards (electoral zones). Bangalore's population rapidly grew thereafter, increasing from just under 800,000 people in 1941 to nearly three million by 1981.[32]

The population growth during this period was predominantly propelled through heavy investments by the state government in industry and defense, especially during the 1960s and 1970s.[33] Ambitious and talented people from across India were drawn by a series of educational and intellectual hubs that were established or were formally labeled as centers of excellence, including the Indian Institute of Science and the Indian Space Research Organization. While the legacies of these efforts are clearly seen in the footprint of the newer frontiers of technical expertise and capacity that is illustrated in modern-day Bangalore, the city in the postindependence era was growing, developing a positive reputation around the country.

The Moorchungs tell a story about how, just after India's independence, a Russian delegation arrived in Bangalore. As they were shown around the city, they wondered aloud why so many postindependence public buildings were designed using European architectural traditions. This spurred the then-state chief minister, K. Hanumanthiah, to champion the creation of the Vidhana Soudha in the early 1950s to house the offices of the state government.[34] The granite building is vast, over five million square feet,[35] and has a huge central dome. As the women in this book recall, it was often fully illuminated on weekends and would draw families to the adjacent green and expansive Cubbon Park to enjoy an evening outside to watch the building light up at dusk. Architecturally, the building is said to incorporate elements drawn from all the major religious influences in the country, thereby embodying the religiously inclusive, secular nature of the Indian government in the postindependence period.[36]

At the national level, India saw the election of its first (and so far only) female prime minister, Indira Gandhi. While her assassination in 1984 resulted in political and social upheavals, the immediate years prior to her death and soon after have been said to be a time when there was a burgeoning people's movement that pushed back against domestic violence, sexual harassment, and alcoholism,[37] leading to a period that "inspired and radicalized an entire generation of women, in their homes, at their workplace, in government offices, in colleges and universities, and in the media."[38] While there is little specific data to highlight the relatively progressive status of women in Bangalore at the time, literacy rates between men and women were relatively stable,[39] and middle-class girls were expected to be educated and seek employment to work outside of the home, both of which were not the norm in other parts of the country.

As Bangalore was about to move into the fourth stage of its historical journey, young people in Bangalore were increasingly finding that they were able to enjoy new freedoms and experiences—ones that might have been commonplace in the West and in other more globalized Indian cities such as Bombay or Delhi but were seldom encountered in the rest of India. To describe Bangalore in this period is to also highlight some of the ways in which a cosmopolitan culture was becoming popular. By the mid-1980s, taking advantage of the growing disposable income of middle-class families and their willingness to let their children enjoy more leisure time, cafés, pubs, and home-grown fast food restaurants started popping up. By the late 1980s, places that became part of the lore of Bangalore's youth population included getting burgers at Indiana's, milkshakes at Macs, hot fudge sundaes at Corner House, beers at Black Cadillac, and anything at Casa Piccola, which was home to birthdays, first dates, breakups, and after-school hanging out. These experiences made the international press where an article from January 1990 in the British newspaper *The Guardian Weekly* described the city's "yuppie" scene:

> The Pub on Church Street, whose owner regularly receives tapes of the latest pop hits from a friend in New York, is Bangalore's most swinging night spot. The decibel level allows for only the most abbreviated conversation between gulps of beer—UB is the best brand, but Export Lager and Kingfisher aren't bad. . . . The unpasteurised beer does not keep for more than 24 hours, so it has to be drunk fast. There is no problem at The Pub, which sells 300 litres a day—400 on Saturdays. At eight rupees (32p) a glass, "business continues to be interesting," says the owner. . . . Bangalore, a city where prohibition has never been imposed, has around 150 pubs.[40]

In some ways, Bangalore was being introduced to the world, and the world was starting to be impressed.

BECOMING INDIA'S SILICON VALLEY: 2000–2024

At the turn of the millennium, Bangalore was the sixth-largest city in India and was considered relatively diverse, with Hindus making up just under 80 percent of the population and Muslims, Christians, and Jains accounting for the other 20 percent.[41] Just over 10.5 percent of the population of the state of Karnataka lived in Bangalore in 2001, clearly making it the largest city in the state.[42] In that year, the city's population was 6.5 million; by 2021, it would climb to 13 million—an increase of 10 million since 1981.

As the city grew, so did its global reputation. By 2007, 30 percent of Bangalore's population were working in the technological sector, and the average Bangalorean had almost twice more disposable income than anyone else in the state.[43] Bangaloreans launched world-famous information technology companies, such as Infosys and WIPRO. More investment in education would lead to the establishment of new types of higher education institutions, including the National Institute of Design, the National Law School of India, and Azim Premji University, a university that was specifically designed to focus on education and teacher preparation. In popular culture, Bangalore was well known enough to be referenced in US television shows;[44] a young student from Bangalore, Lara Dutta, won the title of Ms Universe;[45] and a new youth culture evolved from the pub and café experiences that defined the end of the previous epoch.[46]

Yet the emergence of the city as a cosmopolitan dynamo shifted attention away from the larger gaps that were being created between socioeconomic groups. Infrastructural challenges around water, sewage, and traffic grew. IT firms would come into Bangalore, "plopping themselves down in cow pastures, spinach fields and drained irrigation tanks," expanding the city's boundaries but also urbanizing larger swathes of the semiurban areas.[47] This growth was propelled by nearly US$4 billion dollars a year in investment, the highest figure (in 2007) for any Indian city.[48] But this rapid development left those on the economic margins struggling to figure out how to claim their space, literally. The number of slums was rising, despite the fact that the government was said to undercount three out of every four slums that exist in the city.[49]

Furthermore, the growth of the city came at the expense of the green space that gave the city its earlier moniker of "Garden City." In this poignant description in her study of weather and class in Bangalore, Camille Frazier shares:

> Today, the tension between Bengaluru's past and present is visible and visceral in the cityscape. In the heart of the city, immense trees compete with glass and steel buildings for space along narrow streets. On the city's edges, the few remaining lakes and fields sit alongside massive apartment complexes and tech parks. All throughout the sprawling urban landscape, vehicular exhaust mixes with dust from construction sites to make headaches a normal part of navigating the city. Such daily encounters with urban transformation underlie the rising temperatures narrative, which incorporates a range of visceral experiences indexing diverse transformations in the urban landscape—from the loss of green cover to the exhaust of traffic-clogged roads—in its descriptions of heat in the city.[50]

The challenges posed by such a large population, especially the strains imposed on the city's outdated infrastructure, led to wider divisions. Traffic increased by over 6,000 percent since 1990, and the city suffers from acute water shortages, significant air pollution, and inefficient waste management.[51] Blame for these massive and still mounting problems centers on poor governance and the influx of new residents[52] and fuels divisions between the old and new Bangaloreans.

In today's Bangalore, there are two realities, two populations: those who have been able to benefit from its expansion, and those who are struggling with the urbanization of Bangalore. The people who have enjoyed the cosmopolitan advantages of Bangalore are primarily newly minted IT workers. In her 2011 ethnographic study, Jasmin Mahadevan[53] portrays modern Bangalore IT workers as hardworking and professionally highly sought after but also as "style conscious yuppies" who are not afraid to spend money on experiences such as bungee jumping. This new generation is different from the women—my former classmates—who feature in this book, who came of age and developed their professional identities in the sleepier mid-1980s, before the boom. Mahadevan describes gated communities where IT professionals live in homes with huge SUVs, "roller-skating kids," and "palm trees of the exact same height" as places that are separate from the rest of the city. This is not the Bangalore that was familiar to those of us who grew up in the 1980s where the intermingling of people in neighborhoods exposed people to a wider gamut of human experiences.

But while some are prospering, others see the middle-class life slipping out of their grasp. Prior to the 2000s, disparities in the standard of living between people were far less dramatic. Changes in living habits and increasing urbanization have led to dramatic adjustments at the household, city, and state levels.[54] Castán Broto and Sudhira argue that as the city became more divided, infrastructure and service delivery fragmented, creating a scarcity of dependable and steady supplies of services such as water and electricity. Tensions have since escalated between those who are able to demand access (those with more influence and power) and those who are marginalized (with less influence and power). The subsequent privatization of the delivery of resources from the 2011s, such as water and electricity, has exacerbated "intractable" problems of supply and demand.[55]

At the same time, the city's tradition of high-quality city administrators has eroded and confidence in the city's management is low. The city is managed by an elected body called the Bruhat Bengaluru Mahanagara Palike (BBMP), which is made of 198 "corporators," one from each of the city's wards (grown fourfold since the city's start of just fifty). A survey of residents in 2007 found that access to government representatives was considered unsatisfactory, responsiveness to constituents was unequal across income groups, and cost overruns for public efforts were judged to be rampant.[56] And while the city is dynamic in many ways, the pace of city-managed projects can be glacial. For instance, in light of the all-too-visible increase in traffic, driven by multiple reasons, from the burgeoning population, to the relatively unprepared roads for the number of vehicles, lack of safe and well-designed public transportation and also a desire among middle-class families to engage in the conspicuous consumption of car ownership,[57] the city has sought to build a metro.[58] *Namma Metro*, or Our Metro, which in 2023 has two lines, one running north/south and the other east/west, is due to expand to five lines. Activists have criticized the length of time the project has taken,[59] beginning in 2003 and anticipated to be concluded no earlier than 2026.[60]

Another concern in the city is the use of English as the lingua franca for the general population. A study conducted in 2019 discovered that, as was the case when my classmates and I were in school, many parents still prefer to pay fees and send their children to schools where the medium of instruction is English rather than send their children to free Kannada-language schools, accentuating the divide in the quality of education received by middle-class and lower-class children.[61]

The map of a city changes daily. New homes, roads, and infrastructure are hallmarks of living in a flourishing city, but the dramatic changes witnessed in Bangalore in recent decades have created divisions between those who knew the city before the boom and those who have arrived since the boom began. A chasm exists between the two groups. At the same time, the politics of the city, and of the country as a whole, have taken a turn to the right. The secularism that had been a core value for the country has been substantially eroded. The place, presence, and role of women are subjects of increasingly fierce contention, with the advances in women's rights made in the latter decades of the twentieth century now under attack. Personal experiences of this onslaught on inclusion and democracy are described by my former classmates. In the following chapters of part I, the women recall and reflect on what Bangalore was like while the city was still a bastion of progressive values and a place where young women—among the middle class, at least— enjoyed a sense of independence within the city's private spaces and found support from families and friends within their private spaces.

Chapter 2

Mopeds, Cafés, and Bookstores

Coming of Age on a Public Stage

In his 2003 book, *Public and Private Spaces of the City*, Ali Madanipour, a professor of urban design, calls attention to the fact that individuals interact with cities in both public and private ways. He argues that both types of spaces have distinctive differences when it relates to how we behave, engage with others, and think of ourselves as others see us. He suggests that the action of "watching" happens in public spaces, making us often feel less likely to be ourselves. In private spaces, the intimate circle of self and family are usually the only eyes upon you, which in theory should make us feel more comfortable and safe. In public spaces, the stage upon which we act is much more open, accessible to anyone who might be sharing that space with you. Furthermore, he argues that cities create an environment for people to interact emotionally and psychologically with themselves and others in these locations. How you see others becomes how you see yourself and vice versa, thus impacting your own sense of confidence and worth.

This is an interesting juxtaposition for young people, who often feel worried about the gaze of judgment and expectation in private spaces, whereas public spaces tend to allow more openness to experimentation and creativity. The notion of being watched is linked to the monitoring of one's behavior. Traditionally, in the public space, we are less confident of who is watching us and for what purpose. The state, strangers, and private entities scrutinize an individual and as a result impact how we conduct ourselves in that space, but for adolescents, these eyes seem less restrictive. Not being in the presence of people one is directly familiar with allows for the privilege of anonymity and freedom to test versions of yourself on that public stage. Our levels of comfort with these spaces can also direct our emotions (do we feel safe? do we feel fear?), yet we can adapt what we think is appropriate to share in public and in private, depending on who we think is watching and for our own purposes of exploration.

Cities, Madanipour says, are also meant to provide social cohesion and social capital that can be exchanged for advantages in those public spaces. But for those who cannot access that social capital, their lives can often be constricting, further elevating social stratification and divisions. He also argues that public spaces are meaningful to people both personally and collectively. People remember how they engaged in the space as well as what the space might represent to the community.[1] So while public spaces might not be intimately connected to the individual, they become a component of the story one tells about particular experiences.

In this chapter, the women share the relative lack of self-consciousness they felt in Bangalore's public spaces when they were younger—a sense of freedom from scrutiny that, as the stories make clear in later chapters, stands in sharp contrast to their lives today in the same city. For the women I spoke with, Bangalore was the stage on which the story of their adolescence played out. The city was its own character in many ways, providing not only the settings but also the energy and atmosphere in the minds of the women who grew up there.

Today Bangalore is a vast, sprawling city with an overtaxed infrastructure and a population that is increasingly divided along cultural, economic, religious, and political fault lines. Thirty-odd years ago, the women profiled in this book were leaving high school with a sense of control over their futures in part because of the stability and positive outlook that Bangalore provided. In hindsight, we probably could see the signs of growth that would transform Bangalore into a global megacity, but in the late 1980s and early 1990s, it was in many ways a small, accessible, and inviting city with much to enjoy and little to fear, at least for middle-class girls. Like adolescents, the city was in a transitional moment. Bangalore was neither local nor global but an interesting—indeed, unique—fusion of both, providing both social cohesion and social capital for the citizens who were coming of age at that point of time.

The uniqueness of the city did not lie purely, or even chiefly, in the palaces, temples, and churches constructed by kings and missionaries or in its broad boulevards and picturesque traffic circles laid out by colonists and bureaucrats. The city was inimitable in large part because of the emotional responses it engendered in its residents. As the girls testify, on the cusp of adulthood, their public lives on the Bangalore stage were full of pleasant distractions, with common and shared opportunities to stay busy and active.

There is a differentiation between public *use* of space and the public *space* itself. The relationship we have with the space and the representation of that space in our minds alters depending on how we use the space. Common ways to think about public use of space in urban life are the use of public transportation, parks and recreational facilities, and buildings such as libraries or community centers. In this chapter, the women talk about the *use* of public venues as a way to understand who they were in public spaces. In bistros, bookstores, and movie theaters, all parts of Bangalore's lively and inclusive public stage, the girls graduating from BGHS were offered a chance to enjoy the freedoms the city offered. This was in part due to the autonomy women experienced as being free to be themselves.

Madanipour argues that what takes place in the public space is akin to a theatrical performance, where the city itself is the stage. The actors, or citizens, play their parts and are influenced by the roles they play on that stage. This idea resonates with what the women told me about their lives as high school students in Bangalore. In the late 1980s and early 1990s, the women were not worried about the state watching them, and they operated with a sense of freedom to be who they wanted to be.

A MIDDLE-CLASS VANTAGE POINT

Just before the curtains open on those public spaces, it is important to emphasize that the girls graduating from BGHS belonged to the city's rapidly expanding middle class, and what they saw of Bangalore they saw from that particular standpoint. Around the world, as the middle class grows, their resources, mobility, and access to opportunities like education allow them to gradually dominate life in cities. This was certainly the case in Bangalore in the late 1980s and early 1990s.

Social and economic divisions tend to keep people in specific lanes. Universally, gender is one form of division. Religion is often another. Although this book focuses on how those two identifiers have been impacted by the rise of nationalism over the past three decades, there are other divisions to consider as well. For millennia, caste played a major role in how Indians relate to each other, and this was still an abiding issue in the 1980s. Socioeconomic status also had become increasingly salient as a form of identity to both connect and separate individuals. Studies of friendship among middle-class young men in Bangalore in the early 2000s found that caste and religion were not "irrelevant" but were also not the "primary structuring principles" around which men built friendships.[2] What was unifying was their status as part of the burgeoning middle class in the city.

Since the Industrial Revolution of the late eighteenth and nineteenth centuries ushered the modern middle class into existence, it is that class that has led social, economic, and political change in many parts of the world. This pattern was first evident in Europe, then in North America, and more recently in Asia. In the new millennia, Asia has become a global economic powerhouse and has acquired the world's largest middle class, which today numbers more than one billion people.[3] In India, the middle class expanded significantly in the wake of independence in 1947 and then began to grow prodigiously in the 1980s and 1990s. Yet this middle class is not a homogenous entity. Between urban and rural middle classes, multigenerational and newly minted middle classes, India has not just one type of middle class but many.[4]

Thirty years ago, the idea that India's middle class might grow so quickly to such a size and wield such great economic power might not have been a certainty. But in Bangalore, no one doubted that the middle class was a growing presence in the city, expanding along with the city itself. Bangalore's growth was based on a number of different industries, which meant it attracted—and rewarded—a well-educated workforce. With decent salaries and significant disposable income, those workers and their families began to embrace middle-class values and lifestyles, creating a very specific energy in the city. Like the middle class in other parts of the world, those who made their home in Bangalore embraced consumerism and cosmopolitanism and valued education and personal freedom. This outlook translated into clear decisions for those families about where within the city to live, where to send their children to school, and how to spend their free time. In addition, as parents made those decisions, the youth community in Bangalore also sought to make decisions about how they spent their time in public spaces.

During this time period, the middle class in Bangalore was an influential economic force,[5] even though it was clearly a minority in numerical terms. The middle class was not economically homogenous—with some people owning large bungalows while others lived in modest rental houses, with some families having cars and drivers while others families used their scooters to get around the city—but it was distinct from a small population of wealthier families and from a much larger working class. The working class incorporates those families that make up the service sector outside of household help, including salespeople, office managers, healthcare professionals (technicians, nurses, and physical therapists), and those engaged in tourism and other service sectors.[6] The working class was not included in the spaces that middle-class families were active in but were also not seen as the underclass. The underclass, often coming to the city from rural areas,[7] would make up the invisible population who depended on daily wages for survival, such as construction workers, maids, drivers, and street vendors. The working and under classes would see how the middle class represented themselves in the public and private spaces of the city. In his ethnographic study of youth culture in Bangalore in the early 2000s, Arun Saldhana describes the awkwardness of working-class and underclass youth who were often in attendance at parties hosted by middle-class teens where there would be dancing and drinking among young men and women.[8] Serving as waiters or as household help, or watching from windows, the public and private space of the party would highlight the contrasts of adolescent experiences in the varied classes in the city.

Social class and economic differences exist in every community, but what this chapter seeks to illustrate is that while there was this variance across classes, Bangalore was a city that offered social and cultural opportunities that were unique in part due to the history of the city and the outlook of the people. For middle-class girls, we were fortunate to have the sort of financial and social stability that allowed us to enjoy the diversions that we did. And while some of our families might have been significantly better off than others, we felt a strong kinship to one another, a sense of belonging born of being not only members of the middle class but also of the classrooms of BGHS.

"A SLIGHTLY DIFFERENT ANIMAL"

In reminiscing about Bangalore, the women in this book recalled an energy that was different from that in other parts of the country. Rachna, whose family was originally from northern India, was reminded of her cousins who lived in other cities and states. She saw how they were restricted in Delhi and Punjab, talking about how "strict and patriarchal the society there was." Recalling summer trips to Delhi to see family, she realized that in Bangalore "we lived in a very liberal society," saying:

> Nobody told us not to go somewhere or not to do something in Bangalore . . . you would go and meet your friends for a bit and maybe go out for a walk or just go and have an ice cream somewhere in some corner and do the normal things I think youngsters do.

Bhavna, who worked with her husband in their family business, made this declaration: "Bangalore was a paradise"—which was not as much of a stretch as one might imagine. News articles and features described Bangalore in ways that made it sound almost utopian and destined to become a global powerhouse. An article published in 1989 in the British newspaper the *Independent* described the city as one of the most "efficient and attractive major" cities in India. As the "home of the nascent computer industry, it also possesses fine parks and public buildings which have a curiously Tuscan appearance . . . [and that] combined with its vast symmetrical avenues make it feel like the Versailles of India."[9] While the women in this book spoke affectionately about the city, I doubt that any of us would have traded a trip to Tuscany or the real Versailles to stay in Bangalore, but the point was well made in the article that the city did have a specific charm and character to it.

The boarders in BGHS often returned to their families over vacations and as such had a bird's eye view of other cities during that timeframe. Kiara would reference this, as she lived with her parents in another state in between school terms: "Bangalore has been a slightly different animal compared to the rest of India." We will hear more from Nisha in forthcoming chapters; Nisha was also a boarder and would likewise say that Bangalore never struck her as being the most traditional of places: "It's a slightly more exceptional case. I'm not saying that it was all freedom but comparatively speaking, I think women and girls in Bangalore had it slightly easier in some ways." Oona, who spoke of her "progressive upbringing" and closeness with her father, argued that she thought, channeling her inner Dickens, that we had all lived in Bangalore "during some of the best times":

> It was such a great time because the country was opening up and we were teenagers and we were just getting out and discovering ourselves. I feel like that was a combination. . . . That's probably why I just feel like it was very magical.

Similar sentiments were shared by many of the women, conveying a realization that while Bangalore was different from other parts of the country, their own lives were also different as a result of living in Bangalore. "I think that's one thing that we learnt in Bangalore as a Bangalore girl," remarked Ahana, "just go out and achieve." Ahana and I had both lived outside of India before we came to Bangalore and enrolled in BGHS, an experience that drew us together. Harini, whom I remember as dependable and quiet in school and who had grown into a composed and confident woman, remembered being more aware of the rest of the world than most Indians seemed to be:

> Me and my friends and all of us, we had so much more exposure to the outside world. . . . We seemed to be more in tune with what was going on outside of the country [and that was the same for] some of the people I meet now who grew up during that same timeframe.

Amaya recalled being fifteen years old and enjoying the "golden days" of Bangalore, a judgment with which Daksha would probably concur. Both Amaya and Daksha were in the B section of BGHS, and talking to them as adults reminded me of how little their section and mine interacted, yet how similar our school experiences were.

> Bangalore gave a perfect balance of party-life and home environment. In a very nice way, you could go from one extreme or the other and it would be okay. It gave us the pub culture, it gave us the shopping culture. With the freedom of doing more, parents understood that there was a lot more to life than just being

too traditional, so they opened up a little bit more. . . . It was vibrant, colorful. There was a sense of belonging.

As an aspirational city, Bangalore was in a hurry. Entrepreneurs found creative ways to start a business. From little video stores that rented out bootlegged copies of *Dirty Dancing* and *Top Gun*, to corner shops where you could get a little box of apple juice and a sleeve of chocolate chip cookies while you waited for the bus, people were hustling. As the girls left BGHS and went on to junior college, many of the parents would invest in a "two-wheeler," a moped or small scooter that the girls used to get to their classes. I had what was called a "TVS 50" and would frequently have two girls riding pillion with me on the narrow seat. Saira talked about the standard "Scooty" that was popular in 1992 and that she rode. The mopeds offered freedom and access. Once you were out of the house, you and your friends could head off anywhere, with anyone, and how you spent your free time was a central aspect of growing up in Bangalore at the time—including where you got a bite to eat and drink.

"MEET ME AT CASA'S"

I should have realized early on that in talking to the girls about Bangalore, we would spend an inordinate amount of time talking about food. I had not specifically raised the topic, yet it was fascinating to see how many conversations veered toward and stayed focused on meals and eating out. One café was brought up by almost every single woman I spoke with. While I knew this café was popular, I had not realized how central it was to such a diverse group of my former classmates. The little bistro, Casa Piccola, was nestled in the bottom floor of a three-story building on busy Residency Road. "Casa's," as we affectionately called it, was centrally located near about a half dozen major schools of the time, and students could easily walk there after school to grab a milkshake or a bite to eat. And because it was mostly converted retail space, there was indoor and outdoor eating spaces that were not separate. When Casa's was closed for the night, the owners just pulled down the shutters like one closed a garage, but the outside space was still accessible so we often could stay on for hours after it closed for the evening.

When Casa's closed in 2012, after nearly thirty-five years in business, it made the national newspaper. The *Times of India* reported on the outsized influence this tiny café had on the lives of a generation of teenagers in Bangalore:

Casa Piccola was an everyday chillout zone. A second home, as many like to call it. "Casa's was our favorite haunt in the 80s," says Reshma Gowda, 41, an ex-Cottonian [a student at Bishop Cotton Girls School] and media professional. "Downtown had few options for burgers and Italian food back then, so we converged there in large groups, or when on a date, and even to plot and plan for some inter-school competition. In the late 80s, a couple of bearers [waiters] from the boarding school joined Casa's, which meant we were always served first and we believed bigger helpings too! The Sloppy Joe burger, which came with a little bowl of mayonnaise, was hugely popular." Casa Piccola's piping hot cappuccino, with a dollop of whipped cream sprinkled with cinnamon, and its lemon iced tea, have also been big draws.[10]

The article and the woman quoted in it, Reshma Gowda, highlight three key aspects of life for young Bangaloreans in the late 1980s and early 1990s. First, India had still not opened itself up to the types of foreign investments that spurred growth in the later 1990s and 2000s, but the small city had already turned its attention to a more global world. Casa's blended a cosmopolitan cuisine with an Indian palate and was ready to introduce young people to Indian versions of (spicy) Sloppy Joes and spaghetti Bolognese, profiteroles, and the uniquely constructed dish of half grilled chicken salad and half burger, which was appropriately named the "Grilled UFO." Second, dating, while frowned on in much of India, was not seen as a taboo. There were many locations where young couples went to share an ice cream or milkshake on a first date. Third, interschool competitions were popular. These contests were held all over the country, not just in Bangalore, and facilitated a more dynamic learning environment. They helped to build the confidence of a generation of young people through interschool dramatics, debates, quizzes, and sports events.

Faye connected Bangalore's food obsession with the energy of the city. Talking about a local restaurant, she said:

Just the smell of that place was like a little bit of freedom. [Bangalore] was very much a café culture before we knew what a café culture was. That you just go sit there, you hang out. You chatted. Like we went to Mac's for excitement, but we went to Casa's to hang out and chat and to have their coffee or milkshakes. And the fries were good.

Middle-class girls in Bangalore were well aware that they enjoyed an unusually high level of freedom as compared to girls elsewhere in India. As Ela recalled, "You just could throw yourself into whatever it was that you were passionate about. Whether you wanted to start a club about something [you could]." She goes on to say:

There were some things that were so typically Bangalore in the sense, whether it was going to watch a movie at Galaxy or whether it was going to Corner House or whether it was going to Casa Piccola, for us growing up, down the road from it. And at the same time, I think what Bangalore did really well for me growing up was the balance between the traditional and you still have the rest of the world right there at your doorstep in the sense that you could go get an *MTR idli* [steamed rice cake] and then you could go have a burger.

While eating out was not our only diversion, it clearly was a central component of my classmates' memories. It was not that the girls recalled different places but that the recollections overlapped to a striking extent, with the same types of experiences and similar descriptions cropping up again and again. Many of the girls, for instance, would recall the taste of the store-made mayonnaise at "Indiana's" that was served with the burgers, and, of course, ice cream.

Bangalore had a strong culture of "going out to get ice cream." On warm summer nights, generations of families piled into a car and headed to the main city promenade, Mahatma Gandhi Road, or MG Road, which was wide, brightly lit, and well paved, with shops and restaurants lining one side and the army barracks and grounds on the other. This was the road that national parades went down and dignitaries traveled on every visit to Bangalore. On MG Road, Chit Chat and Lakeview Ice Cream Parlor allowed you to park your car outside. When you rolled down your window, a waiter affixed a stainless steel tray to the side to bring you your order. Eating ice cream in the car with your cousins and aunts and grandparents was a familiar treat for many of the women. My grandfather, in his Fiat Premier, would take his daughter, daughter-in-law, and four grandchildren out after school frequently, and for many families, it was a Sunday evening tradition, a cheap diversion in a growing city.

Some places were illustrative of being "in the know" if you were a real Bangalorean. Koshy's remains one of those places, well known to most "true" Bangaloreans. A simple place that brought a wide variety of people across social classes together, Koshy's served cheap food and good coffee, and there were no frills other than the distinctive uniforms of the waiters, many of whom had served generations of families. Koshy's was the kind of place where you could not be pretentious, but just by being there you felt like you belonged to a special group of people. Local newspaper offices were nearby, and you could eavesdrop on journalists discussing politics; it was a pitstop for local theater groups after rehearsals; and there was always a group of retirees reading their papers. Urmi recalled:

It was very Bangalore in, in some sense, right? Because the menu was very Western except for the *dosas* [rice pancakes with potato filling] that you would get. And the waiters were still dressed in . . . I'm sure it's uncomfortable now . . . they were still dressed in their white outfit with that cap. Somehow the era, these old chairs, these wooden benches, it didn't have the frills of a very hep [fashionable] restaurant, but it had a very old Bangalore crowd which used to rotate through. So you really had to know that place to go there; you needed to be from Bangalore to go to Koshy's.

India's diversity is embodied in multiple ways, but especially through the types of clothes people wear, the different dialects they speak, and the many holidays they celebrate. But most representative of that diversity is the culture of food. In Bangalore as a whole, and in BGHS in particular, students reflected a wide variety of backgrounds and cultures. Many of the women talked about celebrating Christmas at school, going home to celebrate Diwali, and then eating biryani at a Muslim friend's house at the celebration of Eid. And as they went from one feast to another, they would display a familiarity with a variety of languages, not least English, which felt to them like Bangalore's lingua franca.

"SWITCHING FROM ONE LANGUAGE TO THE NEXT"

Language played a critical role in leveling the playing field for the diverse Bangalore middle-class population. Although the state language was Kannada, the student population at Baldwins was made up of girls who spoke many other languages in their families, ranging from Tamil to Telegu, Punjabi, Gujarati, Marathi, Hindi, and Urdu. Ela recalled, "I grew up also speaking Kannada and Tamil, [and] there was nothing, absolutely no difference in like at one moment switching from one language to the next." Even so, it was English that was the unifying language of middle-class Bangalore. As Ela went on to say:

English was such a big part of how we grew up. . . . Most people grew up with that sort of education, even people older than us or even our parents . . . so English was so commonly spoken. I grew up speaking English with my sister. . . . In those days, everybody, even auto [rickshaw] drivers or whatever, had some grasp of English—enough to get by. And I think Bangalore was quite different like that in the sense that it just was easy to experience all these things, without it seeming elitist.

Part of this had to do with the education that students received in convent and missionary schools. Ahana talked about the importance of "elocution," an old-fashioned word today that describes the "skill of clear and expressive speech, especially of distinct pronunciation and articulation."[11] The schools hosted elocution contests, and thirty-plus years later, BGHS graduates still find it impossible to forget the words of certain pieces of poetry memorized and elocuted. Popular pieces included T.S. Eliot's *Macavity: The Mystery Cat* and *Let My Country Awake* by Indian poet Rabrindranath Tagore. Ahana shared:

> We thought [we had] good accents and, and a lot of people, when I speak to anywhere in the world, they're like, "Okay, you're Indian, but you've got such a neutral accent and you know, are you sure you're Indian? Okay. Is it your first language?" So we don't realize it, that English is so important and it helps us a lot. For example, here I'm in China and the Chinese are so clever and everything, but their main disadvantage is English, they can't go all over the world. So for us, yeah, English is a big advantage and somehow they [the teachers at the school] managed to give us that neutral English accent.

It was not just the fluency but also the tenor and the accent that the convent schools developed. While there are important critiques that address the colonizing aspects of ensuring that Indian students learned and spoke English,[12] it is hard to deny that this has helped to give Bangalore its enduring cosmopolitan profile and its openness to people from not just other parts of the country but also other parts of the world. Parul recalled how, despite her parents being conservative, she and her sister would be jabbering away in English until they arrived home. That was when they would slip back to speaking in Tamil. Yashika was certain that her love of language came from her education at BGHS. Farida mentioned the teachers' preoccupation with spelling, adding, "I loved school for things like the choir, and the fact that we all learned such high English, . . . so that was a very cool thing."

While it might be easy to discount this attention to teaching a certain kind of English as a facet of education in a convent school, the reality is that Bangalore had a largely literate population in either English or Kannada. There were daily and weekly publications that provided people with analysis on current news and events that provided people a common understanding of issues and topics. The commitment of parents to send their children to school ensured that most students were taught English as either a first or second language. The national language, Hindi, was far less popular, and although people enjoyed Bollywood movies, Bangalore had at least six movie theaters in the city center that featured a steady stream of Hollywood films. English was generally far more popular in Bangalore than Hindi, and this was the case across all socioeconomic levels. Part of this access was the culture of reading that was fostered by bookstores and libraries across the city.

"SCORE SOME BOOKS"

From the imposing red-painted Central Library in the heart of the city, located amid the greenery of Cubbon Park, to the many local libraries and bookstores, most people had access to affordable reading material. By the mid-1980s, the city was expanding and even new neighborhoods or outlying city "extensions"[13] had local lending libraries and almost all of the social clubs in the city had a reading room with a chance to borrow books, which might range from the latest political biographies to cheesy Mills and Boon romance novels. The 1989 *Independent*'s description of Bangalore alluded both to the rejuvenating rains of the monsoon and to the eclectic nature of the books one could find in the city's bookstores:

> The day we arrived it was raining heavily—a good excuse to explore the local bookshops with their extraordinarily diverse stock. Where else in the world could you purchase a first edition of the collected works of the British painter Paul Nash, a six months' old copy of *Tatler*, plus not one but two books about [British MP] Ken Livingstone?[14]

Reminiscing about the city, the women I spoke to seldom needed prompting to talk about reading and books. Almost every one of the women returned to a memory that was grounded in reading books. Zara was succinct: "Reading was a big thing for me, I loved reading. I got a lot of joy if I could go to the library and score some books." Ela described weekly visits to the Bowring Institute library with her father:

> It [had] really high ceilings with shelves that went all the way to the top, really musty old books in the really old library. There were these really big heavy double doors, and the minute you went in, it's like the rest of the world disappeared. And my dad would let me spend almost an hour wandering around all the different books, read bits, whatever, you know. And they used to have lists of the recent books that they'd got. So I'd love that. And they'd always have a shelf, by the librarian with books that people had just returned. So I always was curious to see what people had been reading. And yeah, if there was anything there that interested me and the fact that if a book was really popular, you had to put your name down and get on a list and get it. It was just so quiet and I just remember, it's not like my dad and I talked while we were in there much, because it was so quiet, but it just was something that I looked forward to. And there was just like this whole world of books and I could get into those worlds.

BGHS itself had a large library, and a few of the girls recalled the influence it had on them. Kiara, who lived like other boarders in the hostel on the grounds of the school, was able to access the school library after school hours. She recalled:

> I remember the library hours after school. I don't think that day scholars had access to the library after school, but I read some of the most amazing books as a young girl. I was very impish, all the impressions of life and love and mystery and murder and everything else came from the librarian introducing us to those books.

Farida also credited the school for fueling her love for books:

> I took a lot of refuge in books, and I read a lot. So I think books for me were like a window to a world that I could enter. I don't know how I was going to do it, because I was academically really poor in school, I think the saving grace was books. So I think that was my first step towards some sort of glimmer of hope that I could better my life in some way, but I just didn't know how; it took me a long time to figure it out.

I had not known how much Farida had struggled in school, which she shared in greater detail as she talked about her memories of one of our teachers reading aloud to us:

> She would sometimes read out stories to us, and for me that was my love, the written word and books and history, but I was never encouraged in that direction, so it was all so confusing for me. I thought that everything I wanted was wrong. Everything I did was wrong. And my dream in life was to be able to buy a book in Higginbothams one day, just to go in there and buy a book—it was just like this book paradise.

One interesting aspect of the memories the women shared about the love they had for reading was the role their fathers played. Ela's recollections of visiting the Bowring Library with her father were echoed by Saira, who recalled her father taking his children with him when he went to a bookstore to buy business magazines. He would then allow them to choose two books a week, including, as she excitedly recalled, "Even comics! . . . So we would all pick up whatever we want. And then from there we would go for dinner." Lipika had similar memories:

> Every weekend, he would take us out to Premier bookstore and buy us a book each, my sister and me, and we used to go somewhere to have a snack, usually it used to be that little place on Double Road. I think getting to choose a book every weekend was very, very special. And even when my cousins came over and all that, even if we just stepped out for a movie or something, [we would

always end the outing going back] to a bookstore and pick up books. It could be
Strand or it could be Premier. One of those bookstores.

This is not to say that mothers did not encourage reading, but many of the
women I spoke with specifically identified their fathers as the primary sup-
porter. I wondered if this reflected the fact that their fathers were the family's
primary breadwinners and the decision makers on what to do with disposable
income or if this paternal support stemmed from many fathers in Bangalore
having nontraditional notions of what their daughters could or could not do.

In all these stories, the women recalled their girlhood as a time when
they were comfortable in the public spaces of their lives. The city was a
stage where props and backdrops played central aspects of their memories.
And as they navigated their lives in these spaces, they clearly did so with
self-confidence and style. They possessed a sense of independence and
agency that was fostered by their access to spaces in the city where they could
be among friends—and among a wider circle of their peers, even if they were
not known to one another directly. It often did not matter who was on the
outside looking in. This notion of "witnessing" feels different as we look at
the private spaces the women inhabited, which, while more intimate, could
also be, paradoxically, more limiting, in part due to the structures of gender,
class, and religion structures exerted control over their lives.

Chapter 3

School, Home, and God

Girls in Private Spaces

On Bangalore's public stage, the girls enjoyed many of the same experiences, but in the privacy of their homes, their experiences could differ significantly. Each girl's upbringing was shaped by numerous influences, the most salient of which seem to have been the state from which the girl's family moved to Bangalore, the religion the family practiced, the girl's birth order within her family, the roles of her parents both in the home and in their professions, and whether the family was a multigenerational household or a nuclear family. It is in the family that Madanipour describes one aspect of the private space we inhabit. He talks about private space as "part of life that is under the control of the individual in a personal capacity, outside public observation and knowledge or state and official control . . . a sphere of freedom of choice . . . protected from the external gaze."[1] The private space encompasses the judgment of others, but how we navigate that judgment depends on the safety we feel in that space. It also, according to Madanipour, encompasses the space in our minds and what we think about ourselves and how we engage with the world through our imagination. The body, the mind, home, friends, faith, and family are all components of this private space, and while there are fewer external eyes on the individual in these spaces, the space foregrounds both our emotions and our psyches. We are constantly making adjustments back and forth between public and private spaces, because what happens in one space can influence how one behaves in the other space and vice versa.

The public spaces in which my classmates grew up in Bangalore were enthusiastically and lovingly recalled as places where they were free to enjoy themselves and what the city offered, but their memories of private spaces were more nuanced. As the yin to the yang of the public space, private spaces are more personal, more intimate, less self-confident, less brightly lit. For teenage girls growing up in Bangalore in the latter years of the twentieth century, they were spaces within which one grappled with one's insecurities and fears while navigating adolescence amid changing times.

The interactions between the public and private spaces exert pressure on expectations on how girlhood is characterized both privately and publicly. Behaving according to social norms and expectations and aligning oneself to the hopes and aspirations of the family are all aspects of how girls are raised.[2] Understanding how the girls engaged with their families, teachers, friends, and religion allows us to understand how they were processing their experiences in private spaces.

Also of interest is how they built bridges between private and public spaces. In that respect, a remark that Kiara made is illuminating. When I asked her what her favorite memories were of growing up in Bangalore, she said, "It's Casa Piccola. I mean, I spent all my time in college sitting at this table. It has to be Casa Piccola and the flower shop and the Sloppy Joes and the many, many sundaes and the soda pops we had." This was her description of how she used the public space. During our conversation, her voice trailed off, she became quiet, and that was when the private space—the influence of the bistro on her mind—emerged: "Yeah, I think it was exciting to be sitting there. It was fashionable to be sitting there, if we had money or no money, the friendships and the memories I have of Casa Piccola [are] solving life's problems all around the pizza."[3]

Solving life's problems around a pizza is a poignant image of adolescence and of the tension between one's emerging public and private selves. For many of these young women, their lives were markedly different both from their parents' lives and from the lives of girls growing up at the same time elsewhere in India. Bangalore's relatively cosmopolitan energy and comparative freedom of movement and thought influenced not only how the city's middle-class young women behaved in public spaces but also how they comported themselves in their private spaces.

THE MYTH AND POWER OF THE ADOLESCENT GIRL

Developmentally, adolescent girls are particularly vulnerable to pressures that are exerted on them by family and society.[4] For much of human history, the marginalization of adolescent girls in most cultures has resulted in limited access to and opportunity within most domains, from education to healthcare and jobs.[5] Since the 1980s, however, as adolescent girls around the world have gained access to education, their roles and positions in families and society have shifted and evolved.[6] While efforts to enhance the status of girls has been growing, and despite the efforts of local and national governments, and international agencies such as UNICEF and UNESCO,[7] there still remain numerous obstacles, both tangible and intangible, that narrow the opportunities for girls' education, empowerment, and success.[8] Over the past thirty years, international organizations and governments have argued that education can lift many forms of historic limitations placed on girls. With girls such as Malala Yousafzai and Greta Thunberg more recently spearheading global campaigns around education and activism, the belief that education for girls is a silver bullet is rapidly spreading. During the past two decades, corporations have launched marketing campaigns that fuel this belief—campaigns such as Nike's "The Girl Effect,"[9] which claims that "adolescent girls have the power to end world poverty."[10] The idea that girls can help reshape their societies has been embraced by many people, and many middle-class women in developing countries such as India have found that to be a resonant and powerful message. Understandably, adolescent girls themselves have responded particularly strongly to the message, seeing themselves as poised to make a difference to globalizing world.

In the United States, researchers have been accused of missing certain signs of economic growth in the post–World War II period by ignoring the significance of the cultural and economic power that girls were acquiring in a deepening and widening consumer culture.[11] By the later decades of the twentieth century, the power wielded by girls was mostly evident within the middle class. For instance, as girls entered mid- to late adolescence, middle-class parents became more amenable to giving not just their sons but also their daughters a weekly or monthly allowance. Middle-class families were also likely to educate their children about how to handle the financial side of their lives.[12] Equipped with an allowance and greater financial awareness, middle-class girls were becoming a source of significant purchasing power,[13] and companies were taking note. In Bangalore, the late 1980s and the 1990s saw new ways for girls to spend their disposable income. These private changes thus impacted how girls engaged in public as well as private spaces.

Adolescent girls were also learning to see their fathers in new roles. As households adapted to the new dynamics of the city, there was an increase in the number of nuclear families.[14] This led to more intimate family interactions undiluted by interactions across three or four generations. With no grandparents, aunts, uncles, or cousins living together in the same household, family dynamics shifted. Mothers were often homemakers and a constant presence in the house, but what the women in this book call attention to is the overall involvement and influence of their fathers in their lives.

Most of the fathers of the girls who went to BGHS worked in business, banking, healthcare, government, or engineering. A few were doctors. The women would often mention the roles their fathers played in their lives; these recollections were almost always affectionate and were occasionally poignant, especially when a daughter recalled that, because she had had no brothers, her father would teach her the kinds of things that he would otherwise have taught his son. For adolescent girls, this transference offered a chance to engage in activities and have experiences that might not have been the norm for other girls.

In this period of life, where an individual is more socially conscious than at any other point in their lives, friendships can have positive and negative ramifications. Adolescent friendships can "buffer against hardships in other areas of life."[15] In private spaces, the relationships between a girl and her friends are complicated and nuanced. School friendships are layered with dichotomous moments where a friendship can signify moments of support and competition, envy and generosity, and solidarity and division within the span of a single day. Religion is either embraced or rejected, and school is a space that helps you begin to define who you are and what you think about as you dream of the future. At Baldwins, girls were offered many opportunities to better themselves through music, performing and visual arts, sports, and academics. These opportunities could often define your own sense of failure or success. How you navigated through those emotions would lead to your own sense of self-worth and value for both yourself and your family.

A WELL-ROUNDED GIRL IN A WELL-ROUNDED SCHOOL

One of the ways the women framed their adolescence was through the prism of their experiences in BGHS. With sixty girls in a class section who usually stayed together through their six years in the high school, and with the same teachers working with the girls from grades 5 through 10, BGHS was an insular community, with a cast of characters that seldom changed, including the school watchman and the office staff. Arriving at school on foot, by bicycle, in a rickshaw, or in a car, a girl would begin a busy school day. Between nine class periods, chapel services, a short recess, a brief lunch break, and extracurricular activities before and after school, the school worked hard to ensure that its students would graduate as well-rounded women.

Every morning began (religiously) with chapel service, which was held either with the whole high school in the imposing Montgomery Hall, or in classrooms (on Tuesdays), or with your house (Thursdays). Hymns were sung based on the season, and a local pastor might visit. Not infrequently, a class was entrusted with designing a service for the rest of the school. In the final chapel service delivered by the girls of the Class of 1989, the fairy queen bestowed gifts on her most favored acolytes—gifts such as confidence, wisdom, sensibility, talent, and kindness—as a lesson in making the most of new beginnings. The ideas for such morality plays were often inspired by adventure and mystery novels we would read, tales of girls who were plucky and independent with strong ethical cores, penned by the likes of Louisa May Alcott, Jane Austen, Enid Blyton, and Carolyn Keene. Ginny recalled:

> I remember a lot of the assemblies and we would get a lot of freedom to run the assemblies in the way we wanted. Of course the content was overall overseen by a teacher to make sure it was not inappropriate . . . but otherwise we had the freedom. We had to do it in between our studies and practices, figure out what play, what messaging you wanted to convey.

After-school sports and band practices kept girls on campus. During the sports season, students marched and marched and marched again around the field practicing being in perfect unison for the Annual Sports Day celebrations. Anything could get you into trouble, even the length of your socks (which had to be precisely shin high). For some girls, this discipline provided a sense of security. For others, it fed a sense of deep claustrophobia. Faye called it a "police state." Oona expanded:

> I'm giving them the benefit of the doubt, but that's what I mean, the focus on things that don't matter, like your socks have to be certain length and your hair can't be on your face and your hair always has to be tied up this way or just the length of your uniform. Like how does it matter in the long run? It doesn't matter!

Up until the late 1990s, the majority of Indian schools followed one of three curricula. As mentioned in the introduction, there were the state board exams, the central board exams, and the Indian School Certificate Examinations board (ICSE), which was considered the most challenging and prestigious of the three. BGHS was an ICSE school, and Juhi spoke of the value she felt she derived from studying in that system:

> In terms of the curriculum, I think ICSE was . . . phenomenal, like almost like a blank [rich] slate of ideas and things to do, because I mean, I subsequently looked at the CBSE (central board) books and I looked at the O-level books and I'm just like, seriously! . . . [It was] not as challenging as ICSE.

She felt that the ICSE "boards" prepared her well for her future, especially in terms of helping her with subjects such as physics and chemistry in which she was less confident.

Ela spent nearly eleven years at BGHS, from nursery school until tenth grade. She talked about how the school had given her a sense of belonging: she felt that she knew everyone, was a part of everything, and carried the traditions of the school with her: "Everything that went with it, the badges, the houses, it was just something that you were a part of. And I think Baldwins was all that." Many of the girls spoke of the rich culture of music in the school, from the choir to the band, which was run by the kindly but fierce Mr. Mitchell, the only male teacher in the school. Ela recalled: "The music at Baldwins was amazing. I don't know whether we fully appreciated what we got compared to most other people . . . but it was just so many things that were so particular to Baldwins and you just took for granted." Yet in Bangalore at the time, the kind of education that Baldwins and similar local schools offered did not seem as privileged as it was:

> I think because there were so many schools like that, whether it was Bishop Cottons or Sacred Hearts, there were so many schools that offered you a similar kind of education. And I think for middle-class kids, that was what it is . . . a difference in the kind of education we had, but there was so many of us, it didn't seem like an elite few.

Memories of school are colored by the personal experiences one had as a student. For several, school was a secure cocoon, a place of solace and refuge. For Lipika, who has daughters who have also attended BGHS, this sense has endured over the decades since she left Baldwins: "It's a place to run back to. I feel like a child, the moment I'm inside the gates, it doesn't matter if I'm approaching fifty now. It really feels good that there's some place to go."

Waida's perspective was a little more nuanced:

> I always felt I really wanted to finish school and get out, you know, to be free. It felt too strict at times. Like everything is very organized and everything had a very rigid schedule from sports day to everything, the lessons and chapel and everything, if you think of all the different aspects on the academic side, they just drove us to the end. And we would always wait, "God, OK when would exams be over?" and we would be finished with school and be out. But as the years go by, you realize how special and how important that is, what they gave us. If they haven't given us that strong foundation, I don't think we would have been where we are now.

Part of the notion of being a well-rounded girl meant that teachers ruled students with an iron fist. There were a thousand ways to get into trouble because there were a thousand rules to follow. Much of this had to do with ensuring an equitable learning environment for all the students. Because the girls came from economically, culturally, and socially diverse backgrounds, there seemed a logic to the wearing of uniforms in ensuring both the modesty of the girls as well as ensuring that economic differences between them were not made evident in their choices of clothes. The base uniform was an ink blue pinafore, with a crisp, short-sleeved, buttoned white shirt. A school tie and belt completed the ensemble. In addition, there were prescribed sweaters, shoes, hair ribbons, and, as mentioned earlier, even sock lengths. Notebooks were to be covered with brown paper, and there were rules on comportment, demeanor, and classroom practices such as standing up every time the teacher walked into the room. Maybe it was the way in which teachers and administrators exercised control over the students that made many of the women remember the ways in which they were reprimanded. In hindsight, the women contextualized their little rebellions, wondering why what today might have felt like a minor infraction provoked such harsh punishments. In recalling their school years, many of the women returned to the ways in which they got into trouble for breaking both stated and unstated school rules. Faye wonders:

> We were really good students. I mean, in the grand scheme of things, we didn't get into a lot of trouble. We weren't on drugs, we weren't drinking, we weren't really skipping class either. What were we doing? I don't know why we were in so much trouble all the time?

Ginny remembered the frequent rule breakers differently. "There were a couple of us who were deemed as rowdy probably, like living as the borderline outlaw." She remembers the girls who would frequently get called to the principal's office and could have been seen as part of this group of "outlaws":

> So anything that we did, we would get called up for, anything. Sometimes a bit unfairly, but I think they just felt that if they didn't control our behaviors, we might just live the fast life or something. So I remember getting into trouble, sometimes silly reasons. I remember that as well as the stress that one went through to say, "Sorry, sorry, sorry," over [and over again].

What was the trouble that the girls got into? One recalled wearing the wrong sweater to school on a cold day, another spoke of bringing the popular photo romance magazines[16] to school, and others reminisced about sock infractions. None spoke of forgetting homework assignments or failing tests, but the policing of behaviors out of compliance with strict school dress and comportment rules was frequent.

Because our teachers, an almost completely female teaching body, taught us the same subject year after year, it created a level of fascination by the girls about the teachers and their lives. From imagining tragic and broken romances for older, unmarried teachers, to expressing a sense of admiration for those who were younger and more independent, recollections of teachers were typically affectionate and tinged with a slight sense of awe. Ahana said this about the teachers:

We were never specifically told, you have to be a strong woman and you have to fend for yourself. But maybe by watching all of them, we all saw that they were very strong women. So maybe that's why all of us were taught not to fuss. You know, if you see other girls [in other schools], the girls were a little more delicate. It was less fuss in our school. You don't wear fancy things, we couldn't even tie our sweaters around our waist. They never came out and said, "Okay, I'm managing on my own." I never ever heard any sob stories from anywhere. Although they must have had difficult times. But you never heard any of that. All we saw was a woman here, doing her job, teaching us. And somehow it got into our minds that that's what women do, right? They're doing everything at home and then they're also teaching.

These memories stayed with the women long after they had left BGHS, coloring—as is clear in subsequent chapters—their attitudes to education in contemporary Bangalore.

CIRCLES OF TRUST

A city is made up of trillions of interactions between people every day. Most of our interactions happen in our homes and with a small circle of people we trust. Far fewer interactions happen in public spaces. In talking about these intimate interactions, the women share how they related to others in those immediate circles, primarily with friends and parents. The women also mentioned their growing interest in boys but from more of a distance because most of this would have to do with teenage infatuations. Relationships with friends and parents played a more central role for all of these women.

In terms of friends, most recollections centered on school. Because the girls came to BGHS from all corners of the city, there was often little or no time after school or over weekends to meet with friends, so the girls had to make the most of their time in school. The biggest chunk of time that the girls would spend time with their friends was during the lunch period at BGHS. School friendships were defined by the lunch hour, which was a time of freedom with limited oversight by otherwise ever-present teachers. Boarders returned to their dining room to have their meals, but day scholars from nursery school to tenth grade were released for lunch at the same time to eat anywhere on the sprawling school campus. A few had a hot lunch from home that was delivered fresh at the lunch hour, while others would bring a packed lunch. I would usually have a traditional dish made with rice and yogurt, and more often that I can remember, the lid of my lunch box would loosen and I would arrive in school with the smell of yogurt and cilantro emanating from my bookbag. The open lunch period meant that little girls often tagged along behind big sisters and their friends. Groups would find and maintain control over a lunch spot, oftentimes for years. If you moved to a new group or blended two groups, lunch spots would shift, but for the most part these locations stayed static. Waida usually got a hot lunch from home, and she loved sharing it with her friends. Brinda ate with two groups, remembering they frequently just stood and ate so they could finish quickly and then talk and play without disturbance.

Harini said:

> I think that with everything that we used to go through in a day, that was something we always looked forward to, that lunch time. It was just us, whether it was sharing food, or [being] interested to see who's brought what, or the conversations we've had, and ideas that we would come up with, and what we need to do over the weekend, or someone's birthday, or whatever it is. I think that is something that I always remember, the lunch time.

With the school emphasizing the importance of each girl finding a niche or developing a talent, it was no surprise that many of the girls had an aptitude for a particular activity. This could be in sports, student government, academics, music, literature, debate, or, as mentioned in chapter 2, elocution and recitation. Bhavna proudly recalled the abilities to be found within her circle of friends:

> I was in this group where everybody was the best in something. One was the best in debate, the other best in English, others best in whatever, whatever. And I remember all of us got 96/100 in computer science in our pre-boards and the teacher came and told us that we were the best batch that she's ever taught. And we were on a level above normal and she sees big things for us. And we had a photo shoot of all of us together, which I still have. And to me that's most memorable because I realized how lucky I was.

Unfortunately, the system was harsh for struggling students, weeding out those who did not meet the school's standards. In their academics, students would have to pass a challenging annual exam to prepare them to take the national board exams at the end of grade 10. These boards would combine results from over twelve different exams, and so every year, students had one week of examinations, with a dozen "papers to sit for." If a girl did not pass two "papers," she was held back. If she did not pass a second time after being held back, she had to leave the school. These painful memories of this sort of trauma were challenging for girls when they remembered friends they had to say goodbye to along the way. Removal from school not only inflicted shame on the girl who failed too many exams but also created a sense of disloyalty and humiliation for everyone who remained. But as Zara remembered, there were few opportunities to reflect on one's social and emotional health, and many of these anxieties were glossed over.

Across the board, the women spoke of their parents as protective but not stifling. Many women were appreciative of their parents making the decision to send them to BGHS. Kiara said:

> I remember before coming [to] Bangalore, it was quite a struggle for them financially to be able to afford to send me to Baldwins and by some good fortune [they could make it happen]. . . . But I also remember my parents talking about how they'd made the right choice because they were giving me the right kind of atmosphere to grow up in.

In a similar vein, Parul remembered that when her parents arrived in Bangalore, one of her aunts was adamant that her parents needed to send their daughters to a convent school: "They [her uncle and aunt] were the ones who told my mom, 'Why are you putting your children in such a small [local/unimpressive] school? Better to put them in a good school.'"

As mentioned earlier, many of the girls recalled their fathers teaching them to be independent. According to Oona, her father "brought my sister and me up like boys. . . . He took us out and told us to drive when we were fifteen, when we were not supposed to be driving. He made us always open the garage door . . . fix our flat tires ourselves . . . that's how he brought us up." Oona's family, South Indian by heritage with two professional parents and two daughters, was different from Saira's family, which was North Indian by heritage and which included brothers and a stay-at-home mother. Yet she too recalled her father saying to her, "If you want to learn how to drive a car, you have to learn how to change a punctured tire." She learned, thinking that she needed to do that "because I was the oldest. . . . So I was the boy of the house. I would drive the car."

Harini's description of her parents echoed many of the women's memories:

> My parents did give me a lot of independence, which I think was a good thing because that made me realize my own boundaries as to what I should or shouldn't do. And they always encouraged me to travel, go somewhere, go to meet friends, and things like that. I didn't really feel restricted, I think that's probably the word I was looking for, restricted, during that time. And I think that's important.

As with the conversations about food described in the previous chapter, I did not ask any questions specifically about relationships and dating, but the subject nonetheless often came up. This was a topic that I had thought might have been limited to a few girls, but to my surprise, a significant number of the women talked about how they interacted with boys despite the limitations of school, parents, and society. Our parents were generally unconcerned if their daughters talked with boys outside and in public places, but we seldom entertained these same boys in our homes or introduced them to our families. Girls and boys might ride home together on the public buses, meet at the local shopping square, or catch each others' eyes in the neighborhood ice cream parlor. More than that was usually off limits. Nonetheless, this was a more progressive attitude than found in other cities, where girls and boys might not be permitted even these sorts of interactions. A few girls might go to the local disco with girlfriends but hope to meet with a group of male friends while there. Ahana noted that there was nothing taboo about these sorts of friendships in general in the city:

> After class, we would be at the parks or in the neighborhood, you know, wherever all the girls and boys would meet, boys and girls would be together. There was nothing like, "Don't talk to boys" or anything. I mean, of course, at the beginning they were like, "You can't have a boyfriend" and everything, but I mean those were just things they said. And all of us grew up very freely.

The boarders were tightly chaperoned. Girls who stayed at BGHS could not receive letters from boys or have male visitors unless they were family members, and boarders were not permitted to leave the school grounds other than once a month, and even then only with tight restrictions on what time they could leave and what time they returned. Despite such strict rules, even the boarders remembered their interest in boys. Kiara recalled: "The church was a very important part of our Sunday life. So that was the time we could meet boys." She paused to correct herself: "*See* boys, *not* meet. . . . We were quite shy, but excited about seeing Baldwin boys on the other side of aisle. They [the girls] made a big deal about it because both schools[17] . . . had to sing songs together, which I thought was really silly."

Ginny reflected on how girls who were immature navigated around the school's attempts to suppress any interest in boys:

> You know how strict Baldwins was about these things. So any little thing of "He stared at me" was a topic to talk about for that day. It sounds ridiculous now, but that was then. So let's say when [we got out] and we could be in someone's house, let's say it was Rita's house, because she had parents who give much more freedom. It was a great home to be in. So, we would hang out. Then five or six of us, you'd just take a random [phone] number, then you will dial it and whoever picks up, say some random things like, "Where's your son? Do you have a son?" And then, of course it was all about boys. And then that person will say yes or no. And then you'll say, "How old is he?" or "Can I date him?" or some dumb thing like that. And then there was one lady who actually gave a good answer back. I mean, she must've been a little older than us, a young

mother or something. She said, "Really, you want to date my son? He's only five." So, yeah. Like I said, it sounds terribly lame now, but that was one awesome memory.

Darika looked back appreciatively on what she regarded as "simpler" times: "I think it was a different time because we didn't have boyfriends . . . it was just us girls and we went to a girl's school and things were simpler. It was just easy. Nothing complicated about it." Faye's recollections resonated with Darika's words:

> I think about how there were no boys and how lucky we were that there were no boys and how much we resented it at the time, but what a great chance it gave us to form like really good, solid, strong friendships and not have to think too much about the way we look or the way we act or waste time wondering who likes us or who doesn't like us. We did plenty of that, but can you imagine if boys were actually in the class?

One troubling memory that the women raised was how often, as teenagers in Bangalore, they were exposed to harassment in public spaces,[18] and how they would avoid, deflect, or try to ignore such unwelcome behavior. While many of the women commented on the dramatic changes around women's personal security that occurred in subsequent decades, their recollections of harassment—of assaults on the private self in the public space—when they were girls were colored more by annoyance than fear. Girls would talk about harassment with their friends, especially because parents, teachers, and other trusted adults did not invite such conversations. This reluctance may have stemmed from parents' assuming that their daughters were too immature or innocent for a frank conversation about sex, or it may have simply reflected the parents' disinclination to talk about such matters. Jasmine recalled:

> We realized there are many instances where, because we are not told these things, but you had experiences. where people like touched you in a funny way or something like that, maybe in a public place or a private place or something like that. Like even in your home or something. You don't know who to talk to and you never go back to your parents for it . . . then you confide in your friends. [Today] you understand and you kind of build your guard and you learn automatically [not to put yourself in that situation again].

Chaya told the story of how she had returned from a trip at 2:00 a.m. She was dropped off by the bus near the school to walk back to her home, which was a five-minute walk away. She remembers "this guy coming on a bike. . . . I think he just thought I was like a prostitute or something, but he was not aggressive. He was just interested. And then when he sort of looked at me and I just walked, he didn't bother me." She goes on to say:

> I think when we were in school uniform, I had a lot more guys harassing me than when I was older. . . . I remember like being brushed against or being touched, when I was fourteen, fifteen, and they guessed rightly, that I would be too scared to say anything. But when you get older and a little more confident, because then you turn around and yell. But I didn't ever feel like I couldn't do things, that I couldn't go out or stay out late or Bangalore felt unsafe.

Was it the confidence of having a progressive education that allowed these young teenage girls of fourteen and fifteen years of age to feel secure in their handling of situations? Was it the comfort with freedom and independence that was fostered by their parents? Or was it that Bangalore just felt like a safe city? These are questions that will be resurrected in chapter 5, but what was evident in their recollections was that they were sure of their capacity to handle most experiences that came their way during these mid-adolescence years.

THE GIRLS AND THEIR GODS

Religion occupies space in both the public and the private spheres. In places such as India that have long tried to make space for the multifaith populations that have made their homes there, there is still a vulnerability to fracture the delicate balance of what is supposed to be a religiously tolerant society when strife and tensions emerge. Frequently in my conversations with the women, we talked about the fact that while BGHS was a Christian Methodist school, our classmates were drawn from many faiths. Many of the women recalled an innocence about the role of religion in schools and the religious affiliations of their classmates. Ahana said:

> I don't think religion was a very important part of our lives in those days. I didn't even know the [religious] difference[s] between [students]. [Did anyone ever of us think,] this girl is a Christian or this one is a Muslim and this one is a Hindu? This one is a Jain or a Buddhist? Never did any of our parents or teachers say, this one is a Christian, so, you know, she's better, or this one is a Muslim, don't talk to her. I don't think any of us really knew the difference. I certainly didn't know.

Ahana contrasts this lack of concern for religious affiliation among her classmates with her husband's attitude. He is a Hindu and far more conscious than she is of his religious identity:

When I got married, I remember, my husband was so much into like "Hindu and this and that." And I'm like, "Really? I mean like I don't care and none of the rituals matter to me." So I think we all got a very open education. . . . We always [were] very open, very receptive to ideas and cultures.

Lipika's comment indicates how much has changed in India over the past few decades in terms of awareness and tolerance of religious difference. She talked about how she perceived her Muslim classmates:

Very well brought-up kids. . . . I don't remember these girls ever raising their voices or fighting and things like that; it never happened. And it was a similar culture across all of us. It didn't matter whether you came from a Muslim home or a Jain or from a Hindu home, I think all of [us] . . . knew what to say and when to say it. Social graces may have been different, but I think the basic sense of values was the same.

Lipika's observation that the Muslim girls did not "raise their voices" or "fight" speaks to the stereotypes that have emerged in recent decades, to the new narratives that depict Muslims as violent and angry.[19] Lipika did not explicitly make this comparison, but she seems implicitly to acknowledge the new narrative as she speaks about the past.

Meher, who is Hindu, talked about the comfort she draws from the religious practices she learned at Baldwins: "When you have periods of stress. I go back to the Bible. I go to a church when I feel I'm going to a bad, stressful period." Parul said, "I am a Hindu. We still sing hymns, still I have my hymn book. If [a classmate] and I come together during the holidays, to my mom's place, we bring the hymn book, we sing the songs." Saira, also a Hindu, recalled that her best friend at school was a Muslim girl:

Even though I was a pure vegetarian, and she is not of course, but still it never affected our friendship that way. She was very comfortable. In fact, on Sundays, many times if she was [at Saira's house], we would all go out together for dinner. My dad also was very fond of her.

Vedhika spoke of her exposure to both secularism and religious diversity:

It was nice. That's why sometimes I find it so weird, you know we all grew up in actually such a secular atmosphere. You know, we didn't think twice about going to assembly and saying prayers and singing hymns every day. And then we would go home and I had to say my *shlokas* [Hindu prayers] at 6:30 p.m. sharp. I had to sit for half an hour in the Puja Room.[20]

Ekta mentioned a classmate whose religion she know only because of her name: "But other than that, I never even thought, 'Oh my God, this girl is a

Hindu, I can't make friends with her.' Or 'this girl is a Tamilian, I can only make friends with her.' It never even crossed my mind." After pausing, she added, "Even today, I don't even know whether they're Hindu or Christian, even 'til now I don't know because it never really mattered." Ila argued that the divisions that were more pronounced were between class sections or school houses; religion itself seemed almost inconsequential.

Faye saw Bangalore as reflecting on a large scale the same acceptance of religious diversity as was to be found at Baldwins:

> I literally never noticed anything. In some ways, I don't know if that's why we were so progressive, if you think about it, we didn't think twice. And we celebrated Christmas, right? We celebrated any Muslim festival where they had biryani. We did Hindu festivals. We did that. I don't think it's that way as much now, but I feel like Bangalore was extremely cosmopolitan. And that was reflected in our school. I think that made us very adaptable. We had to learn about each other's cultures. Within our bubble, we were very cosmopolitan in the sense of being Indian and they really hammered it into our skulls that no matter where you're from or what religion you're from, you're Indian, blah, blah, blah.

To grow up in Bangalore between 1985 and 1995 was to experience the city in both public and private ways as a secular, tolerant, and increasingly cosmopolitan space. The students at BGHS were middle-class girls who expected to see the city continue to be an inclusive and empowering environment. But these expectations came to be challenged in the aftermath of the demolition of the Babri Masjid mosque. That event occurred just over three years after my classmates and I graduated from BGHS. As the 1990s lengthened and then a new century dawned, we watched the rise of the Hindutva movement and what started as the razing of a mosque by a radical fringe movement become a battle cry heard throughout the country. The notion that being Indian trumped many other identities had been instilled in us at Baldwins, but other, narrower conceptions of what it means to be an Indian rose to challenge that ideal and to set the stage for misogynistic fundamentalism to take center stage in India's political and ideological life.

Chapter 4

The Gathering Storm

The Rise of the Bhartiya Janata Party

When politics entered the girls' lives, it was often due to a national event pushing through the activities crowded into their days. In an unhurried and relaxed girlhood, certain events marked moments that stayed with the girls even decades later. In 1984, many of the girls, just ten or eleven years old, remembered the assassination of India's first female prime minister, Indira Gandhi,[1] with fear and apprehension. Memories of parents collecting their daughters early from school and a certain level of chaos as the city hunkered down were common. Televisions were just being introduced into homes in the early to mid-1980s, and the women remembered watching the last rites of the leader, experiencing a form of collective mourning that was a new facet to life. Meanwhile in the northern part of the country, waves of violence marked Indira Gandhi's death, as Hindus extracted vengeance upon the Sikh community, for it was Gandhi's Sikh bodyguards who shot her while guarding her.[2] This religious strife did not have a huge impact on the south. In Karnataka generally, and in Bangalore particularly, things remained mostly quiet and peaceful, albeit mournful.[3]

The second event that cut through our early adolescent days was strikingly similar. In 1991, the death of Indira Gandhi's son, Rajiv Gandhi, who was running for reelection, evoked a different form of trauma. He was, for many of our mothers, the handsome young pilot who was never meant to take office. In a country of arranged marriages, he had married an Italian woman for love. They had two children, a son and daughter, who were both just a little older than many of us and were much admired for their light skin and cosmopolitan outlook. The earlier unexpected death of Rajiv Gandhi's older brother in a plane crash led Rajiv Gandhi to join politics. Rajiv Gandhi's assassination at the hands of another rebel group, this time the Liberation Tigers of Tamil Eelam (LTTE), a guerrilla group out of Sri Lanka, was a body blow to the country. The fact that he was assassinated in a neighboring

southern state brought Bangalore to a standstill. Everything shut down, and
for the girls of BGHS, there was another odd feeling. The woman who assassinated Rajiv Gandhi was just seventeen years old herself, the same age as
many of the women in this book at that time.

So politics intruded with a knowledge that there were currents of anger and
hostility between groups of people. For the most part, girls in convent schools
in Bangalore believed the slogans of a more patriotic nature. Particularly
partial to one that was used over and over, "Unity in Diversity," became a
familiar refrain in our lives. The notion of "Unity in Diversity" came out of
the pre-1947 independence movement as a rallying cry to create a united
India out of a disparate group of kingdoms, principalities, and territories. Yet
the battle between secularism and communalism has been under attack since
the birth of the country, which for the girls of BGHS would ultimately lead
down the road to the events in Ayodhya in 1992.

FROM INCLUSIVE NATIONALISM TO EXCLUSION

Historically, nationalism has been seen as a positive approach to building
a cohesive national identity, especially for countries seeking independence
from colonial powers. This was the situation in India where nationalism was
initially identified as the collective power of a people to exercise their right to
be free of colonialism.[4] As described in chapter 1, similar to Mysore's status
as a princely state, India itself was not truly a unified country but rather a
conglomeration of regions held together by the British. It was the emergence
of a united national front as a single county, India, that facilitated a more
integrated movement that oriented itself toward independence.[5] In an effort to
create a more cohesive identity, intellectuals sought to use the name "India"
as a way to connect disparate people, mostly in an effort to overthrow British
colonizers and gain independence. By decoupling the religion and the people,
Indian nationalists sought to create a new identity for an otherwise sundry
collection of regional powers of varied religions, languages, and castes.
This was strategic, in part, due to the systematic and consistent efforts of the
British to divide India on religious grounds.

For BGHS students, one of the most memorable history lessons we studied
was the story of India's First Battle for Independence, the Sepoy Mutiny, or as
the British called it, the Mutiny of 1857. History books taught us that Indian
soldiers were expected to pull paper cartridges with their mouths to insert
bullets into the rifles provided to the soldiers (sepoys). Coated with a tallow
to grease the cartridges, the Hindus were offended because the tallow was
said to have been made from beef fat. Later, Muslims were offended because
it was said to be made of pork fat. This led the sepoys to plan a mutiny. The

reason many schoolchildren remember this history lesson is not because of the unity between soldiers or the role the mutiny played in history but because one sepoy was said to have gotten the date mixed up and began to shoot the day before the actual mutiny was meant to begin. This historic mistake was amusing to fourteen- and fifteen-year-old girls who could easily relate to how one might forget the due dates of homework and assignments. A young soldier mixing up the date of the mutiny meant he was just like us.

While the events of 1857 united Hindus and Muslims to fight back together, history is full of examples of efforts to foment divisions between Hindus and Muslims as a strategy used by the British to squelch anticolonization movements.[6] Creating divisions between Hindus and Muslims was one way to ensure that disunity between the two largest religious groups. Yet while successfully coming together to craft a movement that went on to capture the world's attention, India's (mostly) nonviolent approach[7] to oust the British was also marked by failure when the British departed, cleaving the region into two countries on the basis of religion, India and Pakistan.

The creation of an independent India, with a separate Pakistan, wounded the country for decades to come. Traumatic especially for Hindus and Muslims in the northern part of the country, much of the south was relatively inoculated from the levels of violence and brutality that emerged during the Partition. In the north, the division left bitterness and hostility from then on. The inclusive nature of nationalism faded in the postindependence period, fracturing amid religious differences. Soon, linguistic, regional, and geographic ruptures further challenged the notion of unity in diversity.

These fissures moved from a more inclusive form of nationalism to a more exclusionary form of nationalism. Furthermore, the shift to more nativist ideologies did not take long to rear its head. India's maintenance of its secular values enshrined in the birth of the country has been one of the fundamental battles over the past eighty years. This is epitomized in the struggle "between those who want to nationalize Hinduism as the tolerant civilization that is the basis of a secular state" and "those who want to nationalize Hinduism as the national religion that makes non-Hindus in India second-class citizens."[8] The 1948 assassination of India's face of independence, M. K. Gandhi, or Mahatma Gandhi,[9] showcases the divisions between inclusive and exclusionary nationalism. While the facts might still be litigated,[10] what was known at the time was that the assassin, Nathuram V. Godse, was a known affiliate of both the Rashtriya Swayamsevak Sangh (RSS) and Vinayak Damodar Savarkar, the founder of the Hindutva movement.[11] These groups and individuals believed that Gandhi was guilty of betraying Hindus in the creation of independent India. This anger resulted in the assassination of Gandhi by Godse who was soon captured after the assassination. After his conviction, Godse was found guilty and hanged for the crime. At the time of his death, he reiterated that he alone was responsible for the murder of Gandhi, yet there are others who argued that he was a politically expedient player to blame in order to protect the larger emerging Hindutva movement,[12] a movement seen even then as a threat to secularism in India.

The tensions between the promotion of nationalism over secularism has been both overt and covert, as well as both subtle and crude. With the BJP's emergence in 1980, there were strains between its initial outward moderate approach and the need to pacify the right-wing groups who promised support in exchange for a political platform that addressed the primacy of India's Hindu identity.[13] Picking their lane, the BJP sought to gain electoral success through the expansion of its Hindu roots and identity.[14] What is clear is that the key moment of the party's ascendancy was the events in Ayodhya. Prior to 1992, the BJP tried to find its place, jockeying for power and flirting with both secular and religious nationalism. Missteps by the predominant Congress Party with Sikhs and Muslims in the 1970s and 1980s propelled the BJP to take a much more rigid turn toward Hinduism,[15] leading over time to ensure Hindutva as the guiding force of the BJP. As this position strengthened, the party shifted from including goals such as the establishment of a temple on the site of the Babri Masjid mosque to more hardened positions, including the creation of a Hindu-first country.[16]

With the changes in their policy platform, as a political force, the BJP has been able to grow exponentially in the postindependence era.[17] For instance, the RSS, the party that foreshadowed the rise of the BJP, started with barely 6 percent support in the immediate postindependence elections. Yet by 2019, the BJP gained more than 45 percent of the electorate with its coalition supporters, the highest vote share of any ruling bloc since 1989.[18] This growth in great part is due to a movement from policies of statism, or how much the government intervenes in social and economic matters, to that of policies of recognition, or how much the government works to redress historical wrongs. This shift toward recognition as well as the rise of the middle class and their apprehensions about their fair share of the economic pie has led to the success of the BJP, altering the national narratives on the country's future. The rapidly growing population, the fear that limited resources will be spread too thin, and the worry that the tenuous hold the middle class has on their lifestyle will be erased allow for the easy exploitation of groups and targeting "outsiders" as taking what might belong "rightfully" to someone else.

Two other aspects of the BJP's rise also speak to the divisional nature of their politics. While further explored in subsequent chapters, the BJP has also found fertile ground in protesting programs that have sought to level the playing field for some of India's most marginalized populations. Caste continues to be another existential conflict in India, where the deeply entrenched and unequal system of social stratification dictates life for most Hindus.

Spanning two thousand years, India's caste system is overwhelmingly complex and intricately entwined in every aspect of the daily lives of India's Hindu community. Caste restrictions can limit what you eat, whom you marry, where you live, and what profession you take on. The hierarchies of the Hindu caste system ensure that there almost always was someone above you and someone below you. The system also supports misogynistic laws to ensure the primacy of men over women.[19] These caste divisions created profound inequities as the country moved further from away from the immediate postindependence period. These differences led to tensions between political parties seeking to balance the power of the state to intervene in social structures and the power of the state to recognize the historic oppressions of minorities, including those who were considered "lower" caste, or from other marginalized groups. The creation of affirmative action–type policies to alleviate the historic and structural inequities in the caste system was one reason people increased support for parties like the BJP, as they rallied against special treatment for historically marginalized citizens.

The other area that the Hindutva movement has also claimed is how gender roles and feminism are defined. For women in India, their status has been relatively mixed. On one hand, this is a country that institutionalized the murder of women upon the death of their husbands in the practice of *sati*. On the other, it was one of the few countries in the world that elected a female leader to serve in the highest elected office for a period of nearly fifteen years. Over centuries, as society evolved and patriarchal structures grew stronger, there is evidence that Hinduism was codified to ensure greater control over the lives of those who were dependent on the head of household, particularly women and children. In her 1983 article on the *Image of Women in Hinduism*, Prahbhati Mukherjee paints a robust portrait of women prior to the establishment of scriptural restrictions as vibrant, intellectual, and engaged with the world.[20] The history of Hinduism will show that there was a point where this changed. The religious text *Manusmrithi* developed a complex set of rules that ensured the increased dependency of women on men.[21] Through myth, epic, and scripture, Hinduism sought to exert forms of control over women, where the primary expectations for women were to get married, have a son, and serve her family.[22] Over time, the BJP has worked to tailor these mythological women into forms of ideal women in an effort to create a more nationalistic narrative for women. While there has been critique, there has also been a significant level of interest in rebuilding the tropes of womanhood to speak to the cause of nationalism. Arguing this point, Soumya Banerjee says:

> In the pursuit of national honour, the demise of women's identity seems imminent in a discourse of militant nationalism that either takes control of women's bodies as vulnerable, or enacts Hindu mythological archetypes of

strong womanhood as protectors of the nation, albeit a nation underlined by a patriarchal order. This promotes the virile, warrior-like image of a woman who fights against evil forces to liberate the nation, while fantasizing her physicality by sensually depicting the Mother nation with all her "grace and beauty" as imagined by the "brave" sons of [Mother India].[23]

Creating a narrative that strong womanhood is aligned in allegiance to Hinduism has been one way the BJP has also sought to create divisions in what was emerging to be a country with strong feminist and female leadership. Issues of caste and gender will be addressed in subsequent chapters. What is important to understand in this context is that as the women in this book reflected on the past, they spoke to the ways in which they saw difference, for themselves as Indians, as women and as girls who lived in the south, in a city that was considered unique in the Indian context.

"'UNITY IN DIVERSITY' IS SOMETHING"

As the BJP shifted right, girls in BGHS spoke fondly of what unity in diversity meant to them. The power struggles of the national government, the fact that India was consumed in the 1970s and 1980s with historic challenges of national emergencies and other forms of domestic terrorism,[24] seemed to be rather distant as the girls spoke of the more idyllic nature of what India as a country meant to them. Ahana brought a lot of passion to this section of our conversations, saying, "But unity in diversity is *something*. It was a phrase that came up very, very often, and . . . in our minds India is a beautiful country, full of different religions and languages."

Furthermore, some of the girls recalled experiences that sought to foster the sort of inclusive nationalism as a way to bring the vast heterogeneity of India together. Students from schools around the country were invited to participate in efforts such as Nehru Bal Sangh,[25] a winter event that spanned four to five days, where students from around the country came together to "Unite India." Sharing camp tents and food, there were organized events to showcase the cultural diversity of the different states. In an effort to build bonds between youth around the county, Faye recalled with fond memories:

> Even when we went for the national integration camp, that was actually nice. It really was nice to meet people from different states. And I think in some ways we were very privileged to be able to see that. Each state has its own culture, each state had its language and their dances and that whole rich and Indian culture and everything, you kind of get that. We were lucky to be able to see that. I think that was great.

There was clearly an effort among young people to see and value the diversity of India, with all its plurality. This was especially important in Bangalore, which was already so diverse. When other school groups arrived at the camps, they usually represented one state, one language, and one religion. When the Bangalore teams went, there was almost no homogeneity to our groups. Often all we had in common was that we were from Bangalore.

Yet coming from Bangalore, while we might have felt sheltered, there was a clear memory of how unity in diversity was not something one could trust in every context. Through the 1980s and early 1990s, there was clearly a difference when the girls recollected their feelings about Bangalore and the ways in which it was different, as a southern city, versus a city in the north. Tanvi recalled that in Bangalore you had "good exposure [in a] cosmo[politan] city. You get to interact with different levels of people, different languages, but the equality is there." For her, moving to Delhi after being in Bangalore for over two decades was a shock.

> I stayed in Bangalore for twenty-one years. For me, it was like, life was a bed of roses. Then we shifted to Delhi and suddenly it was not. North Indians have a very different mentality. Slowly, everything started falling in place, one is [going to have to] fight, it was not easy.

She goes on to expand what she meant by needing to fight:

> In Bangalore, you never felt someone was taking you for the ride, it was all so genuine. When you come to Delhi, you can certainly feel the difference. You are not sure what the person is like. [You are not sure if] your best friend is telling the truth or not. So then your mind also starts working, you need to start analyzing a person so you don't fall into the trap.

Tanvi's larger point illustrated a common understanding among the girls: that life in Bangalore was one where it did not really matter what your background or religion were, nor did you feel like you had to gauge and watch your own interactions with people, because an overall sense of trust existed between you and those around you. This felt different to Tanvi when she moved to Delhi. It represented the larger pattern of understanding that there was a difference between the north and the south. Others said similar things. Ahana said that after graduating from grade 12, she joined an engineering college in a different part of the state, and that was when she heard people ask, "Is this one is a Northie? And this one is a Southie?" and she was flabbergasted, asking, "And I'm like, what is that?" She heard their responses that they were trying to understand where someone was coming from and she went on to say:

I hadn't come across any of that. I don't know if you used the word racism, this is like "sectism," dividing the country into two parts that wasn't about religion. It was about people in the north and south of India being very different in terms of language and maybe culture.

Another area of difference was illustrated in how the girls remembered violence. This might have been a factor of the images of the violence they saw in the north after the assassination of both Indira and Rajiv Gandhi. Darika tried to articulate this, stumbling a little through her words:

I have to say whatever happens in Bangalore is still very, what should I say? Decent and kind of . . . they don't push the boundaries of . . . how do I put this? Like fighting in a physical way. It's very almost intellectual in certain ways. Kids are standing up for themselves. Doing certain things like cleaning up the parks and the lakes and stuff like that. Finding innovative solutions, challenging the government to step up and stuff like that, but it's all done in a non-conflict, non-controversial [way]. Silent protest, stuff like that. Whereas, and this is just my, you know maybe I've got my blinders on, but, I think up north, people are a little more aggressive in the way that they would fight their battles.

So while unity in diversity was something the girls felt was real, there was definitely a sense of confidence that this was something fostered in Bangalore. Yet the tolerance the women had for the north was only slimly reflected in their underlying sense that the feeling of inclusion was not a universally held value. Some of this might have to do also with the ways in which they saw their own girlhood play out in a country that still espoused conservative values for women.

"THERE'S NO WAY I CAN PUT UP WITH A CHAUVINISTIC GUY"

Growing up in India, many summer vacations were spent reading *Amar Chitra Katha* comics. These were twenty-five- to twenty-eight-page comics with vivid colors, iconic typefaces, and rather sexist portrayals of women's bodies,[26] yet they quickly and easily provided young people a sense of the rich and wide array of stories in the Indian context. The stories encompassed history (including comics about many of the freedom fighters in the independence era), religion (sharing the stories of Buddhist, Jain, and Sikh thinkers as well as Muslim rulers), and a vast array of Hindu mythology. These myths would balance the stories of women and men, ensuring that women had a role to play in expressing their own agency[27] with a vast pantheon of goddesses who were powerful and influential in their own rights. With their own origin stories and special powers to bless devotees, Hindu goddesses could influence an individual's future in dramatic ways. From the powerful goddesses Durga (the divine mother) and Lakshmi (goddess of wealth and fortune), to goddesses Saraswati (arts and wisdom) and Parvati (fertility and family), Hindus came to idolize these mythical women as epitomizing the notion of the perfect woman. Unlike the Greeks and Romans, these figures did not fade into oblivion as people adopted other religions. For Hindus, these stories of the gods and goddesses are ever present, existing as true stories of an active religion.

Yet the dichotomous nature of Indian womanhood is epitomized in these stories. To illustrate this conflict, there are the stories of two divergent women who each play a central role in the influential epic poems: the *Mahabharata* and the *Ramayana*. In the *Mahabharata*, Draupadi is feisty, pushes her father to find her a husband worthy of her, is able to summon the god Krishna to her aid, and is willing to criticize her husbands (she ends up being married to five brothers, which is another story). In one scene, she is insulted, disrobed, and mocked in front of her husbands, who gamble her away in a desperate bid to regain a lost kingdom. In front of the royal family elders, she fights, rages, and uses her righteous indignation to foretell gruesome ends to her tormentors. She is fire and her rage is her weapon. In the other epic poem, the *Ramayana*, Sita is kidnapped by a demon, held captive, and in an effort to free her, her husband launches a war between his forces and the demon. After vanquishing the demon, she returns to her husband, who then sends her away because the citizens of their kingdom questioned her virtue after having been imprisoned by the demon for as long as he did. She is banished despite her devotion and loyalty. She seeks out divine proof that she maintained her chastity, but despite proving herself on multiple occasions, she finally gives up and prays to her own goddess-mother to take her back into the earth from where she was found (her father found her in a field, which is also another story). She does not fight or rage but is passive in light of both the accusations and the punishment. Draupadi's passion and Sita's passivity are contradictions, yet they exist in the duality of the minds of Hindus today, leading to a push to encourage women to follow more malleable role models. This would include the self-sacrifice of Sita, who as a matter of fact is the wife of the god Rama, whose stated birthplace is the site of the demolished mosque, in Ayodhya.

The women I spoke with would talk about reading these comics as teenagers and would wonder how the shift from a more inclusive and empowering female narrative devolved into a more passive dependence on male family members from birth to death. This reminded many of yet another event that jolted them as teenager, the death of Roop Kanwar.

In 1987, reports emerged of an educated, eighteen-year-old young woman, Roop Kanwar, in the northern state of Rajasthan, who climbed on the funeral pyre of her husband, immolating herself and performing the ritual of *sati*. This made front-page news, with messages that were quite mixed. In some spaces, people were appalled and shocked. In other spaces, however, people were in awe of her courage and would come to sanctify her for her death. Furthermore, some reports shared that she had done this on her own accord, whereas court documents told a different story, that she was forced. The court documented that Kanwar was forced on the pyre and died while over four hundred people watched her burn alive.[28] Renowned *New York Times* journalist Elisabeth Bumiller, who was in the town of Deorala a few days after the burning, argued in her book on women in India that the village might have even benefited from the act.[29] This sense is not out of context, where even thirty-five years later, people in Deorala believe that their town was consecrated by her act.[30] No matter the reasons, for the girls in Bangalore, it was a stark reminder that educated girls in other parts of the country were not as free and unrestricted as they were. Beyond the shock and the horror, it reminded them that Bangalore was a very different city compared to much of the rest of the country, especially from the north. Ekta would connect this back to her life and thoughts of marriage:

> So my mother used to always say, I think she used to use that as a kind of a threat, "If you don't study, we'll get you married off." That kind of a thing. And I think if both my sister and I were not good in our studies we would have been married off. We wouldn't have had a choice.

Ekta shared that her sister fell in love in medical school and got married, so it added pressure to her to have to work harder to avoid marrying someone her parents chose, remembering:

> They used to bring these really terrible people from my community. These really, not forward thinking people . . . really conservative people from my community. And I was thinking, there's no way, studying in Baldwins, I would ever, ever be compatible with any of them. I just couldn't think of myself like that, because my community is totally chauvinistic, and I thought there's no way I can put up with a chauvinistic guy.

Oona talked about the way Bangalore felt different, especially in light of the kind of lives she heard other girls have to navigate in other parts of the country, saying:

> That's probably why I feel it was such a great time in the city, we were teenagers and we were just getting out and discovering ourselves. . . . There's certain

songs that my daughter was saying that she can't believe I know, or I've heard of. "How would you know? (she asks). . . . And I said, "Well, it's probably because of the schools I went to, the city I grew up in." So I think in Bangalore specifically, also the Western influences were so much more than say Madras [Chennai] where my husband grew up. That's probably why I just feel like it was very magical, very fun time those years.

So while the women worried about husbands, marriages, and felt a sense of freedom in Bangalore, it was the battle at Ayodhya that stayed with many of these women as they moved from girlhood to adulthood. As the BJP began its foray into full-fledged Hindu fundamentalism, it was the images, news, and fear that shaped their emergence from child to adult.

"YOUR PEOPLE DID THIS TO US"

The girls graduated from grade 10 and left BGHS in 1989, going on to junior college or grades 11 and 12.[31] All thirty-five women in this book did go on to a variety of higher education institutions. Some went on to engineering school, others medical, arts, and business programs, but for all Bangalore was still home. And all remembered the events of Ayodhya. They fell into two distinct camps with their memories. The first group recalled the events with worry for family members or were living or going to schools with far more mixed populations, where there were a substantive number of both Hindus and Muslims. They remembered the events and felt a sense of fear and apprehension for friends and neighbors. The other camp was very different. They remembered the event, but there was a sense of disconnect, a sense of separation from the actions of the days and weeks after. My hypothesis is that it was because things in Bangalore never reached the sort of apex that was present in the northern parts of the country. For this group, it seemed like a terrible event that happened in a part of the country none of us were very familiar with. Some might have had relatives in the north, but there was a sense of disconnection between us and them.

Ahana remembered:

Well, I remember, that was '92. Right? Yeah. So I was already in engineering college and we were in class. And then, everyone started buzzing and everyone was like, have you heard, have you heard? And I just remember thinking in my mind that, so what's the big deal? It's a mosque, whether it's a temple, what is the difference? Why would one break down a mosque to put a temple there? Or why would one break down a temple to put a mosque? Why don't you just put them next to each other? How does it matter? . . . It turned into such a horrible thing a killing each other and, and lots of dirty politics and everything.

Ahana's comment was representative of the overall feeling of secularism and cosmopolitanism of Bangalore in those days. Nisha was one of the women who talked about the death of Indira and Rajiv Gandhi as well as the riots in Ayodhya as being pivotal in her development as a lawyer. She could remember all three vividly, but the images from Ayodhya stuck with her, where "these people on top of the dome and sort of hacking away at it" never left her.

By 1992, televisions were a normal appliance for a middle-class family. Chanchal remembered the images of the fundamentalists or the *kar sevaks* pulling down the structure. Her memories focused on the people she knew:

> I had this friend who was from the Muslim community, and suddenly he says, "Your people did this to us." It was like, suddenly being pulled into a whole new idea of life, a whole new sort of an equation that didn't make sense. Because something that is happening somewhere else, can impact our own lives. It can impact our relationships. It can impact the way we look at life. . . . And I'll always remember the 6th of December, because that is so etched in my memory. And just the senselessness of it all. That's the whole thing. And I wasn't there to take sides. It just seemed so senseless. So out of control.

Harini and Ginny raised a sense of fear, but Ila provided one of the most vivid descriptions of what stayed with her:

> Carnage, bloodshed, absolute panic. I remember cringing every time I heard the news and read about what was happening. It was gory. It was really painful to hear and I just kept thinking that, "How can people do this to other people?" I remember reading about this one particular incident. [A report] that this entire mob, they had cut open a pregnant woman's belly, her womb. They had pulled out that fetus . . . those incidents when the looting and the carnage that went on in the name of religion, and Ayodhya, that Babri Masjid was not even being used, it was like a ruined structure. The amount of bloodshed and the amount of inhumanity that came out because of that, is not for me. For what? For a place? Just for a place? It doesn't make sense to me at all, but I remember feeling really helpless at that time, like just listening to what's happening and reading about it in the news, listening to the news. It was really bad.

Returning to the sense of disconnection, the women in the study often said they were unaware of people's religions, that it was private and personal, and something that did not matter to them overall. Oona made this point: "I'm just saying I don't think of religion, I was ever that aware of someone's religion. So this was huge, when people were losing lives and you were scared to [go to] those are places you all frequented." What she meant here related to the city neighborhoods. In most cities in India, there are still neighborhoods that are dominated by either Hindu or Muslim families. While neighborhoods were rather diverse, these pockets of the city were often off limits for girls who might live in other neighborhoods. For most of the Bangalore girls, there were few if any restrictions. But Ayodhya changed that. The areas that were seen as Muslim or Hindu dominated were particularly out of bounds, with parents setting rules to ensure girls were not in spaces that were deemed unsafe. But yet the girls felt a sense of security and confidence in their hometown. Ila made the point:

> Yeah, there was curfew, but I think Bangalore was pretty safe at that time, Bangalore never had communal tensions or anything. In fact, these Ayodhya curfew days, I remember driving around the entire locality, teaching one of my friends to drive. In and out of the lanes in your area was okay. I never felt unsafe in Bangalore at that point of time, I never felt any communal tensions at that point of time.

From the other camp, I heard recollections such as from Saira, who compared her experience with her husband's experience in Bombay, where there were lots of riots. She said, "But I don't remember it of Bangalore at all. Maybe I was very unfazed with what was happening in the world at that time, but I don't remember at all [violence in Bangalore]." Amaya went on to say, "No, it didn't really affect me. I was wondering what these people are doing? Mad [crazy] people. That was running in my mind. That's it. 'What is this Hindu, Muslim? Everyone is same.' That's what I used to think." Yashika made a similar point. Her engineering college closed down, as did most educational institutions during that period, and her northern classmates were worried about their travel back home. She said:

> And they were going back home because it was such an extended break, but a lot of them were worried as to how the situation was. And for me, honestly, that was the first time I really was aware that there was a safety angle. That we really did not consider [that] here in Bangalore.

She went on to say that while she might have worried about catcalls on the street (in India it is called eve teasing), "getting groped in buses, Those were the things that probably I was exposed to, but nothing beyond that." Her recollections of Ayodhya had more to do with the safety of her friends than the riots or violence in the aftermath of the storming of the mosque. Brinda found this less than compelling, in some ways, framing it as history, "a clash between Hindus and Muslims. Which, I think it's almost like, 'Okay, it's another thing that happened between Hindus and Muslims.' It's been going on since independence." Chaya repeated this idea of it being something that had been a part of India's story: "Of course it had been going on for years and years before I realized we didn't think about it as like, 'Who are these people really so desperate for a temple?' Just don't get it, right? I still don't get it."

Ela was recovering from surgery and had been out of school for a few weeks. She remembers being keen to come back to class, realizing that when this happened, she would be further delayed. She talks about how it shifted what she thought of Bangalore and the situation:

> And I remember, but there was a sense of nervousness. It was the first time, I think even in Bangalore to experience a curfew, which was so unreal to me. I'd heard all the stories about the previous [war with Pakistan] my grandfather telling me what things were like during the independence struggles. Never having experienced anything like that. It was really unnerving because for the first time Bangalore didn't feel safe. Just those few minutes, something else from out there was having an impact on Bangalore as well. Whereas Bangalore was always so different from any other part of India I had been to visited. There was a spirit about Bangalore that was just so different. And for the first time, Bangalore wasn't immune to any of that either. And so I remember that very clearly.

Queenie held a rather more unique understanding as compared to many of the other women. She said that she absolutely remembered the day, and she went on to say:

> While I don't justify what the Hindus did, I also think that it was . . . there is no justification for that behavior, but I will say that I thought that the reaction was disproportionate to what had been done to them. I felt that it was that much worse had actually happened in society. Again, I do not justify that, that kind of behavior, you do not respond to something with violence because it only breeds more violence. I don't speak because I'm a Hindu, but how do I phrase it? It got a bad rap in a way that I thought was disproportionate to other events that I had seen happen, which were equally damaging and maybe equally moderate, equally questionable in terms of the intent and what end result it could produce.

Queenie's comments drew from a vast historical context, taking into account events between Hindus and Muslims over a thousand years, but her remarks in some way are illustrative of the ways in which nationalists have started to frame the argument for their followers.

Finally, in thinking about Ayodhya, Ginny was one of the first who drew connections on how her memories framed her understanding of recent times. She remembered being with a group of friends when the mosque came down. Initially, she was more worried about how she would get home if there was a curfew. After that, however, she said:

> But the magnitude of it, what it stood for, I really didn't think or pause to think about it. If I think back on it now, I would say that it was a manifestation. It

was probably the first sign maybe, of things that were changing. But that's only because I'm thinking about it now. And why didn't I think of it even earlier? Maybe BJP was rising, but I didn't [think about it]. I was quite happy with their leader. So I just thought of them as an alternate. In fact, I've even voted for Vajpayee myself. So it really didn't bother me that, I didn't think of it as, "Oh my God! This is going to be communalism in India." And it's going to be this split, Our opinions are going to be [split]. It's not the way, I didn't anticipate that it'd be the way it is now.

"I didn't anticipate that it'd be the way it is now." These words reverberate across the years. Each year, moving further and further away from the riots and demolition at the Babri Masjid have shown a steady chipping away at rights, freedoms, and security. The city of Bangalore, which for a generation of women was not just home but a stage that helped propel them forward, has not provided the same promise for their daughters. The ways in which the BJP and its ilk have impacted almost every aspect of these women's lives allows us to see a much more vivid and dangerous perspective on Hindu nationalism.

PART II

Fault Lines in a Fractured Society

From Past to Present

Thirty years have passed since the *kar sevaks* arrived in Ayodhya, attacking one place of worship in the name of another. Thirty years have passed since the BJP took a stand, unwilling to disallow the narrative of Hindu fundamentalism that represents their party. Thirty years have passed, eroding relations between Hindus and Muslims. And over these past thirty years, a series of fractures emanating from the demolition of the mosque changed the fabric of India.

These fractures have been incremental and oftentimes easy to shrug off as a one-off, an anomaly in an otherwise economically advancing country. It is precisely the growth of the economy, the rising middle class, and the overall financial security of the country that provides a smoke screen to distract from the larger trends these fractures portend. It is easy to divert people's attention when any challenge can be seen as a threat to gains one has clawed to collect. But the fractures have not been completely hidden, and while it might not feel safe to openly critique the concerns, people are noting them, well aware of what it all might mean.

These fractures are driven by the agenda of Hindutva in India. From misogynistic perceptions of women's roles and the need to ensure control through patriarchy to the arrests and murders of activists and thinkers, there is a more threatening and fearful feeling amid people. There is a movement to shift and shape education to lean toward Hindu narratives of supremacy and importance, as well as the proposal of policies and projects that elevate Hindu nationalism in what is supposed to be a secular state. There are narratives meant to be alarming in nature about the influence of the outsider, the non-Hindu, who seeks to change and destroy all that Hindus have tried to grow and build. And there is belief, both stated and unstated, that India is a Hindu country, and that the place for other religions is either below or absent in the primacy of Hinduism.

In Bangalore, as we have learned in the first four chapters, there was a sense of openness and broadminded thinking. Bangaloreans had found a way to balance the global and the local as well as the traditional and the modern. There was a sense of rootedness, despite where you came from. The historic investments in infrastructure and industry led to a middle class that was willing to be adventurous and welcoming to each generation of newcomers that came to make Bangalore home. This feeling percolated into the schools and the local neighborhoods. It infused the expectations families held that their children could aim for accomplishment through education. This was a central concept to the dreams of upward mobility. There was a uniqueness to Bangalore that was noted, both inside and outside of India. And a generation of young women grew up thinking they were unstoppable.

People often mistakenly assume my feminist ideologies are grounded in my early years in the United States. I am very quick to assure them that my personality was crafted on the streets and in the cafés and homes of my beloved Bangalore. I can also guarantee to them that I am not an isolated example. The experiences we had in Bangalore would be pivotal in creating a sense of agency and voice for so many young women. We had our fingers on the pulse of the city; the youth who came of age in the early 1990s were, in fact, and continue to be the heartbeat of that city.

So today, when mobs descend on a bookstore to destroy a Valentine's display, or a young activist is arrested, when classmates are harassed because one is a Muslim man and the other a Hindu women, or an independent-minded journalist is murdered, a generation of people start to wonder, "Is this the Bangalore I grew up in?" In asking myself this question, I was eaten up by curiosity. Is this what my classmates would say is part of the "greater good" in terms of the development of the country? Could the need to develop economically mean that we would have to alienate and decimate those who pushed back against the conformity and compliance that was growing? Could they sleep peacefully knowing that their classmates who were from different backgrounds and religions might be aligned with these changes? And more than anything, how did the lessons of our secular adolescence begin to march to the drumbeat of Hindu nationalism? And for me finally, the critical piece of this was: How were women talking about these issues? How are they grappling with these concerns in the privacy of their families and their friends and in their own minds?

Getting them to talk to me was easy. Returning to review those conversations dozens of times was clarifying. The next set of chapters share their thoughts and experiences in an effort to understand the questions I posed earlier. What they have offered is compelling for a number of reasons. For these women, with the independence and education that they were privy to, the changes to Bangalore have shifted their thinking rather completely. Coming from the types of families they do, these women are not afraid to share their opinion. Coming from the school that they did, these women are worldly in terms of their education. And coming from Bangalore with its freedom and cosmopolitan culture, these women are confident in both their sense of self and of the world. The fractures that might be seen as policy and politics have had immediate and direct implications for them. It has left them wondering: How do each of these fractures fit together? What future is there for a city that was treasured by a generation of young people who found freedom and friendship as the hallmark of Bangalore?

The next five chapters allow us to see how women look at progressivism, rights, and democracy as nationalism and fundamentalism are normalized in governance and politics in 2022. The fractures that they will explore include personal security and public violence, the home and work space, education and equity, secularism, identity and belonging, governance, and politics. Each of these independently would be a cause for concern. Together, they illustrate the different fronts around which the BJP is seeking control. The ways in which the women of Bangalore in this book understand, address, argue, and, in some cases, excuse what they are seeing is illuminating. It allows us a chance to see how issues around gender, education, belonging, intellectualism, and governance are being perceived and to what extent the influence of Hindutva is present in their daily lives, shifting and changing a city that has a long history of progressive and inclusive values.

Chapter 5

Women's Safety and Security

In December 2012, international attention focused on India after the horrific gang rape and subsequent death of Jyothi Pandey. Returning home after seeing a movie with a male friend, Pandey was raped, beaten, and mutilated. Dying of her injuries, she became a symbol of the rising fear among women across the country for their own safety.[1] The story of "Nirbhaya," as Pandey was initially called by the media, shone a spotlight on a pervasive problem. While the graphic and shocking nature of the crime was one reason for the extensive coverage the case received, the media frenzy was also fueled by Pandey's status as a young, middle-class, educated woman living, not in a remote village but in India's capital city of New Delhi.[2] Those markers of identity shifted the narrative of security for middle-class women in India. Rape was no longer something that happened to "them"; it was now something that happened to "us."[3]

In India, violence against women has been growing steadily. According to data from the Indian National Crime Records Bureau, the number of crimes against women rose steadily between 2010 and 2020,[4] from around 200,000 crimes in 2010 to nearly double that in 2020.[5] Data from the National Crime Records Bureau show that 2021 was another record-shattering year, with the number of crimes against women reaching an embarrassing peak.[6] Since 2016, violence against women has risen by nearly 27 percent.[7] In 2022, reports found that a crime against a woman is recorded every three minutes, two women are sexually assaulted every hour, and a married woman is beaten or burned to death or driven to suicide every six hours.[8] Given that crimes against women are typically grossly underreported in all societies, these figures are likely to significantly understate the scale of the problem.

As the politics of the country have shifted to the right, these changing ideologies have reframed the roles of women and girls in society. This is not unusual as most countries with growing authoritarian tendencies also tend to exert more control over women in public and private spaces.[9] Nationalists, populists, and religious fundamentalists have sought to consolidate power by appealing to archetypal forms of patriarchy, often encouraging people to follow traditional gender roles in society.

This return to patriarchal forms of leadership and nation building resonates with people who see themselves left out of narratives of success and growth.[10] Social messaging often pits the working class against the middle class and men versus women. Authoritarian populists, such as Modi and the BJP, tend to find success in arguments supporting strict gender hierarchies by ensuring support on these feelings of victimization.

The term "muscular nationalism"[11] offers a window into the ways in which twenty-first-century nationalism evokes a more authoritarian and masculine version of nationalism than in the past. Arguments that a country thrives when traditional relationships between men and women are maintained is a central facet[12] where men might be asked to live and die for their country, while the expectations for women are centered around on reproductive roles of wife and mother. By encouraging femininity and chastity, both ideas of which are lodged deep in the psyche of hegemonic patriarchal structures of power and authority. This has led to a resurgence of populist and authoritarian leaders who lean into the myth that national leaders must be strong, resolute, protective, and bold, descriptors that speak to the patriarchal vision of the nation.

These messages shape the ways in which people respond to, investigate, or even accept the treatment of those who are most vulnerable in society. By using religion and sacred texts as law, there are often efforts to demonize differences and "prescribe codes of behavior" that either restrict or exaggerate the role of women in society.[13] Furthermore, the rise in "moral policing" where ordinary citizens take it upon themselves to ensure compliance by women adds a sense of justification for people to take matters into their own hands. This is then exacerbated when class, caste, and religious differences intersect with gender. For instance, in the case of Jyothi Pandey, the violence perpetrated by working-class men on middle-class women has also led to a shift in women's trust in the role of authorities and elected officials to ensure their safety, who often see middle-class women as a threat to their power.[14] In addition, because nine out of ten Indians believe that a woman ought to obey her husband and two out of three believe that the obedience is to be complete,[15] there is also limited interest in seeking justice for women in their homes, no matter their class status. The idea of tapping into "resentful aspiration" by the BJP facilitates the "Hindu nationalist agendas" and allows for a "nationalist protection agenda [to depict] the sexuality of middle-class educated Hindu women as a threat to social order."[16]

It is in this complex space where political ideology, religion, and class- and caste-based differences open up a profoundly different city for the women of BGHS. Their experiences of riding bikes, going to get ice cream, and mingling with Hindu, Christian, and Muslim friends of both sexes has changed.

This chapter reveals how women living in today's Bangalore talk about their physical and emotional security. They discuss what has changed since they were young regarding their personal security, the ways that some aspects of their lives have improved but how in others it has grown worse, and describe how the challenges of being a woman have evolved. The city, they say, is regressing in terms of the freedom and safety they felt, and the independence they enjoyed as teenagers and young women is now denied to their daughters, whose lives are restricted and who now face battles their mothers thought were already won.

"NOTHING IS SAFE RIGHT NOW"

In earlier chapters, the women in this book talk enthusiastically about their outings and friendships when they were teenagers. Much of the freedom they experienced had to do with the fact that parents gave their daughters a great deal of autonomy to be out of the home with very little oversight or supervision. For many of the women I spoke with, memories of their own freedom are starkly juxtaposed with the sense that their daughters' freedom is far more curtailed than what they experienced.

Oona raised this, connecting directly back to life in Bangalore:

I don't know that [Bangalore is] a safe place anymore. I don't feel safe when I go out. I feel like I have to dress a certain way to not get the weird looks. I worry about my daughter, she's tiny. She's literally pocket-sized and I shouldn't worry about her, but I do worry about her. I used to walk with my friend . . . from home all the way to Hundred Feet Road[17] and walked back after it got dark. And I don't know if a girl can do that anymore in Bangalore, because there's obviously a lack of walkable streets, but not even that—just safety. . . . It worries me, especially when I hear stories.

She pauses and stumbles, because the stories have been horrendous lately.

I read these news items about little girls being treated, that way in schools, being raped in school. I know my sister is constantly worried . . . if the bus is two minutes late or if her [daughter comes home on] the next bus, she's a wreck. My parents basically said, "Use public transportation" or "Go and come as you please." After a point, they said, "Okay, here's the car keys, go and come, please just be safe." I don't know if we'll get to that point with my niece. I think it's a different world.

After Pandey's death, the government instituted measures to ensure rapists were more stringently dealt with. Yet a decade since her death, the incidence of rape remains high, with reported numbers in 2021 at over 31,000 cases.[18] The government has passed laws mandating harsh punishments for rapists[19] to usher in more efficient judicial processes[20] and to promote reporting by women of attacks, but these have not had the intended effect.

Inara, a practicing doctor, speaks to the fear that percolates through the women of Bangalore when she describes a group of her colleagues going out for dinner in the city:

> So we have a doctors' group, [it] is a big group, One of my friends, after we met, we called the Uber and she was scared to take the Uber and go. She's like, "I'm really scared. I mean, I don't know whether this guy is going to rape me or dump me somewhere. I'm really scared."

Inara goes on to say:

> Because nothing is safe right now. Nothing is safe for anybody, especially [for] girls. You hear about so many rapes. Remember that girl . . . I mean poor thing. What's her name? Jyoti Pandey? Delhi? The gang rape? I mean, you hear about so many of these gang rapes, so many of these things everywhere. It's not safe of late. It was more fun [in the past], looking forward to things. But now, you're scared to send your kids outside, be it your daughter, your son, anybody. You're just too scared. You're scared of any crime that's going to be committed, especially [one targeting] girls, any rape or any kidnapping, anything. It's become more common in not just Bangalore, everywhere in India.

Rape victims are frequently harassed when they report the crime, and justice often takes years (if perpetrators are even charged), further harming the victim.[21] The media has seen considerable debate around the imposition of the death penalty for the rape of a minor. In many of these cases, the perpetrator is within the family unit, and it can impede reporting out of fear of retaliation or the fear that a breadwinner might face the death penalty as a result of being reported.[22]

One thing that has changed is increased reporting of violence against women in the press. Yet this environment of knowing about the high incidences of violence against women stokes anxiety about the day-to-day safety of girls and women in Bangalore. The worry is tangible and extends to even very young girls. Ila remarked:

> I have a niece, she's about seven years old. She studies in Bishop Cottons.[23] I remember in school, we used to play down on the roads on Saturdays, Sundays, because there would hardly be any traffic and we'd play cricket on the roads and stuff. My brother and his wife, they don't even let her step out of the house without company. I think that is one major concern because that area has become so

congested and it's almost become like a main road so you can't really play on the road. But, having said that, they don't let her out of their sight. First of all, she's a girl, right? So they are worried about kidnapping and rape and there's so much happening now. Even for her to go to her school van, they will not let her go alone. My brother goes to drop her and someone is waiting when she comes back to pick her up.

Waida was talking about the street catcalls in her school days and similarly compared the relaxed past to the anxious present:

But it was safe. You could go, there would be "eve teasing" you know, which is a very mild thing that happened then. But compared to that and what happens nowadays, you just think, it's not safe from what I hear from other people. I've got friends, who've got girls and yeah, there's a constant worry of girls going out in the evenings.

Moving from a city where girls would safely and frequently hitchhike to one where children are not sent to school without worries of their safety is one of the biggest changes in how women look at their security. While the cases have been rising, the BJP has also sought to blame women themselves for not behaving modestly or for dressing too provocatively.[24] By allowing men to engage in moral policing, citizens have been emboldened by local politicians to question and oftentimes mete out punishment to women for perceived infractions of rules of modesty,[25] increasing the sense of insecurity and fear that somehow the violence is condoned by those in power.

"SHE WILL NOT GO ALONE"

In 2018, a global poll conducted by Thomson Reuters Foundation was released in which women around the world were surveyed about their perceptions of safety within their home country.[26] The poll found that among 193 nations surveyed, India scored the lowest across all three measures: the risk of sexual violence and harassment; danger from cultural, tribal, and traditional practices; and increased danger from trafficking. Indian women scored India worse than women in countries that are often seen as treating women particularly harshly, including Afghanistan, Syria, Saudi Arabia, and Somalia.[27]

The women of BGHS experienced forms of harassment, but what they said was that those experiences felt like annoyances that they could easily handle because they were often not afraid that things would escalate. They knew that most girls and women faced similar experiences of being groped on a bus or being catcalled in the street. But they also felt that was the extent of it. Oftentimes, I remember we would carry a sharp object in our pockets to jab someone if they tried something on a bus, and that often would be the end of it.

Today, however, it is the escalation of violence against women and girls that has taken a much more dangerous turn. The rise in group violence, from incidents of harassment against women who celebrate "Western" holidays such as Valentine's Day[28] to media reports of gang rapes,[29] there is a more nationalist argument for justifying violence against women. From Hindutva perpetrators arguing that celebrating Valentine's Day promoted loose moral behavior among women and therefore the women needed to be taught a lesson[30] to violence against Hindu women who are in relationships—or are even merely *perceived* to be in relationships—with Muslim men, violence is growing. These interreligious relationships have been called "Love Jihad," where Hindu fundamentalists have imagined a Muslim conspiracy where Muslim men seek to make Hindu women fall in love, marry, and convert them to Islam.[31] In response to this supposed effort, BJP leaders and religious figures have increasingly advocated for greater violence to be inflicted on Muslim women.[32] While international criticism on growing violence in India toward non-Hindu women and girls is increasing,[33] there seems to be little respite for women of all faiths and stripes in terms of worrying about their own safety.

My former classmates talked about the range of issues that were affecting women's and girls' security in India. Many immediately pointed out that they now had to consider their wardrobe far more carefully when it came to safety and security than in the 1980s and 1990s. Ela remembered:

> We used to just jump into autos so easily. I mean, I remember sometimes walking back deciding not to take the bus and the three of us girls walking back quite late by ourselves and not thinking about any of that. It didn't matter. Like even how you dressed, you know, if you were in Western clothes, which we wore most of the time. You never thought twice about any of those things. The only time I remember being conscious of the fact [was] when we went to Madras, [and my mother advised me,] "Oh, don't bring those shorts." And you always thought that [sort of caution] was for other places, it was never Bangalore. You could always be whatever you wanted to be, dressed how you wanted and you never judged anybody on any of those things. I don't think it's the same [today]. I find myself now as a parent, going back,[34] I think you see things quite differently. Like now I'm really hyper about how my kids dress when they're there. And I kind of constantly say, "Well, you can't take that."

Much of Ela's anxiety about what her daughters wore on trips back to Bangalore had to do with the changed environment, such as the lack of safety and the anxiety people would express to her if she considered more freedom for her children (for example, sending them out in an auto rickshaw on their own). Saira blamed these anxieties on the influx of outsiders into the city, which she felt had "changed the face of Bangalore." She considered herself "blessed" to have grown up in Bangalore in the 1980s: "Now when I look back and I realize [that] going cycling to school was such a luxury which no child has now. I can't tell [my daughter] to go cycling on roads now. It's so unsafe." She tells her daughter to always keep her phone close by. "It wasn't like that during our times [at BGHS], it was more free. I feel my mom was more open-minded than I am. . . . She was more free and liberal with me than I am with my daughter."

Technology might help Saira keep track of her daughter, but Juhi saw technology—in the form of social media—as one of the reasons for today's pervasive insecurity. She argued: "It is not very safe right now because even to leave here the children at home, you are scared. Maybe because of social media we are more exposed right now. . . . We didn't know so much [about threats to our safety when we were girls], but nowadays anything happening, [we know about it]."

Ekta chatted about her friends' strategies for minimizing the dangers the city presents to women. For instance, she noted that "my friends [who use Uber] have to pretend that they're speaking to somebody on the phone so that the driver doesn't take them somewhere else." She, like Saira, is quick to blame outsiders for the changes:

> I think it's also because it's people from other parts of India, so they come from places like North India where these kind of things are pretty normal. . . . I think also because they come from other parts, they just want money here. And I think also . . . we were very proud of being Bangalorean, and we used to clearly look after the place and everything. Now, I don't find that anybody takes pride in living there.

Attitudes toward newcomers to Bangalore will be discussed in greater detail in chapter 7, but part of the bias toward the newer arrivals in Bangalore can be attributed at least in part to the fact that the BJP was a dominant northern political party, and there is a sense among the city's longtime residents of guilt by association. Bangalore, they feel, has changed because people who have moved to Bangalore might have brought more conservative ways of thinking with them.

The women talked about the logistics that they needed to keep in mind when ensuring the safety of their daughters and other younger women. Bangalore, said Amaya, was "very safe" when she was growing up there thirty years ago:

I was not at all scared. I think, from fourth standard I used to take an auto rick-shaw . . . I was not at all scared. Nowadays, my daughter's seventeen years. She will not go alone. She will not go alone. Either we have to drop her, pick her up. That too, only during the day she can go out. Those days, we used to come back late also, we had no fear. Now it's not safe. It's not at all safe for girls. You can't trust anyone.

This is not to say that growing up in Bangalore in the 1980s and 1990s was without its flaws and challenges. As noted in earlier chapters, women and girls might often be groped on buses, an experience that many of the victims kept a secret. Part of that secrecy might have to do with the worry that by telling parents, the girls would have their freedoms curtailed. Part of it, as Jasmine noted, was that there was more limited sex education, which she feels is different today. Today, she felt, parents were more open with their children, more comfortable talking about bodies, sex, and relationships; that might not have been the case in the time she was growing up. She said:

Me and all my close friends, now we talk about it openly, but before we didn't realize there are many instances . . . where people touched you in a funny way or something like that, maybe in a public place or a private place or something like that. Like even in your home or something. And you don't know who to talk to and you never go back to your parents for it. And then you confide in your friends . . . and you kind of build your guard.

Today, the stakes felt higher and more dangerous. While the women I spoke with talked about being groped in many ways as an annoyance, they also felt that they had greater control and freedom. The violence young women experience today is juxtaposed against the fact that while they see themselves as more liberated, there was difference between whom they associated with and who they feared:

Well, how horrifying it is and how unsafe it is still. Even though we seem to be making progress, but there are still so many backward people there—people who have no respect for women, at all. And, who think it's okay to assault and be so violent.

It was clear that for the women their physical safety was at the top of their minds. Despite having experienced different forms of violence against themselves growing up, the overall sense of safety was far more pronounced. The ability to balance their own experiences of insecurity and freedom seemed to be far more compromised. This translated to the ways in which they discussed other forms of insecurity, including in their professional roles.

"SO HE PUTS UP HIS FEET AND WATCHES TV, WHICH IS A PROBLEM"

Early in her conversation with me, Zara raised a concern that had not fully captured my attention in light of all the problems women were facing in India, that of workforce participation. Statistics show that the "work participation rate (WPR) of women of India is showing a downward trend in the last few decades." The study goes on to say that workforce participation has declined from 29.6 percent in 1983 to 21.9 percent in 2011–2012. By 2017–2018, the percentage was as low as 16.5 percent. As the study stated, not only is the work participation rate of women declining, "the size of women workforce in absolute numbers is also shrinking. It has dropped from 148.59 million in 2004–2005 to 104.1 million in 2017–2018."[35] This is in a country of over 463 million adult women.[36] This trend has not been lost in the narratives on India. Newspaper headlines from Japan to the United States are asking: What is happening to India's working women? The absence of women from the world of work was in conflict with the ways the women I talked to reflected on the fact that young women growing up today had richer opportunities in school, for their careers, and in terms of general life experiences around travel and leisure that they did not have. Chanchal, who is now a teacher herself, observed:

The girl students are a lot more engaging [as compared to the boys], a lot more enthusiastic, very interested in finding out the whys, and boys take their own time. And then it's language learning, a lot of the left brain, right brain, all of those things come into the picture. It's been very fascinating.

She went on to describe how she has seen boys and girls interact in the classroom:

In the smaller classes, so they know each other very well. And no qualms about expressing their views. I think that's very different from the times when we were back in school. It was sacrilegious to even say something that would seem out of the way to a teacher. [Now, teachers are] far more accepting. . . . A child will question. And I welcome those things, For me it seems absolutely natural to have those questions. That's how girls are now. And lesser inhibitions than before. Some of them I think are going [to go] far . . . I would also think a couple of them, not a couple of them, some of them, are also quite precocious in terms of their behavior whether it be dating, even just a whole lot of behaviors that were very neatly couched [hidden] or masked earlier, is all out there in the open.

Darika saw some of the same loosening of restrictions on women's independence happening in the business world—but she also made it clear that there was still a long way to go in the fight for equal rights:

> I think we've come a long way. When I look at young men and women, when they're out there and they're doing it all at, they're fighting the fight. [Yet] you have a woman that's concentrating on work and she gets reprimanded, or you have a woman that's staying at home and she [gets criticized]. I don't think that's ever going to change . . . I always say when I talk to the corporations, "You're training the wrong people. It's not the women that have to be trained on diversity. It's the guys. It's the men that have to understand it."

While there were not a lot of working mothers in our graduating class, Zara's mother did work outside the home, and as such Zara had a lot to say about where she saw things going. She said:

> I think that the world for women has probably changed for the worse from when my mother was at work. . . . I was horrified to find that like right now the percentage of women who work in India is 24 percent and it's dropped by some 8 or 10 percent. Now we're on par with Saudi Arabia, for example, which means that there's been a hardening of attitudes in so many different places. And I don't feel like life has improved for young women at all. . . . I feel they are stuck where we were when we had our kids fifteen to twenty years ago. And even the promise that was there in my mother's time, that life would be better for you, that the work culture would be better for you, but I think as far as I can see, just seems to have regressed.

The progress that women were able to enjoy in part and the hope that Zara was anticipating were in part due to policies around women's empowerment that were instituted in the late 1990s and early 2000s. In 2001, the central government crafted a national policy on the empowerment of women[37] to give women greater access to social, economic, and political opportunities. But as Darika points out, cultural attitudes have lagged behind such legislative advances, and men have not been socialized to better understand their privilege in society and to be prepared to relinquish or share it.

Ginny, who labels herself "a feminist," said that there are still "very invisible biases against women," but she also felt that this was not particularly just an Indian problem as much as still remaining a global problem. Waida resurrected an acronym that many girls during our school years would use: the MCP, the male chauvinist pig. The MCP "drives me mad," Waida declared, while wondering if the phrase was still even in use. She continued: "It's just that ideology. I've got my old uncles, you know, that generation, like my dad's brothers and things, they expect that it's different rules for men and women."

Ahana pointed to a different explanation for the continued regression: the failure to change the roles that *men* perform in Indian society:

I read a really nice quote the other day that struck home. It said the last generation was so busy empowering woman, they forgot to teach the men how to now deal with these empowered women. I think in India that's really true because the women are now dealing with everything, right? So you're taking care of the house, the children, and then you're going out and you're working [as well]. . . . You're doing a full-time job that requires you [spending] eight or nine hours at work, and then you have to come back home and do your house work or whatever [extra work] you're trying to do outside the office—we're all very driven woman, so we are all trying to get ahead in our careers, So you again have to come back home and answer all your emails or whatever. And on the other hand, the man comes back home and it's not his job, right? He doesn't have to take care of the house. He doesn't have to take care of the children. So then he puts up his feet and watches TV, which is a problem.

Her words highlight the larger structural issues around the relationships between men and women. When women seek new roles in society, they often have to compete with men in spaces they did not traditionally occupy, but they are not permitted to neglect their domestic duties. The women raised an interesting contradiction. They frequently spoke of their fathers encouraging them, as Ahana says, to "get ahead in our careers," yet Ahana often meets men who would hear from their mothers that they should not have to lift a finger in their homes, either as sons or as husbands. Farida made this point vividly, talking not about the ways in which men need to step up but how challenging it is when women did not raise sons to be more responsible in domestic work. She said: "A lot more women are educated. I just find it quite a . . . how to say? Contradiction. On the one hand you have many more educated women, but the treatment of women is still . . . " She then gestured with her hands to signify "Who knows?" and then shook her head in disappointment. She continued:

So you have the MeToo movement, but at the same time, on the other end you still have domestic abuse, you still have women bickering about other women. I think in India, the other problem is that women do stand up for women in public demonstrations and shows, but I think under the surface, women are still against women in India. I find that mothers-in-law still put down their daughters-in-law. And I find daughters-in-law still don't get along with their mothers-in-law.

She continued by talking about the ways in which people would blame a woman if she was attacked outside her home:

I don't think I talked to a single person who did not say that it was the girl's[38] fault; everyone said, "What was she doing outside so late?" So I find that, yeah, a lot of people in India blame people that are outspoken. And if you're a woman, "Why on earth are you inviting this trouble? How can you change the world, how do you hope to change the world with your little opinion? You're just a woman." That still continues in India.

In these comments to me, the women were quite clear that their experiences were formed in the safety and privilege of their middle-class experience and that this privilege extended to young girls and women today who also might reside in the same social strata. They were also clearly aware of the *lack* of privilege that girls from poorer families must contend with. Vedhika pointed out that while all women were still expected to get married, young women from low-income backgrounds were expected to marry earlier, live with fewer resources, raise children with no help, and struggle against a number of different odds. She said: "Girls are still expected to marry and have kids and especially if you come from a poor family or from the minority community. . . . It's easy to say we [women] have so much freedom and stuff but how much of it is actually trickling down?"

As fewer women work less outside of the home, they are often left with little or no income of their own, and they are vulnerable to isolation and violence. Inara had a good deal to say about this:

Girls coming from good social status, good families, going to good schools and studying at good colleges, they have a better life, they have a better education, [they have choices], you can be a homemaker or you can be a doctor, whatever your professional life, a professor like you or whatever. . . . And you get to be more confident, you experience life, you can deal with anything because you're more educated. But again, kids coming from a lower background, lower socioeconomic status, the poorer kids, I mean those kids or those girls who are dropouts or because they don't have money to continue with school or something going on in the family, the poorer kids and all, they are the ones who face more trouble compared to us.

She goes on to predict their path:

Because those are the kids who lack education, lack money, lack self-confidence, lack everything in life and they are like, "This is my life. I get married at fifteen. Okay, my parents chose this guy. I listen to him, I'm . . . " You know, [they must endure] . . . domestic abuse. You hear a lot of all this. And that I feel because I think they're not educated well enough. . . . Domestic abuse and stuff, it's there even in educated people. But at least being educated, you're aware of it. These [poorer, less educated] kids are like, "This is my life. Okay, he tells me he is my god. I can't get it out of the system. I'm here."

While she mentions this in passing, Inara's use of the phrase "he is my god" illustrates the findings from the Pew Research Centers shared earlier where two out of three people (both men and women) believe that a wife should obey her husband. This attribute of obedience is grounded in doctrines in many religions.[39] In India, the BJP has sought to capitalize on these notions by arguing that ensuring traditional roles for men and women in religion can in fact also be patriotic:

> Religious fundamentalisms offer women a sense of belonging and identity. They also offer security to women and their families by promising to fight against corruption and crime. At the same time, religious fundamentalisms convince women that the fight for gender equality is secondary to the fight for religion.[40]

While hypothetical, the absence of women in the workplace could be due to the rise of nationalist ideologies and the belief that men and women ought to aspire to traditional roles in society. This aligns with data from the Pew Research Centers that finds that 43 percent of the country still believes that men should be the primary breadwinner and that in times of high unemployment priority should be given to men over women for jobs (56 percent). India scores second highest in this category among thirty-four countries.[41] This allows men to not have to be inclusive of women, as Darika pointed out, and prevents women from seeking their rights, as that would run counter to the needs of a nationalist agenda. Because a person's primary allegiance should be to their religion over their gender, the inculcation of religious ideology percolates across a number of different domains, including taking center stage in education, as we explore in the next chapter.

Marching band at the Annual Sports Day at Baldwin Girls High School

Graduation photo of the senior class for the yearbook: author and friends

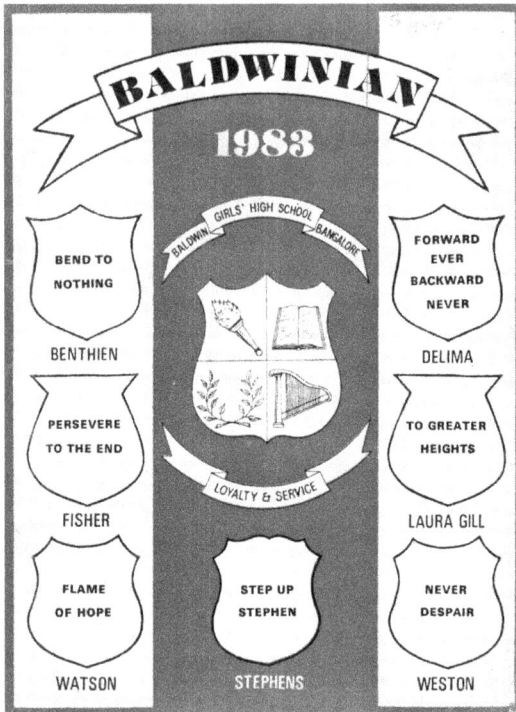

1983 scanned cover of the BGHS yearbook

Author and friends at local café Casa Piccola

Republic Day celebrations at BGHS

Torch Passing Ceremony 1988

Conference of Vice Captain Badge Ceremony 1988

Winners of the Captain/Vice Captain Race—Sports Day 1988

Chapter 6

The Battle for Education

In 1991, I went to Delhi to study for a year at Lady Shri Ram (LSR) College. Spending that time in the capital city, 1,333 miles north of Bangalore, was an eye-opening experience for me. I had left the cocoon of home for a city with wide avenues, people who spoke a language (Hindi) I did not know, and a culture that was very different from the slower and softer pace of my beloved Bangalore.

LSR is an all-women's college. In the 1990s, it was relatively well-known college for middle-class young women, and I was admitted—or given a "seat," to use the vernacular term—largely because of my debating skills and community service activities in Bangalore. The head of the college gave me a welcoming pep talk and told me that much would be expected of me as an LSR girl. Those words have stayed with me for thirty-plus years.

Today, LSR is far more renowned. It is second in the national rankings for colleges,[1] and many of its degree programs only admit students who scored 100 percent in their high-stakes twelfth-grade exams.[2] While it is considered a far more elite institution than it was thirty years ago, it continues to espouse the values of feminism, social justice, and egalitarianism,[3] much as it did when I studied there. I do not tell this story to highlight the meteoric rise of the profile of the college but to illustrate one startling statistic. On a visit back to LSR in 2014, I was speaking to Dr. Meenakshi Gopinath, the same woman who inspired me thirty years ago, who was preparing to retire from LSR. She told me that LSR was admitting approximately 450 students per year, yet the college received nearly 450,000 applications per year. In other words, only one out of every 1,000 applicants would be admitted to the college. By comparison, Harvard University admits around 2,000 students a year out of nearly 60,000 applicants,[4] a ratio of 1:30. The LSR odds are astronomical, and it remains a mystery how an admissions committee could review nearly half a million applications in order to identify fewer than 500 women who would be considered good enough to start at LSR. There was no way that the student I was in 1991 would have made the cut by today's standards. On the positive side, it was exciting to think that every year, nearly 500,000 women seek to enter a college famous for its feminist and progressive ideologies. Even so, the odds were startling—and a sobering illustration of the scale faced by middle-class and aspiring middle-class families who want their children to access education in India today.

Education in India is a story of feast and famine. While there are vast numbers of people to educate, the country's system of elite science and technology universities has created a cadre of professionals who have been instrumental in supporting global technology companies. The development of the preeminent Indian Institutes of Technology (IIT) have been well recognized in the United States where the reputation of IIT graduates has been considered "brand India" for many Silicon Valley employers.[5] As such, getting your child into an IIT (there were initially six such institutions, today there are twenty-three), in part due to its reputation but also for its affordability as it is heavily subsidized by the national government, is the goal of parents "who are doctors, engineers, lawyers, senior executives, school teachers and government employees (the traditional Indian middle class)."[6] Preparing their children for the entrance exams has become a central goal for middle-class families who see admission to the IITs as a ticket for their children to ensure continued financial and professional success. From private coaching to ensuring their children are admitted to high-quality primary and secondary schools, middle-class families' focus on educational access is a central concern.[7]

Yet despite such pockets of success, India's demographics present a much more complex picture. The share of India's population that is under the age of twenty-five is nearly 40 percent. The median age in the country is twenty-eight.[8] Demand for education continues to outpace supply. Families face frequent rejections when they seek to admit their children into "good" schools, and the deck seems to be stacked against those who have limited resources, live in less urbanized parts of the country, and have little social capital when it comes to educational experiences. Furthermore, according to OECD data, only 61 percent of three- to five-year-olds are able to access early childhood programs (compared to 83 percent across other OECD countries), and India continues to have some of the lowest levels of educational attainment at secondary and tertiary levels as compared to other OECD countries.[9]

The large numbers and the desire and need for education have been a central focus of different Indian governments since independence in 1947. Between developing and implementing ambitious five-year plans for educational growth, expanding access to free education up to the age of fourteen, and ensuring that schools follow one of three approved "boards" of education[10] to guarantee quality of education, the Indian government has tried numerous strategies. One particular policy has been a lightning rod, with large swathes of people adamantly for and against the impact and outcomes of the "reservation system."

Much of the access to high-quality educational opportunities tends to be mostly available to middle-class, "higher"-caste, urban residents of India. Government efforts to create a more equitable playing field for historically marginalized groups has led to the establishment of the "reservation system," an affirmative action structure that sought to ensure that those who had experienced generational mistreatment, such as the lower castes and the tribal communities, would be provided "reserved" quotas to ensure they were able to benefit from education and employment opportunities.[11] The reservation system seeks to guarantee that in employment, education, and politics, a representative selection of the population will be included, particularly for women and other minority or marginalized groups.

Yet the implementation of these policies has been inconsistent.[12] In education, the reservation system comes into play chiefly in the admissions policies of colleges and professional schools.[13] As the anxiety of families to access education has intensified, frustration and resentment has grown among non-marginalized (historically privileged) groups that they are forced to play by different, if not more demanding, rules. Early on, the BJP was able to capitalize on the discontent by consolidating the upper-class vote by arguing that the establishment of the reservation system would weaken their position and threaten their "dominant position."[14] By 2014, this discontent was clearly a way to pander to middle-class voters, who were encouraged to feel like they were competing against people who were not as deserving. There were feelings that the groups who were to benefit from the reservation system were gaming it to take "seats" in schools and colleges that they might not otherwise have offered purely on merit. By creating a division between these groups, the Hindutva movement was able to "challenge the legitimacy" of the reservation system[15] and galvanize middle-class voters on an issue (education) that was central to their hopes and dreams for their children.

In 2014, when Modi won the elections, the BJP capitalized on the support of "upper"-caste Hindus in part due to the lack of support for caste-based reservations systems.[16] Yet by 2019, the growth in support for the BJP came from "low"-caste Hindus, whom the BJP courted by introducing a number of programs designed to make their lives easier on a day-to-day basis while also maintaining the support of "upper"-caste Hindus.[17] The party focused on different messaging and a less overt criticism of the reservation system, allowing Modi to make inroads with the groups to gain votes.

As this chapter unfolds, we will see how the current system of education from early grades to higher education have been influenced by the changes in the political environment and the rise of the BJP over the past decade. While prior governments focused on access, affordability, and equity in terms of reaching and teaching both boys and girls of all castes and classes, albeit with inconsistent results, the BJP has, in addition to its back and forth on reservations, sought to dismantle the independence of educational institutions, control the content of the curriculum, and direct educational institutions to align with Indian values, which is often a code for "Hindu" values.[18]

Recognizing that colonial values and models have influenced how India's postindependence leaders have structured the nation's education system, the BJP has sought to make education the "centerpiece of the Hindu revivalist campaign"—a campaign that seeks to build a "Hindu nation out of what is officially a secular country with rights accorded to religious minorities."[19] By reshaping the education system, the party has been able to set the stage for what some commentators have called the "indoctrination" of young people in Hindu fundamentalism.[20]

The BJP effort to impose its control and ideology throughout the country's education system has taken three main tracks. The first is the establishment of Hindu schools in which activities and school culture reflect and promote Hindu ideologies. The second is to redirect classroom content toward a more Hindutva curriculum that is at odds with India's postindependence commitment to secular values. The third relates to the complex dance between balancing access to education for middle-class and lower-class families ("high" caste and "low" caste) in an effort to create wedges between voting blocs.

"THIS IS A VEGETARIAN SCHOOL"

In 1947, as a newly independent country, India was struggling to identify what to keep, discard, disavow, or dismantle as the shackles of the colonizing country were removed. This was the "dilemma of modernity in India," where it created a "profoundly confused notion of national identity" that furthermore struggled under the "the manipulative pressures of colonial rule,"[21] which would manifest itself in a complex relationship between what was local, what was imported, and what would ultimately stay or go according to the political leaders of the time.

In the realm of education, finding the balance between what is local knowledge to be valued and what is global knowledge to be taught has been difficult and highly contested. Soon after independence, the ruling party, the Indian National Congress (generally referred to as the "Congress Party" or simply "Congress"), sought to focus on "their vision of development, which, in spite of their anti-imperial rhetoric, did not represent a radical departure from colonial-era ideologies about 'progress.'" Arguing for a "linear model of development similar to the industrialised societies of the West," the Congress

Party ensured that education for the most part remained aligned with the structures set by the British, albeit with more focus on universal access.[22]

Determining that India would take a secular path, unlike its neighbor, Pakistan, which opted to make Islam its state religion, India's leaders sought to maintain a separation between religion and the state in the education system. Today, India has the one of the largest school systems in the world. Yet ensuring that all students have a high quality of education continues to be a challenge. Some 250 million students are enrolled in K–12 schools,[23] split relatively equally between attendance in government-funded schools and privately funded schools.[24] In India, there are two kinds of privately funded schools: those that have some government support and those that are independently managed and require no government support to exist (such as BGHS). These independently managed schools depend on fees to survive, and as middle-class incomes have grown, the number of fee-paying schools has also grown exponentially. According to some estimates, there are over 400,000 such schools today.[25] Researchers have found that with the growth in demand due to the burgeoning middle class, the market share of such schools increased from 9 percent in 1993 to 25 percent in 2017.[26] This increase has been driven not only by the expansion of India's middle class but also by the growing perception among that increasingly prosperous group that private schools are the only vehicle that can deliver the quality of education that will enable their children to enjoy a financially comfortable life. There is little trust in the ability of government-funded schools, which are poorly resourced, have less well-prepared teachers, and tend to have fewer extracurricular activities, to provide the quality of experience the middle class is expecting and demanding. This has led to the robust growth of private schools in India despite the tuition fees and hidden costs (uniforms, extracurricular fees, and social events for instance) associated with sending children to such schools.

Because most middle-class families were primarily sending their children to schools that were set up by missionaries prior to India's independence, and in an effort to meet the growing demand, the BJP and its larger umbrella organization, the Rashtriya Swayamsevak Sangh (RSS), launched a network of schools under the name Vidya Bharati, which has expanded dramatically over the past two decades. These schools are meant to be grounded in Hindu values, to contrast with the Christian values that have been perceived to be "un-Indian" and colonial. The RSS is clear about the mission of the schools:

> To develop a National System of Education which would help building a generation of young men and women that is committed to Hindutva and infused with patriotic fervour; physically, vitally, mentally and spiritually fully developed; capable of successfully facing challenges of life.[27]

Since its establishment in 1977, by 2019 the schools number over 12,000 across India, with nearly 3.4 million students enrolled and nearly 200,000 teachers working in the system.[28] Its success is defined through its growth, defining itself as "the largest educational organisation in the world."[29] The schools are affiliated with the Central Board of School Education and follow the curriculum prescribed by that board.

The growth of these kinds of schools spurred some of my former classmates to talk about the ways in which religion and education are intertwined. Most of the women, if not all, would remember the hymns we sang in BGHS. While the school espoused Christian values, the students came from a variety of religious backgrounds. Ahana reminisced:

> We sang and did our hymns and I don't think religion was a very important part of our lives in those days. I didn't even know the [religious] difference between [her classmates]: this girl is a Christian or this one is a Muslim and this one is a Hindu. This one is a Jain or a Buddhist. No, there was no discrimination. Never did any of our parents or teachers say, "This one is a Christian so she's better, or this one is a Muslim, don't talk to her." I don't think any of us really knew the difference. I certainly didn't know.

This resonates with the thoughts of Indian legislator, writer, and diplomat Shashi Tharoor, who says in his book *Why I Am a Hindu* that in part due to the "paradoxes and contradictions" inherent in Hinduism, there has always been a "willingness of Hindus to accept other faiths and modes of worship—indeed embrace them for themselves." In fact, he goes on to say that it is rather normal for Hindus to show respect and carry "relics or sacred objects of other faiths."[30] I would strongly agree with this, as even my mother and her Hindu friends would go to the local Infant Jesus Church in Bangalore, a shrine dedicated to the Infant Jesus of Prague, on Thursdays (deemed by the shrine to be the most auspicious day to visit) to pray and ask for blessings even though they were devout Hindus.

In BGHS, other than the morning meetings, where students would gather for inspirational speeches from a variety of people, to the singing of hymns, the curriculum itself was secular in nature. Girls celebrated Hindu, Christian, and Muslim holidays with their friends, and personal preferences of diet and prayer were equally respected. "I'm still a very strong believer in the fact that there's no room for religion in two places, and that is in politics and in education," commented Oona, who went on to say:

> And it just bothers me that it still keeps making its way into those two things that make or break any country. [She recalls a particular classmate of ours.] You remember her? So she lived just a few houses away from me and we were good friends. We used to go to school together and things like that. Some of my

really good friends from Baldwin's were Muslim. And that was never a factor, you know, growing up; it just never was. I'm just saying I don't think about religion, but I was never that aware of someone's religion. So this was huge [the riots during the demolition of the mosque] when, when people were losing lives [everywhere] and people were putting fear in, you don't step out, don't go to this area, don't go to Commercial Street. Those were . . . [our] hangouts. Those are places we all frequented. That there is a concentration of a certain religion population there or here. I never thought that way until Ayodhya happened.

Ahana talked about her sister's children, who were attending a Hindu school. She worried that the development of such schools would continue the process of unravelling the fabric of secularism that she valued. My former classmates seemed to share the view that while convent schools in the 1980s and 1990s espoused some Christian practices, the schools were not trying to deny the secular nature of the country. Vedhika described how this has changed, citing the example of

a very conservative school, in that sense it's very Hindu oriented. . . . [When you are deciding where to enroll a child,] nowadays you always think of who the owner of the school might be. Who are on the board of governance? Who is it run by? Is it run by a Muslim? Or is it run by the church? . . . The concern doesn't come up when it's Hindu.[31] . . . but you do sort of see, what is the hidden agenda? One is always looking for the hidden agenda unconsciously. Does this school come from a very conservative background?

For some of the Christian women I spoke with, school lunches had become a space that was fraught with tension for their children, given the BJP's ban of the sale of beef and the wider Hindutva movement's opposition to the eating of (sacred) cows and (unclean) pigs.[32] Ginny shared the experiences of her Christian daughter, who is in a Hindu school. As a mother, Ginny found the school to be of high quality overall, and by the standards of Bangalore, the commute to the school was easy, which is critical. Her daughter had a good set of friends, but she described an episode when her daughter was in fourth grade, of how her daughter felt ostracized due to her religion:

I remember somebody making fun of her when she was new. She took pepperoni pizza to school and they said, "Yuck, it's pig." And you know, she started crying and someone said, "Oh, this is a vegetarian school. You should not bring and so on." And then there was a formal set of rules that were sent out saying that don't send non-veg [nonvegetarian food]. So I just stopped [including meat in my daughter's school lunches].

The growing influence of the Hindutva movement on education is not confined to the Vidya Bharati system or to other conservative Hindu schools.

Hindutva factions may have had limited influence over the education system during the BJP's first two periods in office in the late 1990s and early 2000s, but since the BJP won a landslide victory in the general election of 2014, both the BJP and the RSS have accelerated their efforts to control what Indian children learn at school through the use of centralized curriculum planning.

"AN ALTERNATIVE NARRATIVE OF WHAT'S HAPPENING"

In 2020, in the early stages of the global COVID-19 shutdowns, the government sought to trim the curriculum for the board exams that were supervised by the central government. Announcing that the Central Board of Secondary Education (CBSE) would initially cut 30 percent of the syllabus to "relieve stressed-out students who have lost valuable hours in the classroom to COVID-19 and are trying to adapt to online learning," things changed when families saw the specific adjustments. Government schools could now, on the pretext of supporting students, ignore "chapters on democratic rights, secularism, federalism, and citizenship"; not surprisingly, many commentators expressed "concerns that the omissions are politically motivated."[33] Further, Prime Minister Narendra Modi began to identify people with negligible relevant expertise but strong links to Hindu political movements to take on critical policymaking and managerial roles in the sphere of education. Dinanath Batra, the leader of a conservative pro-Hindu group, was quoted in the *Washington Post* as saying, "What we need in India is value-based education, education that will build character. . . . We can't do that without religion, so religious studies must become a part of school curriculum."[34] He noted that his group, and others like it, would advocate for Hindu religious texts to be taught to all students irrespective of their religious identification.

The changes in the curriculum were something the women would try to rationalize in their conversations with me. Meher, for example, said:

> Education should be something that focuses more on how you're going to be a better person and how your life is going to influence the people who are around you. It should not be based on religion. Religion is something that is very personal and it is something that you're brought up with and you have certain beliefs, which your parents brought you up with. And that should not change; someone should not change that.

Part of the changes in curriculum come from a shifting of Indian history to promote a narrative of Indian primacy prior to the arrival of the Mughal leaders. *Akhand Bharat*, or the notion of "unbroken India," refers to the belief that culturally and geographically, India stretches from Afghanistan to Burma and would encompass island nations such as Sri Lanka and Maldives.[35] Students are taught to see a new picture of Indian history—one from which key secular freedom fighters have been erased. At the same time, Hindutva speeches and Hindu scripture are being included in core subjects such as history and geography in many states, including Karnataka.[36]

The scholar Lars Tore Flåten traces the history of the rise of the Hindutva movement in education from India's independence. He argues that while some of the more organized nationalist efforts around education emerged in the 1970s, incremental successes grew more visible after 1998 and when new history textbooks were developed as part of a national effort to update syllabi, curricula, and textbooks.[37] An example of such shifts is discussed in chapter 1—namely, how history textbooks in Karnataka have moved to the right in the tone and language they use to describe Muslim rulers, such as Haidar Ali and Tipu Sultan. Similar changes have been made in states such as Gujarat, Maharashtra, and Rajasthan, where textbooks have been rewritten to "downplay Islamic contributions to Indian history and culture."[38] In Maharashtra, lawmakers "scrapped an entire chapter on the Mughal Empire."[39] A 2017 article written by the Indian journalist Betwa Sharma on how Muslim students are learning to live with the Hindutva changes cites the example of a textbook in a morality class that begins with the lyrics of a song that declares, "the one culture and the blood that flows through our veins is Hindu."[40]

The women I spoke to were well aware of these changes to the curriculum. While Nisha did criticize some of the gaps in her own education at BGHS, she expressed concern about recent patterns in the national BJP government interfering in educational content. She noted that although she did not remember studying evolution, she felt that, in hindsight, her education was much more of an "absence of" rather than an "alteration of" sensitive topics, which she felt was different from today where things were in fact actively being altered:

> I think that there are some deficits with how [our BGHS] curriculum was structured . . . [but these days] I think there's a lot of that sort of being slipped into prescribed textbooks and things, which is quite dangerous. An alternative narrative of what's happening.

Darika, too, brought the changes to the textbooks up in our conversation. "From what I understand," she said, the threat is that "people are rewriting textbooks." She also noted the threats to artists possibly referencing news articles in early 2020 where BJP supporters painted over graffiti that was in solidarity with Muslim students, despite the fact that it was on private property.[41] She stumbled a bit over her words here, trying to articulate a larger idea and the general sense of worry about doing things outside the approval of the Hindutva movement:

> I think it does have a huge impact, because for me, education is not just the curriculum, it's everything else. . . . I think this polarization and this constant rhetoric that you get, has got to have a huge impact on education as well. I still have a lot of friends in the arts and the theater and they tell me just levels of censorship that they have to wade through, the kind of struggles they have just to go through. It's almost like you can't be creative or you can't be original anymore.

Extracurricular activities are also affected by the rising tide of the BJP and the RSS. In July 2017, the state of Rajasthan renamed a prestigious scholarship program, discarding the name of former prime minister Indira Gandhi and replacing it with the name of the Hindu goddess of knowledge, Saraswati (also known as Padmakshi). The "Indira Priyadarshini Puruskar Yojana" had been established to honor Indira Gandhi, India's first and thus far only female prime minister. The change of name to the "Padmakshi Puruskar Yojana" had both strong political and religious associations. The politics relates to the fact that Indira Gandhi was a member of the secular Congress Party, the BJP's most formidable political rival and currently in opposition to the BJP government. The religious overtones represent both an implicit and explicit connection to BJP's Hindu ideology. An article in the (secular) *Hindustan Times* explains the link to Hinduism:

> Padmakshi, meaning a woman with lotus-like eyes, is another name of Goddess Saraswati, the deity of wisdom and knowledge. The award will be given on Basant Panchami . . . celebrated as the birth of the goddess . . . [and which] marks the beginning of spring and falls on the fifth day (Panchami) of Maagh month in the Hindu calendar. Hindus worship the goddess on this day and wear yellow—the colour of spring.[42]

The award, given to girls who score the highest in the district board exams given at grades 10 and 12, includes both a monetary prize and a certificate. With the change, eighth-grade girls also became eligible for this award, which was then touted by one BJP minister as a "positive" change, while ignoring the request for a response to the name change for the award.[43]

Changing the curriculum and infusing Hinduism into school programs and policies are tolerated in part due to the fact that the growing middle class worries that the odds of getting a good education are more competitive than ever. The odds, such as the ones at LSR, keep parents up at night anxious about the opportunities that might not be available to their children. Being perturbed about getting a smaller piece of the pie allows for wedges to be driven between groups, and making cultural issues a central focus is a key political strategy of populist parties everywhere.[44] The establishment of Hindu schools and the changes in curriculum are issues that can divert attention to the larger worry of middle-class parents fighting for a space in school.

"WHAT ARE THEY GOING TO BE DOING?"

India's youth population is immense. India has more young people than any other country,[45] with half of its 1.3 billion population under the age of twenty-five.[46] While some see this as a tsunami of transformative potential,[47] the competition for any access to education is a challenge, but for a high-quality education, it is particularly brutal. In this regard, the women were conflicted. They recognized that access to education was something that was a long-term challenge and could be a struggle in a variety of ways. For many, getting a foot in the door of a good school is difficult. Inara pointed to the ways in which those students who could not access a good education would be hindered:

> You get to be more confident, you experience life, you can deal with anything because you're more educated. Kids coming from a lower background, lower socioeconomic status, the poorer kids, those kids or those girls who are dropouts because they don't have money to continue with school or something going on in the family, the poorer kids and all, they are the ones who face more trouble compared to us.

The better the school, the greater the likelihood of one's child moving forward, first to college and then on to a well-paid job. Government schools, whether they were state supported or lower quality CBSE schools, left Inara in no doubt that they were far below the level of quality of the private schools to which she was accustomed:

> I visited a government school, I think, nine years back. I was shocked. In Bangalore, this is in Bangalore. There were like 120 kids in that class. I was shocked. I was shocked. [The classrooms were] literally cramped. And I don't know what education they're getting. I mean here, we speak of smaller classes, [with more] one to one . . . you know?

She was referring to the fact that middle-class families are seeking schools that are better equipped than government schools, with more facilities and curricular and extracurricular opportunities and endowed with that key measure of quality: a low teacher-student ratio. But these features come at a cost. Bhavna commiserated, "So education today is not what it was, inexpensive, anymore. It's extremely expensive. It's almost impossible for a normal child to get admission or pay these kind of fees." Even if they do get into a school, the sheer numbers can exacerbate a student's sense of insecurity and lack of confidence. Vedhika explained:

> I don't know where to start; there is so much to say. So I think the root cause of all of India's problems is its population. Yes, we do laud ourselves, saying that we have the youngest population in the world and stuff like that. But so much of that population is actually unemployable. We are not giving them the support, the education, the literacy that they need in order to actually move forward in a meaningful way. Yes, we have a huge population, but what are they going to be doing? You know, if you walk into any store, yes, there is an eighteen-year-old sales girl. But she's not employable in that sense [for advancement]. They're not being given the soft skills to be better employees. So there's this whole bunch of people who are not going to be able to move forward, to move past this, because they have not been given the education, which is of a certain quality.

Ginny recognized that India's schoolchildren are not only competing with one another but also, to some degree, with students globally. The fallout results in students working to the point of exhaustion to ensure they get high grades. Ginny comments, "I think it's very competitive now and that's across the world," she said. "[Almost] everyone is in the 99th percentile. And if your child is in the 85th percentile, she wouldn't get any admission anywhere." Ekta similarly voiced concern about the fierce competition facing Indian students::

> It obviously has become way more competitive. . . . I think because obviously the population has grown so much and there's more people for fewer seats. I remember getting 60 percent [on one's exams] was good enough and we were there, and now everybody is scoring 90 percent [and still do not get a seat in a college they want to go to]. And I'm thinking, how is that even possible?

Chanchal, herself a teacher, sounded disgusted about these situations: "Given the sheer numbers of students in the college [she used to teach at], we had to come up with a system [to teach so many students] . . . and some of the senior teachers decided to sift out some of the students." After giving them a test, the teachers grouped students into different sections based on perceptions of income disparities, creating a system where the sections made up of lower-income students were considered a second-tier environment. Chanchal also complained about the "one-sided" nature of the instruction she was expected to deliver in the classroom:

> As a teacher it was so one-sided, because all I did was go there, explain something, dictate answers and that was the end of it. At the end of it all, I just don't

know how much learning took place. . . . We had to spend time figuring out how best we can support [our students] outside of class. And so it was quite a tough task trying to be a counselor and at the same time be . . . an orthodox kind of a lecturer. . . . Just go in there, disseminate the knowledge—whatever, I don't even call it knowledge. Just give them information and get out.

She explained why she had stopped teaching in larger institutions:

It wasn't a very pleasant experience in that sense. And I realized that in a class of 120, 130 students, what kind of qualitative change can one bring in? That really became the challenge for me. That sense of injustice. That sense of, "So what if they're in a mixed class? So what if there are some terribly brilliant students? And so what if there are some stragglers? Why can't they be in the same class?" We have a whole bunch of people who are struggling to make their way up. There were many things that I just didn't agree with. And those in the department who thought along the same lines, we tried to convince the senior teachers to consider changing it and try something new. But somehow that didn't work.

The demand for education is fueled by the desire of a large population to use school as a vehicle for upward social and economic mobility. For a lower-class family, providing a good education for their son means that he would be more likely to get a white-collar job in an office, elevating the family's status in society. For a middle-class or aspiring middle-class family, educating their daughter would make her both financially independent and more attractive in the marriage market.[48] In a country in which arranged marriages are still the norm, the choice of a spouse in middle-class families is driven by both the quality (Does the prospective bride or groom have a professional degree and if so where did they receive it?) and the quantity (What are their potential future earnings based on their degree?) of education of the potential partner.[49] Therefore the demand for education continues to grow, but the need to compete with nearly 68 percent of the population who identify as one of the protected categories under the reservation system[50] is a point of contention for many middle-class families. Saira talked at length about the impact of the reservation system on middle-class families:

See, we have reservations in colleges, in engineering, [in] medical [schools]. Now we have reservations in jobs. Again, I'm talking from my point of view, which is very narrow. You will have to just take that into focus, because my view is very narrow.

She continued, candidly describing the tension she feels between wanting to be fair to historically marginalized groups but also wanting her daughter to have a fair chance of being admitted to a prestigious college:

I don't know how it is in rural areas, but [in] urban areas [we suffer]. When you've given so many benefits [to people covered by the reservation system], specifically maybe for education. Okay, you give it to them, fine, I agree. You've been doing it for so many years now, sixty, seventy years. They say, "We have been downtrodden for hundreds of years, and for seventy years you're giving it to us, and you're feeling the burden of it? We have been stamped upon." I agree. But when my daughter goes for admissions to IIT [a premier engineering college], or any other colleges, like even LSR or something like that, 50 percent, 60 percent of the seats are reserved for those quota students. And we just fall into 5 percent, and my daughter's [scored in her board exams] 98 percent and those students are coming from 70, 80 percent. It shocks me. And especially for medical seats. Medicine is something you don't do that. Somebody's life will be at stake because of that. There are all reservations for those students. It's very insensitive of me to think like that. But when it comes to your own child, it really pinches you. I'm like, "What is this?"

Waida described the pressure on middle-class students who do not score as highly in their exams as Saira's daughter:

It's so unfair to expect that from all the children. . . . [What about] those in the mediocre stage, you know, 60 percent, 70 percent children, what will happen to all of them? I think that education has gone for toss [gotten worse] in India. It's just too much pressure. . . . The amount of pressure is just overwhelming. Education has to loosen up in India, that's for sure. It's still severe, strict. I think children have to be children. They're not allowed to be children at the minute; they are expecting too much of little ones. You know, once they go to senior school, you start pushing them. It's one thing. But when they are in [grade] one . . . they start with that many books and exams and expectations from the children is way too much.

In any country, the education system can have a major impact on the attitudes and beliefs of those who pass through that system. The power of education to influence can either nurture independent and critical thinking or it can foster conformity and compliance—and such attitudes, of course, will influence how, as adults, the former students engage intellectually with their society and participate in its democracy.[51] The next three chapters explore my former classmates' attitudes toward inclusion, intellectualism, and governance, attitudes initially shaped by their experiences at Baldwins and more recently buffeted by the policies and practices of Hindu nationalism.

Chapter 7

Chipping Away at Belonging and Secularism

On a cold December day in 1986, eight thirteen- and fourteen-year-old girls boarded the first of two trains that would take them to the northern city of Ranchi, in the eastern state of Bihar. With two teachers as chaperones, we were representing BGHS at what was being called a Unite India camp, organized by the alumni of the St. Xavier's High School, in Ranchi. After thirty or so hours on the trains, and arriving to a type of cold we girls from the south were unaccustomed to, we spent four days with students from all over the north (we were the only group of students from the south). Before we arrived, we had been asked to write an essay about the value of the principle of "Unity in Diversity" (a phrase coined by independent India's first prime minister, Pandit Jawaharlal Nehru) for the program book. Our early adolescent words were full of lofty rhetoric:

> What can we, the younger generation do to promote the idea of oneness? . . . We should forget our minor differences of languages and . . . customs and manners. . . . We should regard everyone, irrespective of their different religions . . . as our brothers and sisters.

Adolescent idealism? Of course, but in essence, we were echoing what we had been conditioned to believe we should do to help stitch together myriad ethnic, linguistic, and religious groups into a single country, one that was not quite forty years old at the time. Politicians, teachers, and journalists celebrated the notion of unity in diversity, so at the camp, we sang songs in Kannada and performed dances and discussed things such as the food and culture of Karnataka in an effort to build bonds across the diverse states. As mentioned in chapter 4, Faye recalled appreciating the opportunity to meet people from different states, seeing it as a privilege to get a sense of the whole cloth of the diversity of India.

What, in hindsight, was rather ironic was that our group of eight girls was by far the most diverse delegation. The groups of students from Gujarat, Maharashtra, and Bihar, among other places, were far more homogenous, claiming deep roots to the states that they were representing. But for our group, while we sang songs in Kannada, it was the mother tongue of maybe only three of the eight girls in the group. When we performed dances from Karnataka, all of us had learned those in rushed lessons about four weeks before we left for Ranchi. When we talked about food and culture, we did so from the perspective of cosmopolitan Bangaloreans, whose regular diet included staples of global cuisine: burgers, pasta, milkshakes. Not only were we a multilingual, multicaste, and multireligious group, we were also a multicitizen group, because a few of us who attended also had non-Indian passports, having been born outside of India. If my memory is accurate, four languages and three religions were represented in our group. This diversity solidified our thinking that Bangalore was different. And, as official statistics for 1991 confirm, we weren't wrong: in 1991, only 35 percent of the population of Bangalore spoke the state language of Kannada; others spoke neighboring South Indian languages (25 percent speaking Tamil and 17 percent speaking Telugu); and 13 percent spoke Urdu, the language of the Muslim population in India.[1]

In many ways, what we in Bangalore represented was nothing other than the unity in diversity that other cities, if not the country as a whole, was trying to emulate. Every day, Indians deal with people of diverse linguistic, regional, and religious backgrounds, and the ability to communicate effectively within and between these communities fosters social cohesion. The close proximity of such a wide diversity of groups can breed discord, leading to intercommunal violence becoming one way of handling difference.[2] Communal violence, or "violence involving groups that define themselves by their differences of religion, ethnicity, language or race,"[3] has been a facet of Indian life for over a century.[4] And while modern Bangalore has not been immune from this persistent evil, one journalist tallied eight "major riots" since 1986.[5] While the number of fatalities has historically been lower, seeing communal violence as a problem in the central and western parts of the country, there has been a parallel rise of such violence in Karnataka, as there the BJP has been increasingly present.[6]

The causes of these riots have been varied. In 1986, for instance, the publication of a short fiction story in the regional paper, the Deccan Herald, about a boy who commits suicide was seen to have taken Prophet Mohammed's name in vain, leading to the death of seventeen people during the riots. Other outbreaks of communal violence have been fueled by the death of a movie star and by antagonism against settlers coming into Bangalore from other parts of the country no matter their religion.

Growing up, we were not entirely sheltered from these tensions, but it tended not to affect us directly. While there were certain city neighborhoods our parents would warn us not to spend time in, this was not unusual for any person in cities and towns across the world. A few times, certain areas of the city would be off limits because religious tensions might be running high. Muslim girls recalled being asked not to go to Hindu-dominant neighborhoods and Hindu girls would be warned not to travel into Muslim-dominated areas during sensitive times. Meher recalled:

My parents live in a place that is 50/50, 50 percent Muslims and 50 percent Hindus—basically we live in a Muslim area. And right in front of our house, we've witnessed a guy being killed. That was the worst thing I can remember, how he was killed with a bicycle, being hit with a bicycle. That was so horrible, horrendous, [the most] horrendous scene that I can remember.

Despite this, for the women, secularism and belonging were hallmarks of how they perceived the world around them. This was something that they remarked on frequently. Garima, for instance, said:

Bangalore is peaceful in that way. There's minorities but I think everybody has their own space. Generally, I think everybody is tolerant to each other's faith and I don't remember any incident where things were shut down for a certain reason, or certain religion, or certain riot. I don't remember that. I think even in school, I know we had everybody from different religions. I don't remember religion interfering with the way we interacted with anybody or anything like that.

More recently, however, the idea of who is a Bangalorean has shifted. The changed political landscape has altered conceptions of who belongs in the city and how inclusive the city is and should be. My former classmates spoke extensively about how religious and regional tensions are interwoven today and how issues of identity and secularism now intersect in a city that was once seen to be the most cosmopolitan of all Indian cities.

"INFILTRATION IS THE WORST"

One point that the women would keep circling back to was that the city where they grew up rarely required them to think about or navigate through the sorts of differences that divided people in other parts of the state and the country. And while families were relatively unconcerned about who our friends were, religious, caste, and regional differences would rush to the foreground of their concern if we ever considered marrying someone from across these lines. But as classmates, we encompassed a wide range of communities and seldom saw the differences in our identities as barriers.

As my classmates have grown older, and as the influx of migrants from the north has continued to increase, their consciousness of the differences between being from the north or the south has grown. Moreover, they have come to resent some of the newer transplants to the city. Ironically, perhaps, the women grew up in an inclusive city—a city in which most residents were accepted as "Bangaloreans"—but that sense of inclusivity has contracted as the size of the migrant population has expanded. For longtime residents, it is the influx of new people to Bangalore, especially people who have come from the north, that has generated the city's worsening problems with traffic and personal security, and the associated loss of the city's beloved bungalows and green spaces.[7]

Vedhika pointed out that "actually Bangalore's always been a magnet for outsiders" and that Bangaloreans have always had multiple identities in terms of caste and regional backgrounds. But almost all the women voiced concern about how the city's culture and quality of life have deteriorated because of the arrival of so many North Indians. Even women whose families had historical ties to the north did not consider the recent immigrants "Bangalorean."

Ginny reflected on the city's changing demography and economy:

> Survival has changed in more [ways] than just the political climate. Bangalore has also changed, because there's a lot of other people, non-Bangaloreans who are here. So there's a lot of people from North India, from Bombay. There are a lot of job opportunities here as well. And as a result, Bangalore has changed. So, it's not the same population that was there, say twenty years ago. It's grown and changed.

Specific figures for newer North Indian arrivals are hard to come by in part due to the fact that internal movements of people are not tracked closely, but one report in the *Hindustan Times* claims after Mumbai, Bangalore has the highest number of nonnative settlers of any city in the country.[8]

The relationship between longtime Bangaloreans of all backgrounds and newer arrivals continues to be tense. Part of the reason for this charged atmosphere is the competition for scarce resources such as water, electricity, housing, and education and the implacable problems that have descended on the city with the exponential growth of its population. Bhavna talked about what she saw as different:

> All these big people come for these computer software [jobs] and move from North India. Infiltration from North India is the worst. . . . It's really sad. North Indian friends . . . talk about how they came to Bangalore [and criticize the city], and I want to seriously punch them in the face and get them [to go] back.

Oona, too, felt that her local pride was offended by recent arrivals. She noted that while Bangalore had never been a city with a dominant Kannada-speaking population, there was enough exposure to that language that reminded you that you were still in Karnataka. She continued:

> Bangalore is not a Kannada place [anymore] and it kind of pains me. I feel sad. It's overrun by folks from other places. Sometimes it bugs me, and my husband calls me a prude, but when people who've lived in Bangalore for two years, come to me and say, "Oh, Bangalore. I know this is how Bangalore does it." But you don't! You cannot claim that! It's very different. It's more of a transient population [now]. And you can still pick out a hardcore Bangalorean just talking to them or meeting them, and you can say, "Okay, you have Bangalore in your blood."

The paralyzing traffic problems are a constant reminder of how many people have come to Bangalore in recent years. The city, designed to be a modest, middle-class city, with broad boulevards and tree-lined roads, has become unrecognizable due to the vast number of people who now drive along its streets. According to one report, Bangalore has the worst traffic congestion in the world, with the "average Bangalorean spend[ing] 71% extra travel time stuck in Bangalore traffic."[9] Saira linked congestion and migrants:

> I feel very sad for Bangalore when I look at the traffic situation, and I look at how the city is crushed under all of that weight. The influence of other people, mostly North Indians maybe, or whatever. So you feel that dying culture there. I don't see many Bangaloreans anymore.

Ekta talked about her perceptions of how the changing demographics of the city led to changes in her:

> Especially the people who are not from Bangalore, who have come from other parts of India. I think [the city] has really changed. You have to be aggressive these days in Bangalore, because if you're still laid back, that's it! Then people will just walk all over you. . . . I think it's because of the times, basically isn't it? And it's also because it's people from other parts of India, so they come from places like North India where these kind of things are pretty normal [she felt that being more aggressive was something more common in the north]. . . . And I think also . . . we were very proud of being Bangalorean, and we used to clearly look after the place and everything. Now I don't find that anybody takes pride in living there. . . . I feel they just come there, they make as much money [as they can], they get the lifestyle. They don't really think of Bangalore as their own place, they're just there as a temporary place for them to work.

From being residents in a city where your outlook and your commitment to inclusion were hallmarks of your Bangalore identity, the women now are as conscious of who does not belong in the city as they are of those who do belong. Part of this shift in attitude is driven by the inescapable fact that the city has become much larger and more congested, but it is also fueled by the women's exposure to larger messages being telegraphed through the political changes about inclusion and belonging in India as a whole and the ways in which religion is becoming a primary determinant of belonging.

"THE RADICALIZATION OF AN ENTIRE MINDSET"

While the women were aware of communal flareups during their adolescent years, what they were beginning to note was the more systematic and overt political efforts increasingly being used to marginalize those who were not Hindu. A number of laws from local to state and national, both proposed and passed, have sought to elevate Hindu issues over non-Hindu issues. These laws have ranged from those proposed to prevent religious conversions to bans on the sale of beef. In addition, there are other rules and practices that discriminate against people in areas such as housing and education.

The policies of a militant Hindu national government with widening control at the state and local levels have created new social and religious divisions and widened existing ones, leaving some groups feeling increasingly vulnerable and rocking the former relatively peacefully coexistence. The examples shared by the women on how they now saw exclusion, alienation, and difference were eye opening. Interestingly, while they did not welcome the newer arrivals in Bangalore, they were dismayed by the lack of welcome in the city for people who are different, especially those whom they regarded as part of the "original" population of Bangalore.

Non-Hindus around the country have been the target of increasing hostility in recent years, which has been expressed, for instance, in threats of attacks on migrants from the northeast parts of the country to a rise in attacks including violence, smearing dog feces, and direct threats of rape and death made against Christians.[10] Historically, although minor eruptions of violence did occur between different ethnic, religious, and other groups in Bangalore, the city was not as volatile as other parts of the country. The intercommunal tensions would generally remain "under the surface," as Nisha said, especially as far as the middle class was concerned, because middle-class families were usually sheltered from the types of communal disharmony. Furthermore, any outbreaks of violence could quickly be quelled by the local security forces in a city that was overwhelmingly middle class. Nisha remarked that while some tensions were always visible in other cities, in Bangalore, "we seemed largely, at least on the surface, to be getting along." She wondered if the Ayodhya riots "just kind of tore open [the mystique of the city] and showed us everything that was simmering under the surface?"

Yashika, shared a similar reflection. As a Hindu, she recalled she had a boyfriend who was from the northern part of the country. His uncle was a member of the Rashtriya Swayamsevak Sangh (RSS), the precursor to the BJP, often viewed as a right-wing Hindu paramilitary organization. Her uncle was introducing his nephew to ideas that were very different to those she embraced, and that was when she realized there was this "majority that was very different from the way I thought." She went on:

> But I never realized they felt victimized, because they were in the majority. They got everything that they wanted. I don't like the way things are manipulated. I don't like the way things are pushed in a certain way, and I especially don't like the way Muslims are put down. even though I'm not a Muslim. And Christians, you know are not comparatively, really pushed down, [but] there is a certain level of antagonism, but it's not as awful as it is against [Muslims].

One worrying development in recent years is the increasingly common practice of restricting who can live in apartment buildings or rent homes in certain neighborhoods.[11] More and more frequently, landlords are actively discriminating against people who are non-Hindus by screening for tenants who are either "vegetarian—which is code for 'higher'-caste Hindus[12]—or explicitly stating that Muslims should not apply."[13] The national newspaper *The Hindu* highlighted the widespread use of such practices in Bangalore. The report, titled "India's IT Powerhouse Mired in Social Prejudice," described the situation:

> The most guarded areas in the city are also those endowed with the best infrastructure. House owners in Jayanagar, Basavangudi, Malleshwaram, Sadashivnagar, Indiranagar, Rajajinagar, Upper Palace Orchards, Koramangala and J.P. Nagar hold some of the worst prejudices, says Seven Raj. "In these localities, neighbours gang up against an owner who dares to rent his house out to somebody from a lower caste or a minority community," says M. Paari, a former Bruhat Bangalore Mahanagara Palike Corporator [that is, a local legislator].[14]

This unsettling trend was unknown to the women who grew up in Bangalore in the 1980s and early 1990s. Where they went to school, caste and religious differences had little to no bearing on who they shared lunch with or whose house hosted sleepovers. As Yashika commented, when discussing the treatment today of non-Hindus:

That is such a shock because that is something [treating people differently because of their religion] we never ever did. We had lots of vegetarian friends. But I honestly don't remember any of my friends by whether they were vegetarian or not. That wasn't even a factor that we looked at. Religion, the way you live, all that, it is now considered important. So there are these different buildings, for example, where they say only Jains can live or things like that. So, in that way, the people themselves have changed. So that's how Bangalore has grown. It is no longer that little city when I was growing up. Once that clicked in my mind, that I need to think about Bangalore more like Bombay, because that is the very stereotypical thinking, and there are different kinds of people over here. That's just something that I needed to wrap my brain around.

She ended by sounding this disquieting note:

We have always had protests in India because it was a country that had two or three sides for everything, but it was hardly, at least the way I saw, [this tradition of protesting], it was not [intended] to split the country into one side and the other side. But now I think all of these [government policies] are really [designed] to make all of us say which side you belong to.

Rachna talked about how it sickened her to witness the growing divisiveness. She said that while she understood the role religion played in people's lives, religion was something that ought to remain private. In her mind, the religious motivation that was infiltrating almost everything was disturbing. She mentioned that in her job she had come across an advertisement for a Hindutva Information Technology conference. She said:

I've heard of IT, which is information technology. I don't know what Hindutva has to do with it. I don't know how you can club [those two things] together, and it just scares the daylights out of me. And we're living in a democracy.

Chanchal, who works as a teacher, shared some of the same concerns. She feels that society has changed insofar as many people are now ignoring the mistreatment of those who are marginalized in society, paying very little attention to unfair or exclusionary treatment:

Whether it be the kind of treatment that has been now meted out for the migrants that are suffering, or women, cutting across all strata of society, a girl child, the LGBTQ+ community. It's like the whole patriarchal setup has its blinkered approach, and that's it. . . . It's just radicalization of an entire mindset of a community for years, then you start imposing a certain idea, little by little, [which] percolates down into little pockets. And it's always one against the other, or one that is more divisive than anything else, building on all the old hurts and old wounds, which have always existed in certain communities, a sense of victim-hood is just being reinforced. It's very distressing to see all of that.

Another way in which Christians and Muslims have been marginalized in recent years is through measures introduced to ban the sale within India and the export abroad of beef and beef products that are taken from cows. While there are all forms of cattle in India, from oxen to buffalos, cows are considered sacred in Hinduism, and the cow slaughter prevention movement has been gaining ground in India since the mid-2000s, despite the fact that beef has been a cheap source of protein for millions of people in India.[15] During the early days of the Indian independence movement, there were increasingly calls for banning the sale of beef, in part due to the fact that beef was a large part of the British diet.[16] During the postindependence period, efforts to ban the sale of beef continued, but by the time the BJP began its political ascendency, the issue was well ensconced in the political rhetoric of the times. By 2017, the BJP also sought to reduce the export of beef and leather—a potentially expensive step given that India is one of the world's leading exporters of those products.[17] The government's attempts to clamp down on those who sell or buy beef has been supported by Hindu vigilantes.[18] Between 2010 and 2018, violence against people who butchered or bought beef grew; of the 123 recorded attacks, 98 percent occurred after the BJP came to power in 2014.[19] The government often avoids punishing those who have instigated such violence, by ensuring that courts either limit or ignore prosecuting such crimes, or handing down light sentences, thereby emboldening perpetrators of future actions.[20] In Karnataka, the Karnataka Prevention of Slaughter and Preservation of Cattle Act, passed by the BJP in 2020, "has decimated the business of those in the beef trade"—namely, Muslim butchers. Cow slaughter, including calves, was banned even before this new law, but the new law also bans the slaughter of bulls, bullocks, and oxen.[21]

This recent prohibition was frequently commented on by my former classmates. Although many of us eat chicken and lamb, most avoid beef and pork for religious reasons, but in our youth we did not see any reason to condemn those who did eat beef and pork. The BJP, however, has made this a front-page issue. Rachna talked about how the ban was affecting people who depended on the cheaper meat and were finding it increasingly hard to find, even before the bans. Ginny enjoyed eating beef and said that although beef from cows was seldom available, she could until recently find beef from buffalos until the ban. Now that it was impossible to find, she explained the problem confronting her as a Christian:

If they say you can't eat beef in Karnataka, what do we do? Just conform, I guess. My husband can't [conform, because he likes it], we go back to Kerala [another southern state to get beef]. I feel that it is an invisible bias. I feel I'm a minority. You really don't want to draw attention. . . . [She shares the story of an activist she admires who is Christian and protesting these changes.] She speaks up, but you can see the ire it draws, and the reaction to her. I'm sorry to say, but I'm not that bold [brave]. I wish I were. So I just don't speak up.

The chipping away at inclusion through policing where you live or what you eat aims directly at feelings of safety and security. Jasmine said, "There are undercurrents of 'I'm a Hindu,' 'I'm a Muslim,' 'I'm a Christian' kind of a thing. And, you know, people feel insecure in their own ways." Vedhika said:

> Everything is so polarized now, and you have to be careful as to what you say, as to whom you say [it] to. Everybody's under this impression that Hinduism is under threat, it's under siege. And so that is leading to every religion saying, "We are under siege." It's so stupid and, you know, frankly, as a practicing atheist, it doesn't matter to me. I have married a Christian, we follow everything [are inclusive about all religions], we celebrate everything [both Hindu and Christian holidays]. But it does worry me in a sense because my son does have a Christian surname. So I feel like, "I don't know what it's going be like," in that sense. So I have to keep shutting people down every so often [when they say intolerant things].

The housing and beef bans seem to be aimed at elevating Hindus over all non-Hindus. The prohibitions may also be intended to radicalize moderate Hindus and push them closer to the BJP's brand of Hindu fundamentalism. But while all non-Hindus are in the fundamentalists' crosshairs, Muslims seem to be the target of particular animosity.

"NOT A FAIR DEAL"

In his article "Terrorizing Muslims: Communal Violence and Emergence of Hindutva in India," Jayanth Deshmukh clarifies the ways in which ideology is at the heart of the rise of the Hindutva movement in modern India. Citing Karl Marx, he says that "ideology is a false consciousness that favours the ruling class . . . [where] the consciousness of the elites thrives on the oppression of the vulnerable and provides justification for engaging in those [oppressive] actions."[22] The creation of the Muslim "other"; the condemnations of Islamic "invasions"; and the claims that Hindu culture, history, and faith are being lost and the growing the political power of the BJP[23] helped inspire more attacks on Muslims than on any other minority group in India.[24] Political hate speech has been growing as well, and politicians are perceived as being rewarded when they marginalize Muslims.[25] In 2016, a Karnataka state political representative, Anant Kumar Hegde, declared, "As long as we have Islam in the world, there will be no end to terrorism. If we are unable to end Islam, we won't be able to end terrorism."[26] Eighteen months later, he was named to the central government as the union minister of skill development and entrepreneurship.[27]

Such words and actions have not gone unnoticed by the women with whom I spoke. Ila remembered:

> When we were studying and even when I was in college, the fact that I'm Muslim was never in the forefront of any conversation. It was never even up there in my thought processes. But now, sometimes when I introduce myself to somebody, I can see them gauging, "Okay, what is she?" They're trying to figure out what religion I belong to, which is not required. You don't need to know. I don't need to know what religion you are, I just need to know what kind of person you are. It's something which is happening right now in our country. People are looking at one another and gauging them based on their religions, which was not there earlier.

Islamophobia is a worldwide phenomenon,[28] and the women sought to place recent developments in India within the global context. Ela, for instance, remarked:

> I mean it's not just India. A lot of it is everywhere, but I think I feel it really in India because it almost seems like a betrayal, because it almost feels like an India that I don't know. It's like somebody just replaced the India I knew with something else.

She reflected on the contrast between attitudes in Bangalore now and when she was younger:

> I find that really, really disturbing. Now it's almost like we have to fight to hold on to that Bangalore. . . . The thing is it's not just Bangalore; it's all of India, isn't it? Growing up in Bangalore, I don't think I thought, "Oh, so and so is a Muslim." So you knew people's names or whatever, you took it for granted that some people went to church and some people went to the temple and it didn't matter. It didn't affect your relationship with that person.

She told me a story about a Muslim friend of hers whose father was in the Indian Air Force. The friend told my former classmate that she had always felt proud that her father was serving in the Indian Armed Forces but that her ten-year-old son was told by one of his classmates to "go home [to Pakistan]." Ela ends her story:

And that's unbelievable to me. Unbelievable. That it could come to that. And I can't imagine as a ten year old ever speaking in those terms to other kids. Not that we were perfect; we were, at times, mean, but not about someone's ethnicity or religious beliefs or any of that. That's so hard to get my head around, but then I realize India is not isolated. Yeah. It's happening in so many places.

Another facet of the growing intolerance among Hindu fundamentalists is their fear of relationships between Muslim men and Hindu women. According to a conspiracy theory commonly known as "love jihad," Muslim men are actively seeking to convert Hindu women by making the women fall in love with them. Internet trolls and gangs of vigilantes are using this red herring as a way to vent their Islamophobia and deepen divisions between Hindus and Muslims.[29] Gruesome murders have been committed against Muslim men who are either in a relationship with or even merely perceived to be in a relationship with a Hindu woman.[30] There are laws already on the books in some states in India that make it illegal for a Muslim man to marry a Hindu woman, and the BJP-led state government is considering introducing such a law in Karnataka.[31] Kiara, a Hindu, did not talk explicitly about "love jihads," but she did say:

There is a sense that if I was a Muslim living in India, I would be resentful of the fact that for some reason, even though we call ourselves a democracy, the Muslim folks around India have not been given a fair deal. If you're talking to a Hindu and Muslim who have been Indians, . . . I think the Hindu guy is feeling a little more secure than the Muslim guy, because there is a sense of this Hindutva being the sort of driving force behind the government.

The driving force of the government was on full display in the early days of the COVID-19 pandemic. Following an international religious gathering of Muslims from around the world in India in February and March 2020, news reports spun a narrative that "foreigners" were responsible for the spread of COVID in India.[32] With people filing court cases against Muslims whom they thought responsible for transmitting the virus, the decisions from the courts found that there was no merit to the cases and that in fact the media played a role in creating a false narrative against the Muslims in order to identify a scapegoat.[33] In the decision, the High Court sought to defend the international visitors:

There was big propaganda in print media and electronic media against the foreigners who had come to Markaz Delhi and an attempt was made to create a picture that these foreigners were responsible for spreading the Covid-19 virus in India. There was virtually persecution against these foreigners. A political Government tries to find the scapegoat when there is pandemic or calamity and

the circumstances show that there is probability that these foreigners were cho-
sen to make them scapegoats. The aforesaid circumstances and the latest figures
of infection in India show that such action against present petitioners should
not have been taken. It is now high time for the concerned to repent about this
action taken against the foreigners and to take some positive steps to repair the
damage done by such action.[34]

International presses quickly picked up the story, with National Public Radio,
the BBC, the *Washington Post*,[35] and other major global outlets documenting
the ways in which the government "scapegoated" Muslims as the reason for
the spread of the virus.[36] As an article in *Foreign Policy* commented:

> India's television news channels, already notorious for spreading hatred against
> Muslims, were quick to attack. Anchors accused Muslim missionaries of
> "deliberately" spreading COVID-19, dubbing them India's "virus villains" and
> "human bombs."[37]

One article described how the sister of an Indian movie star "called for the
shooting of Muslims . . . [and] a hospital in the northern Indian state of
Uttar Pradesh said it did not admit Muslim patients."[38] One of the women I
spoke with, Harminder, found this appalling and then connected the government's COVID-related lockdowns as a way to further restrict the movement
of Muslims, especially during the month of Ramadan. Observant Muslims
would break their fasts at dusk and the restrictions seemed particularly
restrictive at a time when they might be traveling to celebrate with family
members. She said:

> Even in a lockdown, they're relating it to the Muslim, because [one of her
> friends] was discussing that the reason why they're having a lockdown [start-
> ing at] seven o'clock [when Muslims can break their fast during Ramadan] is
> because the Ramzan is going on. Otherwise, all the Muslims are going to come
> out, a lot more. They say the spread of the viruses [is happening] because of
> that. They are trying to get some connection to religion in this, which I definitely
> don't think it's the right thing to do.

Bhavna echoed Harminder's discomfort with the attempt to make spurious
"connections to religion." She spoke articulately about her family business,
and said that with 90 percent of its workers coming from Muslim families,
she was "very much toward [supportive of] the Muslims being safe." She herself grew up in a Hindu family, but in her conversation she seemed to describe
a less strict connection to any religion. She remarked:

This bringing religion, dividing these people is not correct. It's not correct at all. We've never followed it before. . . . Bangalore has a lot of Muslim populations, right? We're not going to break that bond for politics. It's very sad to bring religion in this because nobody practices our own religion [meaning many of us celebrate many holidays of varied religions].

As she continued, Bhavna began to get emotional: "I feel sorry for what they must be going through. . . . We're a hundred-year-old company and we've never ever brought religion into this. Anybody [is] safe with us." She explained how she had to reassure her Muslim employees when they asked her if they might lose their jobs because they are Muslim. "We tell them, 'Boss,[39] no. Nothing's going to happen. We'll see that nothing happens to you guys.'" After a few more minutes discussing her concerns and her commitments, she ended rather matter of factly: "And I don't want religion to separate all of us because frankly none of us would even practice our own religion."

The fractures that have emerged in India over the past thirty years have created a country that is a far cry from the vision of unity in diversity that eight thirteen-year-old girls carried with them to Ranchi. Yet their youthful idealism in themselves has largely survived as they have grown older, their sense that there was an India that would respect and value, not just tolerate, differences had eroded. The loss of that vision has been accompanied by a parallel loss of hope, as became apparent when they assessed where the city and its citizens currently stood. While the women did harbor resentments, much of that resentment was grounded in the fact that there was an old Bangalore and a new Bangalore. They recognize that migrants coming to Bangalore has long been the story of Bangalore, but they have no confidence that these latest waves of newcomers are embracing the values of the old Bangalore. Rather, as the city has expanded in recent decades, there has been a shift away from the progressive spirit and easygoing attitude that characterized Bangalore when the women were young. This, in tandem with the ugly efforts to marginalize minority religions, has created a well of sadness and regret. Similar emotions rose to the surface when the women discussed the challenges—some of them brutal and violent—facing intellectuals and freedom of speech.

Chapter 8

The Backlash against Intellectualism

The obituary read:

> Her commitment to a casteless society was unparalleled. She reduced religious institutions to rubble with her sharp and witty questions. Her ideologies were pro-people with great focus on the welfare of the minority communities. Her struggles had a long way to tread before they reached the finishing line. At 55, Gauri Lankesh is gone too soon. This cold blooded murder of journalist-activist Gauri in a city like Bengaluru, that was so far considered the "safest," has left a lot of minds numb with shock and pain.[1]

The profound depths of emotions that Bangaloreans felt upon hearing the news of the death of Gauri Lankesh in September 2017 cannot be overstated. The *Times of India* described how she was murdered outside her house:

> She was shot from 10-foot distance, indicating that the shooters were professionals. After she was fired at, she ran to the door and died instantly, police said. "Usually, she would drive back home late at night. Today, she returned earlier and we heard gunshots and rushed out. For a few minutes, we could not understand what had happened. Then, we realized Gauri had been shot and she was lying in a pool of blood near the door of her house," a neighbor told police.[2]

Killed at the age of fifty-five, she was a decade or so older than the women featured in this book, an adult when the events of Ayodhya occurred. She was the publisher and editor of a magazine that was openly critical of the BJP and the rise of the right-wing Hindutva movement. Coming from an old Bangalore family, with deep roots in the community, her death was personal and heartbreaking to many of the city's residents. After her death, thousands of people protested in the streets,[3] seeking a strong response from politicians and police for a thorough investigation into her murder. The vehemence of these demands was prompted due to the fact that a similar killing had occurred in another part of the state and was as yet unsolved at the time of Lankesh's death: eminent scholar and historian M. M. Kalburgi, who had also been shot at his home, with the reason for his killing ascribed to his beliefs in rationalism and critiques of both organized religion and the Hindutva movement. Three or four other killings around the country had led many Indians to suspect that intellectuals were being targeted because of their opposition to the BJP and their rationalist stances.[4]

This backlash against intellectualism has been growing steadily since the 1990s, especially among those who are ideologically aligned with India's political right.[5] By trying to create a lack of confidence in or disdain for experts, right-wing politicians have created an environment in which vast numbers of voters respond based on their emotions or prejudices.[6] This rising tide of antiintellectualism seems to be a global trend. Recent explorations of the phenomenon can point to numerous manifestations, from skepticism about what reputable newspapers report to conspiracy theories about vaccinations.[7] Antiintellectualism movements are increasingly associated "with 'strongman politics,' anti-immigration sentiments, anti-globalization and local protectionism, [and] is often anti-women and anti-environment. It is a kind of national populism that builds momentum on emotion and blind faith rather than fact, reason or argument."[8] A 2019 op-ed in the Indian newspaper *The Hindu* bluntly stated that some of the world's most stable democracies—namely, the United States, the United Kingdom, and India—now "worship at the altar of anti-intellectualism."[9]

Nationalist ideologues argue that a country is weakened by those whom they label "elites"—and intellectuals are seen as natural members of that despised group.[10] Painted as disconnected from the "everyday man," often discounted as overly sensitive "snowflakes,"[11] and condemned for not exhibiting "true" patriotic qualities, there is a sense that intellectuals should not and cannot be trusted. In India, this view has helped fuel attacks on influential thinkers and led to the imposition of restrictions in higher education and on academic freedom,[12] a growing fear of speaking up, and an uptick in arrests of activists and thinkers.[13]

Despite the fact that nearly four years had passed since Lankesh's death, the women I spoke to were still clearly shocked by the manner of her death. While I initiated a number of conversations through my questions, my former classmates would often bring up the situation of Lankesh on their own as an example of one of their concerns about the city. They would usually begin by sharing their reaction to her death, and then quickly move to the connections to the other killings. This would in some cases lead them to voice other anxieties, from restrictions on freedom of speech and ideas, to concerns that the condemnations of "elites" were designed to divert attention away from other problems that the BJP had not solved, such as infrastructure or corruption. Many women also spoke about the environment and the culture that was being fostered by the violence manifested by her death three years later. What had not yet happened in 2020 when I spoke to the women was the arrest of a young Bangalore activist on sedition charges. This occurred a few months later when I had begun writing this book. The activist was a young woman, Disha Ravi, who attended the same college as most of the women in this book and in many ways traveled a similar path to the women in this book. My classmates had warned me that things would continue to get worse, not just for them but for young people as well. Ravi's ordeal helped to confirm the veracity of their grim predictions.

"THIS LADY STOOD UP FOR SOMETHING"

One of the first ways the women discussed the death of Lankesh was to connect it to their own worries about security in Bangalore. Some of the women were well aware of her death and would associate the murder with the other concerns they had about the city, not least the overall lack of safety for women in the city. Parul told me that the murder was "really shocking. Really, really shocking. [The city is] quite unsafe for women, it's quite dangerous for people." Inara was shocked for a somewhat different reason, having believed Bangalore to be free from such violence. She said that while she might have expected such a murder to be committed in a "backward area," for such a thing to happen in Bangalore, "being a city, being so forward, being educated, it was quite a shock."

Amaya and I discussed the subject at length, and she took the conversation beyond the safety issue:

> I know about that case. That was a wrong thing. This lady stood up for something. She was a very bold [courageous] lady. This Gauri Lankesh was a very bold lady. My dad tells me about her. They must have thought she's going to be a threat to them.

I, of course, had to ask, "Who were 'they'?" She replied, not fully answering my question, "Somebody against whatever she had written. Something she had written on the paper, or in the news we saw. Maybe she was a threat to them, so they must have killed her."

Farida spoke to me about being "horrified." She knew of Lankesh, calling her a "celebrity." She went on to say:

And that was just such a blatant act, I don't even think the perpetrator was [caught] . . . or somebody else was framed or something, but I don't think the killer was really caught. Yeah, but I find that this whole right-wing mentality, I see it among friends and family in India, and it's really scary.

If Lankesh did not come up initially in the course of the conversations, I would usually begin to ask more neutral questions, such as, "Did you hear about the death of Gauri Lankesh?" If they started to show a sense of recognition, which was almost always, I would follow up by asking, "What did you think about it?" Farida directed this conversation to her worries about the rise of right-wing factions in India almost immediately. She was not the only one who would take that conversational path. Kiara, for instance, explained that she was familiar with Lankesh and her work:

See, she was one of the old, respected writers. Especially for us old girls, we knew her, we read her. So when it happened, the way it did, it left a sort of a distaste in your mouth. [You couldn't] believe it, you couldn't believe that she could have been targeted for her political views.

Shaking her head later, she said, "It doesn't happen in Bangalore. Right? Right? Garden city? It's a very cultured city? So that whole episode is such a tragedy."

It is a tragedy that is compounded by the fact that journalists in India are currently facing harassment from the government and a variety of new legal obstacles to reporting on some issues. The international human rights organization Amnesty International has called on the Indian government to stop such activities, arguing that journalists have been detained and arrested on false charges of terrorism and sedition, have claimed the government has searched offices and installed spyware on computers, shut down the internet, and operated in many other ways to hamper the role of the free press in India.[14] According to the Committee to Protect Journalists, thirty journalists or media workers have been murdered in India between 2014 and 2022.[15] The motives for some of these murders are clear, but for others they are not, and it is this uncertainty that has fueled a volatile and insecure situation for those involved with the press in India.

Nisha spoke about the press and the government early in our conversation, bringing Lankesh up even before I raised the topic of her killing. When Nisha was reminiscing about Bangalore early in our conversation, she said:

I don't think it has that sleepy Bangalore flavor anymore. It's like a big mish-mash of all sorts [of people]. We have such a large population from the north and from elsewhere and I'm not quite sure what their views are, but then sometimes when I see what's happening in Bangalore, it upsets me because we haven't had the best of government formations in many ways. I don't know. I think the politics in Karnataka haven't really been conducive to stem the flow of extremism. You know that woman journalist, Gauri Lankesh, she got murdered.

She began to get emotional and stuttered a little:

It's really very upsetting for me that there are contract murders on women journalists in the middle of Bangalore. Of course, it can happen anywhere but you have people locally who know everything and are willing to do this? And obviously there is. The character of the city has changed and there's a lot more. A lot more radical views going on as well.

Only one person made a comment that seemed to reflect a different view. Queenie seemed to downplay Lankesh's death:

Well, I think, frankly, the reason that it made the waves in the United States was because of how much of sanctity the press has there. And so I think that that probably was predominantly the reason why it was [so present]. It's because it's what is it? The whole journalism and the media, fourth estate thing.

Queenie's comment resonated with the views she expressed on related issues such as the challenges Modi has in governing and her sense that the BJP's motivations were misconstrued. It certainly set her apart from her classmates, most of whom were well aware of the Lankesh case and felt that her death was an unpleasant sign of the times. As Rachna said:

We grew up just saying whatever we felt like saying. We weren't scared. Now, people are scared. Now, people actually realize that you can either live without getting into the bad books of the people that actually want things to go their way and Gauri's case in point [that is, you can get killed for having other opinions]. I mean, can you imagine being from Bangalore, where we said what we wanted to say, we did what we wanted to do? It's not like people are just stopping us right now, but there's a subtle inherent need to just censor yourself. Don't say too much, especially when you don't know the people around you.

As the BJP has acquired more power, so right-wing extremism has taken a more violent and confident turn.[16] The investigations into the death of Lankesh led to forensic connections to the deaths of other intellectuals across India. In 2019, the *Indian Express* reported:

The arrest of a lawyer, Sanjiv Punalekar, and his assistant, Vikram Bhave, by the CBI [Central Bureau of Investigation] in Pune on May 25 in connection with the killing of rationalist Dr Narendra Dabholkar, have underlined, again, the alleged links between this murder in 2013, and those of the leftist thinker

Govind Pansare and Kannada scholar MM Kalburgi in 2015, and journalist Gauri Lankesh in 2017.[17]

The attacks on Dabholkar and Pansare in Maharashtra and Kalburgi and
Lankesh in Karnataka have been reported to be linked to groups connected
to Hindutva movements.[18] While those groups have denied any connection,
the fact that it had taken more than two years for progress to be made on the
investigations into her death were troubling to the women I spoke with. In
addition, social media efforts to threaten and challenge journalists in general
and female journalists in particular have grown.[19] This has both muzzled the
press in some ways and made ordinary citizens more careful about saying
things that are controversial or openly critical of the Hindutva movement.
Chanchal alluded to all of these issues when she spoke about Lankesh:

> The fact that she's in a democracy, in a so-called democracy, [and yet] you're
> not even allowed to express your views freely. That was the whole shocking bit.
> And the fact that everything happened in a manner that was so, it seemed like
> the complicity of the law, the defenders of the law or whatever, there seems to
> be a kind of a nexus. Everything seems to be tied in very closely with every-
> thing else.

This idea of self-censoring oneself, especially in public spaces, was evident
as the women started to discuss the other killings. While there were two other
notable deaths in the state of Maharashtra, just north of Karnataka, the death
of Kalburgi was clearly something these women were aware of and concerned
about. Their focus on his death was related to the ways in which the journalists, independent thinkers, and others were being targeted for their ideas.

"LET HER SAY WHATEVER SHE HAS TO SAY"

Chanchal's comments about the nexus of political and social issues showed
that she paid close attention to politics. Indeed, it was striking to discover
how many of my former classmates spoke about threats to freedom of expression, to the press, and to the discussion of ideas the BJP finds unpalatable.
This was clearly a group of women who read the local media, who were
informed about politics and business issues, and who had a sense of what
democratic values looked like. This level of awareness, while not uncommon among many middle-class women in a city like Bangalore, also seemed
to reflect the sort of education we had all received. BGHS was an unusual
school in that it had an elected student body organization, the Baldwin
Democratic Organization (BDO). In most schools, students were usually

tapped by teachers to lead school organizations, but BGHS had student elections, and this helped instill in us a belief in our rights to vote, run for office, and engage in local governance.

The press has been under pressure throughout the rule of the BJP,[20] and the practice of persecuting people for their ideas has seeped into society at large. Ela mulled over this in her conversation with me when she talked about journalism in India generally and in Bangalore specifically. While she moved away from Bangalore in 2015, she returns frequently to see her parents, who still live in the city:

> I mean, it's just, it's just, I don't know, it's beyond belief. I don't understand it at all. One thing that I have to say that has really changed is newspapers in Bangalore. You know, like even the quality of writing or it being balanced or being really informative, the language, everything has changed. You look at it and it's all like tabloids almost. And the headlines scream at you and it just seems so shallow in so many ways. I think it adds to everybody's hysteria over all of these things and having to pick a side. And you know, there was never any of that [in Bangalore in the past]. You never felt before that you have to pick a side. Now, if you're not on somebody's side, you very clearly, according to them anyway, are on the other side. It's almost like you can't be balanced about anything anymore. And I feel that's shifted where you constantly can't freely speak your mind anymore because you never know [if people around you] think completely different to you and then that can become a huge issue.

This fear of speaking one's mind, and of succumbing to self-censorship, was voiced by several women. It was inspired in part by the rising intolerance among the BJP hardliners who had been amassing political power and taking over the state government. It also stemmed from a sense of helplessness among ordinary people who felt they had few or no ways of holding anyone accountable. Jasmine, for instance, remarked when we were talking about Lankesh:

> Politics is such a dirty game that everything just gets hidden. And you know, for that moment in time, the media picks up the news and it's big news for some time, but then everything just fizzles out and whoever's in power can influence the cops, can influence investigations. So the common man can do nothing about it. Except for the activists and the people who are working to raise the issue, they can do something. But the common man, we don't know what to do about it, we just have opinions. We know that she was killed and the criminals have to be brought to justice, but that's all we can hope for, right? What happens after that is not in our hands at all. So it was quite a sad thing. And you could see, it was kind of a vengeful murder. But we, as common men, couldn't do anything about it at all.

Zara was also frank about how she saw the government, her worries about using her voice, and the impact this had on women:

> I mean it's kind of like a thug government in some sense You say something and you are killed for it and then it disappears from the news. Women who are not murdered are vilified [instead] because they share their point of view which is not pro Modi. It turns out it's the women who have the courage to say these things [but they are then] trolled, doxed—and in that sense, it is very dark time. And that's why it is people in journalism and people who write books, who are really courageous

When Zara talked about people who write books, she was beginning to reference the growing attacks the BJP was directing toward higher education institutions generally, and one particular target specifically. The Jawaharlal Nehru University, commonly known as JNU, has been a thorn in the side of the BJP, especially since 2016. JNU was established in 1966 and describes itself as a "young university" emerging from the "vision that ideas are a field for adventure, experimentation and unceasing quest, and that diversity of opinions are the basis for intellectual exploration."[21] Considering itself to be a "place for the intellectually restless, the insatiably curious, and the mentally rigorous,"[22] the university is housed on a lush green campus in Delhi that gives one a feeling that one is walking among the best and brightest in the world. The campus has a long and storied history of protest,[23] and active political participation is a vital aspect of the campus community. According to some estimates, more than 70 percent of students participate in some sort of political organization.[24] Interestingly, participation among those considered "minorities"—a label that encompasses not only those who come from castes designated marginalized but also Muslim and Christian students—is among the highest at JNU. Those who come from the most privileged sections of Indian society seem to play a less active role.[25] JNU emanates activism in most aspects of its organization, particularly in its governance and curriculum. Members of marginalized groups are encouraged to be vocal about the changes they are seeking.[26]

In 2016, JNU students participated in what had become an annual event: a protest about the two controversial cases in which people had been sentenced to death and then executed. The first case involved a person who had been executed on charges that they were part of a terrorist attack on the Indian Parliament in 2001. The other cases involved a separatist from Kashmir, the Muslim-majority region in the northwest of the country whose control that has long been contested by Pakistan and India. Authorities at JNU had initially appeared to have given permission for the annual protest to be held on the campus in 2016, but later reports said that this consent was revoked before the protests took place.[27] However, JNU students went ahead with the protest in February 2016, with students delivering what some might consider passionate, and others incendiary, speeches. Soon afterward, the Indian government arrested students, some on charges of sedition, which carried harsh punishments of life sentences. Among the students arrested was a man named Kanhaiya Kumar.[28] Interestingly, Lankesh had met and become close to Kumar, whom she came to call an "adopted son."[29] After her death, Kumar tweeted that Lankesh had taught him to "speak truth to power." He went on to say that she was "fearless in her fight against hate. We resolve to carry on her struggle."[30]

Scholars who work at JNU have argued that the events in the winter of 2016 were initially no more than a right-wing attempt to intimidate a small group of JNU students. Over time, however, the events were coopted to align with the political strategy of the BJP in three ways. First, the protest and the arrests reiterated the ways in which the "current regime [the BJP] has sought to redefine Indian nationalism in decisively illiberal and authoritarian ways, in accordance with the RSS[31] Hindutva philosophy of nationalism." Second, criticizing the students allowed BJP politicians to discredit the university as a whole, thereby adding fuel to their arguments that the government should not be funding public higher education. Some scholars argue that the BJP attacks on JNU are part of a larger "war waged against public universities in general, and against the social sciences in particular" in an effort to promote Hindu-dominant worldviews in higher education spaces.[32] Finally, the attacks led by the BJP and through its partners such as the RSS allowed them to intervene and to usurp the autonomous power of institutions and engage in a larger project of "Indianising education."[33] These are patterns that many of the women I spoke to could clearly recognize—even if they used different terms to describe them—as creeping ever more rapidly into their day-to-day lives.

When I spoke with my former classmates about their reactions to the death of Lankesh, many of them connected her with the events at JNU. They knew about Lankesh's connection to Kanhaiya Kumar and that Lankesh was writing about the larger issues raised by the protests at JNU.[34] Rachna spoke about Lankesh's vocal critiques in the context of Rachna's own fears about where things were going:

[Lankesh] was very vocal. She was quite in your face. I didn't agree with a lot of stuff that she said, but some of it made sense. [When I heard about her death, I felt] that you cannot [do that to someone]. I mean, you're taking away a person's right to speech. Let her say whatever she has to say. Even with the WhatsApp groups in India today, everything is being monitored and you can't speak against the government in such a way. I mean, there are so many examples of people who've spoken and they've been silenced. So I was shocked that actually somebody would kill her. It's terrifying to be in a country where you have to be very careful.

Rachna went on to say that she, too, had been told to be less vocal or tone any political opinions she had down in her own professional life. "We didn't grow up like this," she noted.

She also referenced WhatsApp in India, which has over 250 million subscribers. WhatsApp has been critically influential in elections,[35] as well as in terms of mobilizing groups. This mobilization occurs in a number of spaces, including social and religious ones. One example of this would be the political right's use of WhatsApp to identify and harass Hindu women in non-Hindu relationships by directing groups of Hindutva activists to locations where "mixed" couples might be spotted.[36] The use of social media to inflame prejudice and spread misinformation has been another way through which Hindu nationalists have sought to control the nation's ideology and curb intellectualism.

"IT'S JUST REALLY REGRESSIVE, BUT THERE'S A MARKET FOR THAT"

Rachna was blunt: "My God, you should see the kind of shit that's going on in the world on WhatsApp." Indeed, social media in general, and WhatsApp in particular, is rife with incendiary content and misinformation. Moreover, despite much of that content seeming too far-fetched to believe, it exercises a major influence on popular opinion. Understandably, this phenomenon has drawn the attention of scholars who have sought to document and analyze the role, influence, and impact of WhatsApp in India and the ways in which the Hindutva movement has been able to exploit the highly popular platform.[37]

One study examined a large population of WhatsApp users in four states, one of which was Karnataka. The study's findings documented that since 2015, there have been over one hundred episodes of violence or "lynchings" that have been meted out to individuals in minority groups (Dalits or those historically considered "lower" caste, Christians, Muslims, and Adivasis, or those from the tribal regions of the country) due to the sharing of false information on social media platforms among Hindu fundamentalists. Many of these incidents centered on the beef bans and information being shared around the cow protection acts. Apps like WhatsApp allowed people to "spread lies about the victims, and use misinformation to mobilise, defend, and in some cases to document and circulate images of their violence."[38]

They also found that many of India's WhatsApp accounts are dominated by people sharing disinformation and misinformation. This is especially rife in networks of "upper"- and "middle"-caste Hindus, who are more technologically connected. Both male and female as well as rural and urban residents were already predisposed to believe false claims, but it was their social class and the subsequent messages that were designed with them in mind as the audience that promoted increased sharing and forwarding. For instance, memes about taxes or about national security are more aligned with the issues middle-class people are concerned with.

Finally, the false information is designed to incite people through incendiary messages being shared. For example, a message about a suicide might actually say that it was a murder committed by a minority community member. In another example, damage to a temple caused by lightning was said to be caused by Muslims who were seeking to destroy the temple. Another example of frequent misinformation would be the labeling of violent images from somewhere else, as if they were from the local community.[39] Such lies create a narrative to raise tensions in local communities between the different groups. The truth in these stories is often easily confirmable, but the trust levels in the networks (because you think you are receiving a message from someone you know) makes people easily absorb and believe the misinformation.

Only Parul spoke positively about WhatsApp. She felt that "people are coming together because of WhatsApp," and she described it as a space where people could join together to "create a petition or share opinions to support their cause." But even she could not fully ignore the dark side, commenting that "too much of stupid things happen" because of what's posted on WhatsApp.

Many of the other women spoke about being unnerved by social media. Nisha recalled receiving a "WhatsApp forward," which she described as "just basically propaganda." Ahana described "videos that pop up on your WhatsApp. They'll show a child getting into an elevator, even a boy, and then a man in an elevator will be touching the boy." She found these images disturbing, but she was also worried about the larger problem of targeting people via digital means to arouse interethnic and interreligious tensions and to encourage mob violence. Yashika explained her concerns about social media whipping up strong emotions by spreading lies. She noted first that she was not active on Facebook:

> I took a kind of decision that I'm going to keep that as the positive place, even when I had friends who really became very negative about certain things. I stopped following them because I didn't want to get pulled into any kind of discussion when I was on Facebook.

She was uncomfortable that often things were posted that were not true:

I prided myself on India being a free country, and then it's not that free. And then you wonder whether it was always like that, but probably I didn't see it. That is the question that came up in my mind: [Was] the sense of fairness something that was there? I don't know whether it was part of our Baldwins, our upbringing, education, all of that?

Nisha was similarly uneasy about the spread of lies, but she focused on the people who were disseminating such material:

It's like somebody had spent some time writing it up [the misinformation], and it was written with spelling mistakes, you know what I mean? Somebody has actually written this and then you had some actress or somebody saying [it was true] and I'm being forwarded this by somebody who's studied medicine who was a doctor, somebody who studied law. And it really upsets me. I don't know. Maybe I'm just . . . I don't have the patience anymore. It upsets me.

She later described the process of how misinformation is spread and leads to a type of indoctrination:

This is being put out there. Every time, it is like an F.A.Q. [Frequently Asked Questions] kind of thing. All their talking points, basically in a question-and-answer form, just reproducing this on social media, forwarding it and nobody bothering [to counter the lies]. . . . People who have been lulled into this thing, [feeling like] they're doing something positive, asking, "I don't see why everybody's so upset about it," right? You know that it is dangerous because they're getting the narrative out and these things get into people's heads, and it's at the back of their heads. They've read it somewhere. And then at some later time, that's the view about it because they haven't read any further or scratched the surface or gone into it.

Nisha was most upset about the fact that educated people were forwarding her material that was incorrect. Besides their overall concerns about social media, some of the women spoke about the ways in which science and critical thinking were under attack. A few of the women would sheepishly share some of the more recent news stories that embarrassed them to even consider sharing. One story they brought up with me was a report about a speech given by the state minister of education for the state of Rajasthan to scientists at the opening of a new regional science center. He was quoted in the media as saying that India "is a leader of scientific development." Given the technological and engineering contributions of Indians both in the country and within the diaspora, this statement should hardly have been controversial. But he supported his assertion by describing India as the country that conducted the world's first successful completion of a head transplant, where the head of an elephant was placed on a human. He was referring to Indian mythology and the creation of the beloved elephant-headed god Ganesha. According to the report in the *Times of India* newspaper, he gave no scientific evidence for this "transplant" operation and instead quoted Hindu scripture.[40]

Science, the flagship international magazine of the American Association for the Advancement of Science, ran an article in 2019 titled, accurately enough, "In India, Hindu Pride Boosts Pseudoscience." The article cites other examples of outlandish claims. For instance, G. Nageshwar Rao, a scientist and the vice chancellor of a university in another southern state, claimed Indians had mastered the use of stem cell research centuries ago, in part due to the fact that a female character in the epic poem *Mahabharata* had given birth to one hundred sons. In chapter 4, I mention my affection for the *Amar Chitra Katha* comics I began reading when I was a girl. I knew that somewhere in my thirty-five-year collection there would be an issue that features the story of Gandhari, the mother of the one hundred sons. Sure enough, I found the story, which is compassionate and romantic, and which also touches upon the mystic. The myth tells the story of the princess Gandhari, who was married to a powerful but blind king (how he lost his eyesight is the central theme of a different myth). After she bears a child that is described as "lifeless [with] neither shape nor features,"[41] a sage arrives in the kingdom and feels sorry for her. He asks the palace staff to fetch large pots of ghee, or clarified butter. He asks for one hundred pots to give her one hundred sons. Gandhari privately wishes that even with one hundred sons, she would be grateful to have one daughter. The sage reads her mind and agrees that they should bring 101 pots of ghee. He divides the dead baby into these 101 pots and tells Gandhari that in two years she can open the pots and she will find her children. While the story is captivating, as myths are wont to be, the idea that the birth of 101 children in clay pots is scientific evidence of India's expertise in stem cell research is unfathomable.

Yet such claims are increasingly becoming part of the national conversation. Chaya mentioned the Karnataka-born Jagadish Vasudev, otherwise known as Sadhguru, a yogic guru of sorts. She said:

> It's too depressing. I really think that the country's taken a turn for [the worse], like towards superstition or being okay with it. Like Sadhguru, saying the woman's breasts will give different milk.

When I looked bemused, she asked me, "You did not know?" She explained that Sadhguru was extremely popular and that social media groups were abuzz because of his claim that if a woman gives birth to twins, she will "have specific milk coming out of each breast for each twin." She elaborated:

He says these regressive things, what he says he truly believes. So the other day he got invited to a conference of gynecologists where he says that if a woman has twins, that one breast will give specific milk to one baby. And the other breast give specific to the other baby. I don't know if it was a gender thing as well [if one baby was a boy and the other a girl]. He has said that women [should be] put into a different room during their periods, because otherwise it would attract wild animals. It's just really regressive, but there's a market for that. That is what I'm saying.

Chaya connected these ideas to the killings of Kalburgi and Lankesh, who, as rationalists, abhorred dogma and superstition. People like Sadhguru "are hugely threatened by people who are calling them out on it—[people such as] Kalburgi." Although Kalburgi and others like him are just critical of superstition, in the current environment "somebody feels okay killing them." "You should see the comments on WhatsApp, because it's all out there," Chaya said. "People think she [Lankesh] deserved it and that's what's horrifying."

Such observations about the level of intolerance among BJP supporters are grim but apparently accurate. So, too, were the women's concerns about a government that seems ready to stoke prejudice and eager to repress independent voices. As if to confirm these views, just as I had wrapped up my conversations, a young woman named Disha Ravi was arrested, in many ways reiterating the concerns raised by the women I spoke to.

"THEY GET THE FEAR"

On February 13, 2021, police entered the home of a young college student in Bangalore to arrest her on charges of sedition. According to the national newspaper *The Indian Express*:

> In a closely-guarded operation, the Delhi police special cell on Saturday reportedly "picked" up Disha Ravi—a young student climate activist and one of the founders of "Fridays For Future" (FFF) campaign—from North Bengaluru for questioning for allegedly disseminating the "toolkit" related to farmer protests in Delhi through social media sites, said sources.[42]

Fridays for Future is an international, youth-led climate change organization founded in 2018 by Swedish teen activist Greta Thunberg.[43] Ravi, who at the time was twenty-two years old, had just graduated from Mount Carmel College, where a large number of Baldwin girls tend to go when they complete their education at BGHS. This middle-class girl was the daughter of an athletic coach and a homemaker. At the center of what was soon referred to as the "toolkit case" was a Google document that was "edited" by Ravi and was said to be seditious in nature. The toolkit was a document to help identify ways to support the Indian farmers who were protesting governmental regulations that affected their livelihoods. The charge of sedition was predicated on the argument that Ravi was instigating external (foreign) violence against India. The farmers' protests were a political liability for the BJP government.[44] Ravi was remanded to policy custody in Delhi for nearly five days,[45] after which she was granted bail. Headlines soon after accused the government of paranoia,[46] of being afraid of independent thinking,[47] and journalists described the entire country as being on shaky foundation if a college student was a threat to national security.[48]

The exchanges I conducted ended just a few months before the arrest of Disha Ravi. Some of the women I spoke to commented—often when speaking about the death of Gauri Lankesh—on the need to use one's voice to speak out against inequity and to highlight the lack of accountability for the powerful, but they also worried about the ramifications of doing so. Kiara remarked that many public activists were quieter than they used to be. She talked about the "circuits" of activists and artists who had often been at the forefront of social movements. But from theater groups to civic leaders, things were different now. "Some of us who've been here longer," Kiara said, "we sort of expect these to be voices heard. [She names some well-known activists.] This was the old order, right? And even if they don't influence you much, [you still hear them]." She turned to the fate of Gauri Lankesh:

> The fact that she stood for something and she was brutally murdered for it—that was something that I think at least the old Bangaloreans may have been shaken up by. Even though I didn't know her personally . . . she was very effective with her vocal [blunt] writing. And you'll find this, even in Pakistan or in some of these countries where somebody is vocal about something, they've tried to shut that voice down . . . but I know that she was a threat to them. I know that her views was strong enough to be heard.

Meher echoed these sentiments:

> I feel that such things create a negative atmosphere for kids because she [Lankesh] was a person who spoke out and because she spoke out, she got murdered. So the kids . . . they get the fear; it creates a fear that you'd rather keep your mouth shut and not say things. It's dangerous for your life. Mind your own business and don't support anybody, you know? That's the thing that they get, the impression they get, which is not good.

This might have been one reason why Ravi was working on the toolkit in what she might have assumed was the safety of her home computer.

Meher went on to report what she had been hearing about the death of Lankesh:

> It occurred after the BJP government came [into power], and people do say—at least when I was in the North, when this occurred, they did say—that there was a lot of political support for this [murder]. I don't know if it's true, but this is what it is.

Chanchal ended her conversation by talking about how Lankesh's work had put a target on her back:

> It comes back to this whole aspect of radicalizing societies. The intolerance, the growing intolerance, there's anger. It's seething. It's like this underbelly. You have this India with this . . . sheen that talks about culture and this and that. And then heritage. And then you have this dark underbelly which suddenly rears its ugly head up. The kind of intolerance, this patriarchal mindset, this really rigid right-wing nationalism. These are some of the things that really are difficult to deal with sometimes.

The attacks against thinkers and activists, as well as the atmosphere that has been created that makes people uncomfortable and unconfident about speaking their minds, constitute a blow to the functioning of a country that is supposed to be both secular and democratic. People start to feel that it is normal to intimidate and muzzle women, outsiders, and thinkers. The consolidation of power that comes from fostering an environment of fear and trepidation makes it easier to craft policies that formalize restrictions that until then had been potent but unofficial. This is what we will explore in chapter 9.

Chapter 9

Politicians and Patriotism

Over the past four chapters, the women of Bangalore spoke about how they perceived their freedom and security, raised concerns about the direction of education and secularism in India, and revealed their fears around the repression of intellectualism and free speech. Their words often represented an emotional response to what they were seeing and hearing, but there were also specific policies or practices they could point to that affected their thinking. For instance, the beef ban or the practices around real estate were some of the ways in which the government was formalizing exclusion and reverting to narrow-minded or oppressive tactics in support of its Hindutva ideologies. There were also other significant national issues taking center stage that the women spoke about.

The demonetization policies of 2016 and the Citizenship (Amendment) Act (CAA) of 2019—both crafted in a political environment of heightened nationalist rhetoric—were front and center in the minds of the women. The outsize personality of Narendra Modi, the prime minister and leader of the BJP, was another topic the women felt they needed to address. These were some of the most conflicted conversations the women had with me. Often contradicting themselves, many of the women went back and forth between criticizing and condemning the BJP, sometimes trying to create a logical narrative for why they supported at least some of the BJP's policies. These subjects also brought out their worries that they might be seen as being insufficiently Indian or that, by criticizing their country, they were in fact not being patriotic. They had good reason to be concerned: BJP politicians would often attack people for criticizing India and its leaders, condemning such comments as betrayals of national pride.[1] What was being demanded was vocal and unwavering expressions of love of country and its political leadership. The BJP's attitude was reminiscent of George W. Bush's statement during his speech to the U.S. Congress after the bombings of the Twin Towers on 9/11: "Either you are with us, or you are with the terrorists."[2]

The women feared that a nuanced vision of patriotism would be misunderstood in the prevailing environment of hypernationalism and "mandatory patriotism."[3] The latter is a form of forced allegiance gaining popularity among right-wing politicians around the world. It targets a wide array of behaviors, such as not wearing flag pins[4] or failing to sing patriotic songs.[5] Expressions of "true" patriotism include showing unequivocal support of the government and its actions. In India, one form of mandatory patriotism emerged after a 2016 Supreme Court ruling where movie theaters were mandated to show an image of the Indian flag and moviegoers were required to stand at the start of every film during the playing of the national anthem. This decision was reversed in 2018,[6] but not before a disabled man and a non-Indian citizen, in two separate incidents, had been beaten because they either could not or did not stand. Such examples of violence against people who did not express the appropriate degree of patriotism in both public and private spaces led the women who spoke to me to worry that their patriotism might be questioned if they were too critical of government actions.

Even so, demonetization and the CAA came up frequently in my conversations. The demonetization policy was put into effect in 2016 to eliminate larger currency bills in an effort to reduce "black money," which is money that people have earned but have not paid taxes on. There was a mistaken assumption that people who hoarded black money would hold cash assets in large currency banknotes. In reality, most people who had untaxed income normally held it in noncash reserves, such as jewelry, gold, or land. According to the BBC, only about 5 percent of black money was held in liquid form, and as such the policy was considered an "epic failure."[7] The people it did affect were those who used cash on a daily basis, mostly in the working and underclass, and for them the introduction of the policy created complex challenges. Despite this, the policy met Modi's political goals. He was seen to be directly addressing India's significant problem of corruption, a widely shared concern, especially among the middle class.[8] For many in this group, the mere idea that Modi was even trying to tackle the problem won him plaudits and support.

The reception for the Citizenship (Amendment) Act (CAA), however, was more mixed. It was enacted in December 2019, just a few months before I began to reconnect with my former classmates. The act was presented as a pathway to citizenship, revising the Citizenship Act of 1955 by adding a specific amendment whereby any resident of India who considers themselves Hindu, Sikh, Buddhist, Jain, Parsi, or Christian and who has previously lived in Afghanistan, Bangladesh, or Pakistan would not be "treated as illegal migrant for the purposes of this Act."[9] In the rationale provided in the bill, framers first argued that there has been a long history of "trans-border migration" of people between those regions and the territories of the Indian subcontinent (modern-day India). They also argued that because the three countries named had Islam as their state religion, "many persons belonging to Hindu, Sikh, Buddhist, Jain, Parsi and Christian communities have faced persecution on grounds of religion."[10] They claimed that the goal of the amendment was to ensure that if non-Muslims came to India to escape persecution, they would be entitled to the opportunity to seek Indian citizenship rather than be treated as an illegal migrant. In the eyes of its critics, the act was clearly trying to create a narrative that Muslims were not true Indians. This view was bolstered by the fact that the act did not address the status of the Rohingya in Burma and the Tamils in Sri Lanka, both of whom are marginalized populations in neighboring countries but who were either themselves Muslim (the Rohingya) or were not in a country where Islam is its state religion.[11] This anti-Islam agenda was one of the two main reasons the women cited as reasons to be critical of the act. The other had to do with the linking of the CAA to the National Registry of Citizens (NRC). The NRC was established in 1955, together with the original Citizenship Act, in an effort to keep a register of all Indian citizens, a mechanism that seemed especially important in the wake of the tumultuous process of Partition and the birth of an independent India. While the NRC had been only sporadically maintained since its creation, Amit Shah, the minister of home affairs and former president of the BJP party, who is frequently considered the heir-apparent to Modi,[12] had strongly recommended that it be reconstituted.[13]

In talking with the women, there was a sense that the combination of the passage of the CAA and the renewal of the NRC created both fear and anger that the government was seeking to marginalize and isolate India's Muslim population. In a country where legal documentation is unreliable and older generations often have no records of when and where they were born, some of the women suspected that the government was looking for a way to expel Muslims who called India home. The requirement to register, alongside the fact that Muslims were being told they were not welcome in light of the new laws, provoked widespread protests.

One of the most powerful protest movements that emerged against the passing of the CAA happened organically at a small park in New Delhi called Shaheen Bagh.[14] Muslim women took an active and visible role pushing back against the CAA. Taking over the Delhi park, the "women of Shaheen Bagh," as they came to be known, peacefully protested for their rights for nearly one hundred days.[15] Described as "a non-violent, creative and an inspiring movement led by women—a movement against fascism, a movement of reckoning based on the ideology of humanity to protect constitution and its values,"[16] they were a visual and daily reminder of how the government was choosing to elevate some religions over others in what is still, constitutionally at least, supposed to be a secular country.

Just as the women in this chapter were aware of the CAA, they were also aware of the women of Shaheen Bagh. There was a sense of respect and sisterhood, and some of the women I spoke to had Hindu and Muslim friends who had traveled to Delhi to join the protests. They were eager to talk about the CAA, as it was one of the first pieces of business conducted by the BJP as it consolidated power in its second term, after winning reelection in 2019. The CAA also seemed to formalize the rhetoric and the ideological groundwork that the BJP had been laying in an attempt to shift India away from its historically secular roots.

"YOU CAN'T SUDDENLY DISOWN THEM"

The establishment of the CAA inspired mixed emotions among the women. On the one hand, they argued that this was unequivocally *not* the India they knew. On the other hand, they seemed to feel a need to justify the introduction of the law and pointed out that this was how most countries sought to protect their borders.

For instance, Ahana said she was not "comfortable" with the act, especially as she had grandparents who had lived through the trauma of India's partition. She said:

> So now, if somebody tells you that we're only going to accept citizens who are Hindu, who are not Muslims, and when we have so many Muslim friends, immediately your mind goes to, "Oh, but what would happen to this friend of mine? You mean his mother or her mother is going to suddenly get kicked out because she doesn't have a paper?" It doesn't sound fair. And that's not India. We never were a country like Pakistan, which says that we only accept Muslims. . . . I've heard my grandparents telling me about how my grandfather had one hour to leave the house in Pakistan, and they said, "You're a Hindu and you have to get out of here." So they gave him one hour to collect whatever he could put in [a bag] and then he was thrown out and he had to flee to India. India is not like that. We never asked, as far as I know, or I hope we didn't ask the Muslims to get out in one hour. But our constitution says that regardless of religion, you are welcome to stay in our country. So I don't see now how it can be, how a political party can say that, how the government of India can say something unconstitutional like we will only accept refugees from a certain religion. They have to accept everyone.

Ahana was emotional through this conversation. Being close to her grandparents and understanding the trauma of India's Partition, she felt a great deal of empathy for people who might be forced to leave because they did not have papers. This history and those experiences made some of the women keenly aware of the challenges the law created and how it echoed the trauma of the past. The combination of targeting innocent residents while discounting India's secularism was troubling. Garima tried to make this point:

People are working, they're paying taxes and they're part of society. You can't, once you make changes like that, you can't suddenly disown them just because of an amendment to a law. So, that is the part I don't agree and I think, again, growing up, I thought India was many religions together. If you're starting to exclude certain religions to promote something, that's not the India I remember, and I don't think that should be the India moving forward as well. Again, going back to school, we had so many friends from different religions and we worked well together and we're still in touch and we've formed really, really good relationships. So, I don't think we should bring religion into any of the other aspects of life.

Saira put the blame squarely on politicians, saying, "Ah, the big debate. The NRC and the CAA Law. This is total politics." As she delved further into the topic, she started to explain that while she was a Hindu, she was not religious and had many friends from different communal groups. She felt that Muslims suffered because they often had a "bad reputation" (due to international perceptions of terrorism). Nonetheless, she did not see anything wrong with the CAA, at least for now:

See, Muslims have their lot of states or countries where they can go. Jews have Israel. Christians is wherever. Muslims have a lot of their own countries. Whereas, there's not a single Hindu country. So if they made a law that any Hindu who's being shunned from their country wants to come and settle into India, you can come in, it's okay. What is wrong? I'm not telling Muslims to get out of my country, I'm not doing that. So why are the minorities getting offended, or why are they getting insecure? Maybe they think we are going like how Hitler [treated the Jews]. . . . But if you look at it, point blank, from Modi and Amit Shah, right now it doesn't seem like anything is wrong. How we will misuse this in future, I don't know.

Jasmine said something similar:

See, it all depends how you look at it. If you say, all Muslims are not allowed, it's not a right thing. But if every country has a limit, they don't allow everyone to walk into the country. You have to have certain kind of control on your citizens, you can't let anyone come in and give them citizenship. . . . So they want to get a rule . . . I say that every human has a right. But when you see citizenship, I just can't go to some country and say, "I want citizenship here." Same thing with India; India has to have some kind of control. Otherwise, our poverty rates would increase. And that's how it is. But for me, everyone has to be treated equally. That's my argument. Can't differentiate between religions or sexes or whatever. Each person is a person that has to be treated equally.

While some women worried about the ways in which the policy could be weaponized in the future, there was also a sense, as articulated by Saira and Jasmine, that this policy reflected what other countries were doing and it might be that this was something India needed. Future problems could be dealt with as they emerged, but getting something on the books was still needed.

For another group of women, messages about how the CAA would counter terrorism resonated. Politicians claimed the act would tighten India's security, like politicians the world over who are pushing for hardline defense- and security-related measures, seeking to instill fear while ignoring evidence that the threats of which they warn rarely come to pass.[17] This approach seems to have worked with Lipika, who talked about how the government was justified in ensuring safety:

I think the government is in a perfectly good place, and we should have had it in place a long time ago. We would have had not had this kind of infiltration and people just floating around without identities. . . . This is a country with 1.3 billion people. Imagine managing a country like this without documentation. . . . Because if you read what the government has put together very clearly, it says that it is about protecting our land from people who want to infiltrate and come and settle. So if there are people like that, they need to go through a process. That's all that the bill is saying. Right? So that's what every other country is doing. Why don't they [those protesting the CCA] object to that?

Ekta provided a more nuanced view:

I feel sometimes there is a reason why they've done it. Obviously, when they give citizenship to everybody, they're not able to do background checks as to who they're giving citizenship to. So you never know, there could be some terrorist coming in from Pakistan, and that is always a possibility. . . . But in places like India [and] other developing countries, it's very difficult to do background checks because people don't even have identification documents, so what background check can you do? So I have mixed thoughts about it. I'm not totally for it and I'm not totally against it.

Amaya was the only one who admitted that, until recently, she had known little about the CAA legislation. But then she heard more details from her daughter: "My daughter told me. She explained to me, 'They want these immigrants, everyone to go back to their places, like these Bangladeshis. They want proof [of citizenship].'" Amaya then shared her opinion:

One way, it is good. See, you cannot enter other countries. Our political leaders are right, sometimes, but they took it in a wrong way [designed and implemented the legislation incorrectly]. People took it in a wrong way. See, we cannot enter any other country. Can you go to Bangladesh? No. Can we go to Sri Lanka? No. How these people are coming into our country? They want to stop that, basically. That is a good thing, but they are asking to show all the records. People are thinking, "How will we get thirty years old records, fifty years old records? Where we stayed? What we did?" . . . They are insecure now. That shouldn't happen.

Waida was not sure that people had the full picture:

It is unclear if they intend to send everyone back [to Muslim countries]. So, I don't know. Really. It's just, there's more to it. I think there's more to it than meets the eye. There's many more issues involved there. There's religion. There's other aspects there. There's the political side. There's a lot more going on there. It's unfair on the people being involved. If they've been in one place for too long and then they have to move, then it's unfair because you're uprooting them. Isn't it? It's unfair for those people.

Nisha articulated the domino effect the policy was beginning to have and the ways in which it was opening the door to other policies being used to restrict people's movement. One such example was the recent developments in the northern state of Jammu and Kashmir (J&K). Wedged between Indian and Pakistan, the state has had a complex history during the post-Partition period. At the time of India's independence, the region had a majority Muslim population with a Hindu ruler who opted to align with India. This has been a flashpoint between the two countries for the past seventy-five years.[18] In 2019, Home Minister Amit Shah proposed a change to the Constitution by amending the status of J&K from a state to a union territory. There are a number of union territories in India, which are governed by the central government and have limited autonomy. By revoking Article 370 of the Constitution, which guaranteed statehood, the central government, and the BJP more directly, can now intervene in J&K's affairs. Since 2019, there have been significant restrictions on communication systems (cable, cellular, and internet services) and civil liberties (gatherings, press freedom, and speech) there.[19] The communications blackout lasted nearly 550 days, the longest in any active democracy; nearly eight million people lacking access to many of those communication services.[20] Because much of the rest of the world considered this an internal matter, it led to limited or negligible diplomatic responses.[21] In addition, nearly "500 protests and stone pelleting incidents . . . took place since the day quasi-autonomy of the state was revoked . . . [and]

more than 4,000 people including children, elected political leaders, business-men, activists and civil society members have been detained."[22]

The situation in Kashmir was on Nisha's mind. "That's part of their agenda, isn't it?" she said. "I mean, if you look at the Kashmir issue and then you see, that's their first thing." She goes on to describe her recollection of a tweet posted by Amit Shah, prior to Article 370 being revoked.[23] His tweet flirted with the idea of repealing statehood status, and when there was limited backlash to the suggestion, it was soon put into practice. Nisha went on to say that he "kind of got away with it":

> So, they had a little clever trick about Article 370. . . . Amit Shah, he is too clever by half. . . . And, you know, there was a little bit of outrage. Kashmir is still on lockdown many months later. . . . What I find alarming really is again, friends that have had similar education to mine, who then say, "Actually, this isn't discriminatory at all." You know? And then they sort of send you a WhatsApp forward or post on their Facebook or something. And it's just basically propaganda.

While having a positive or negative view of a politician is normal and everyone expects politicians to use the force of their personalities to move their pet projects forward, it was the discomfort the women had with trying to be fair that led to the final topics of our conversations about politics: the BJP, Narendra Modi, and the future of India.

"WE WANT AN EASY LIFE"

Analyses of Modi's electoral success point to a couple of key elements. His focus on corruption and being an outsider was one narrative that made inroads with some voters. His willingness to stand up for India resonated with the middle class, who had grown tired of apologizing for perceived failures of infrastructure and India's second-tier status at the global level. Modi also pushed for tangible changes that people could see, which then allowed them to excuse excesses elsewhere. One example was Modi's "Clean India" campaign, which promised to end "open defecation by 2019."[24] This effort led to the building of over 110 million toilets, a move that was warmly welcomed by the middle class, who found public urination and defecation embarrassing for a country that had global aspirations.[25] While the toilet program was not considered a success due to larger infrastructure issues with water shortages and upkeep challenges,[26] people applauded Modi for trying to tackle the problem. Oona, for instance, strongly supported the toilet program:

Those are huge steps towards progress. And those were always things that always brought me down. This is such a great country. Why can't we get our act together? Why is it, why do people have to use the streets? Why are there no public restrooms that you can walk into without thinking you're going to catch something? I saw [some toilets on the side of the roads], and I was impressed. I was blown away by some of that progress.

Oona continues to talk about the greater purchasing power she was seeing. "Everybody has a car and that's progress. . . . the malls are all so crowded means people have buying power. There was just a handful that could afford stuff when we were growing up. So all that, I think, is fantastic." But as she wraps up the conversation about the progress, she says, "I do worry about how much religion is influencing the current government knowingly or unknowingly."

Parul said something similar:

I don't know how to say, I'm not actually anti-Modi; some of his policies are really good. I think, Hinduism is being given more importance, which I don't like. I think that people should live where they are, things should not be forced on anyone.

She made a related point later in our conversation:

Is it so important that we build a temple there [in Ayodhya] now with so many people being affected? There's so much poverty, there's so many people who don't have basic amenities. So many people are not educated now. There are so many people on the roads [homeless]. So many people are suffering a lot. So, is it so important that . . . we have so many heritage cases across India, so many temples, Why do we need to spend so much of money in building a temple there?

All of the women I spoke with expressed deep frustration with Bangalore and its crumbling roads, the traffic nightmares, and the overall lack of high-quality infrastructure—all problems that are seen as tied to corruption. In their day-to-day lives, the women frequently encountered corruption, and they were clearly infuriated by it. Bhavna, who had voted across multiple party lines for a variety of candidates in the 2019 election, said:

It's very sad. See, we only want our surroundings to be working well. We want good roads and good air. We want good schools. We want good public transport. We don't want to bribe people to get things done. We want all of this to work smoothly for us because we need to have a life to live. We can't be dealing with struggles at every point in our life. Everything is a struggle to get something done. Today's almost impossible, right? Because you have to bribe, you have to follow up. Follow up is the key word today. You can't do anything without 100 follow ups. I have to get windows done in my house the last three years. I phoned the guy every day and it's still not done. Can you imagine how difficult our lives are just following up? That's what we all want. We just want our simple day-to-day lives being easy on us. Who cares who is the politician?

"Who cares who is the politician?" Some, in fact, did care deeply, but others argued that no matter which political party was involved, politics was always the same game. Chanchal, a teacher, bemoaned the "sheer lack of leadership that exists." She went on to say that she could not think of any "kind of true leadership," and she believed there were always "political games being played out there."

The lack of consensus about whether the identity of the politician matters manifested itself in two completely different views of Modi. Daksha gave us one view:

I'm a huge fan of Modi, and I'm making a political statement right now, but I think what he's done, especially in this lockdown period, the kind of leadership he has shown, and the simplicity that the man brings to the table . . . I think it's been phenomenal.

Farida gave us another:

I'm completely anti Modi, I don't have a good word to say about him. So I just think it's a tragedy. I really think what's happened to India is really. . . . I mean, my husband and I always talk about, that I don't think there's a country more rich and varied and beautiful and diverse as India, but it's really all the way, it's going downhill.

The women said a great deal not only about the politics of today but also about the future of the country, especially in light of what they had lived through since leaving school. Much of what they saw, they connected to the Hindutva movement and the ways in which personalities and politics were intersecting.

"I THINK WE NEEDED A DICTATOR"

Would the BJP be as successful without the charismatic personality and savvy political operations of Narendra Modi? Modi came to power focusing on the neoliberal policies that were important to the burgeoning middle class, but once in power, he was able to move toward more populist policies in part due to his ability to use language to deepen social and religious divisions in the country.[27] It is his use of the media, of social media, and of the power of narrative through the use of his life story that have in many ways given him cult status in India. The "Modi myth" is one of the reasons that the BJP has done as well as it has over the past decade.[28]

Since his early political days, Modi has crafted his story in ways that appeal to a vast number of people. In the run-up to the 2014 elections, the BJP and Modi were considered to be the party of the middle class, particularly those voters who were both male and "high" caste. By 2019, his landslide victory showed that the BJP had expanded its appeal to encompass marginalized castes and women voters. His roots as someone who had sold tea on the streets was a rags-to-riches story that was almost a made-in-Bollywood storyline and appealed to poorer and more rural communities.[29] In 2019, more women voted for Modi than in the previous election, and women outnumbered men among his supporters among all voters.[30] Some of this has to do with his overt focus on "women's issues" as a calculated response to the lack of support in 2014.[31] Others have hypothesized that his eagerness to draw attention to his fifty-six-inch chest has created an appealing narrative for some women who like his "overt masculinity and tendency to be seen as a man's man."[32] This was surprising to some observers, who were aware that there were conflicting stories about his abandonment of his wife at a young age.[33] Studies of authoritarian leaders and their followers find that a blend of certain forms of masculinity, personal charisma, and paternalistic policies can exercise a powerful appeal for many voters. The "man of the people" narrative allows the politician to argue that they are saving people from "corrupt elites," which then permits them to rely on "religious majoritarianism, moral policing, intolerance of dissent and a nativism that combines nationalism, xenophobia, and muscular religiosity" as ways to protect people.[34] It is this complex cauldron of issues that the women I spoke with would sit with uncomfortably as they ended their conversations with me. A few spoke with great affection and admiration when they discussed Modi. Urmi tried to skirt some of the things she did not like and instead discussed how she welcomed his "iron fist":

> Okay, so let's take the religion part of it because, I really don't know the truth behind the religion and politics in this government. I haven't seen, so I don't want to believe, but I think we needed a dictator to bring in some discipline in this country. You need someone with a very iron fisted policy to run . . . because there's no alternate. Look at the other political parties, you have nobody there who can run India, given the population, given the density, given the way we are as a country. So, I am quite favorable to the current government. . . . It has its huge negatives as well in terms of [the] current finance minister and so on. But I don't see an alternative.

Queenie sympathized with Modi, given the scale of the task he was faced with:

> I have to comment on the political situation that I would say that frankly I think
> Modi-ji [Modi-sir, a term of respect] gets a really bad rap for either promoting
> Hindutva or so-called Hindu nation. Because to me, he is probably one of the
> most hard working and a leader of true integrity. Who he's surrounded by and
> what kind of organizations he came from or he's affiliated with [and] what they
> are doing is . . . [she trails off]. Frankly, there's only so many hours in the day
> and there's only so much that he can do.

Others were far less impressed by Modi and far more worried the political
direction in which India was heading. Ginny admitted that she had not realized in 2014 where Modi's BJP would lead the country:

> But the magnitude of what it [the BJP's election victory in 2014] stood for, I
> really didn't pause to think about. If I think back on it now, I would say that
> it was a manifestation. It was probably the first sign of, maybe, things that
> were changing. But that's only because I'm thinking about it now. And why I
> didn't think of it even earlier? But I didn't. I was quite happy with their leader
> [Atal Bihari Vajpayee, the previous BJP prime minister, who was in office in
> 1999–2004]. So I just thought of them as an alternative. In fact, I've even voted
> for Vajpayee myself. So it really didn't bother me. I didn't think of it as, "Oh my
> God! This is going to be communalism in India. And it's going to be this split."
> I didn't anticipate that it'd be the way it is now.

Although Ginny remembered the controversies in Gujarat when Modi was
chief minister there, and that gave her some pause, she was frustrated with
the Congress Party. When Modi came to power, however, Ginny, who is a
Christian, began to feel like a "minority." Today, she is grateful to "Hindus,
who speak out against him. . . . It's in a way quite heartening to know, that's
probably how we're able to survive in this country. If everyone were right
wing, I think we would have a really difficult time."

Ginny shared a wide range of concerns with me over the course of her
conversation. Most of her comments, from her worries about being seen
eating beef to feeling concerned about her daughter's reception in school
as a Christian girl, reflected her status as a member of a minority religion.
Chanchal, a Hindu, was spared such concerns herself, but she could see the
anxiety felt by minority groups and recognized that an "ugliness" was spreading through Indian society:

> There are some policies which appear very draconian and very stiff, but I don't
> know the complete picture. I don't want to be an armchair intellectual and say,
> "Okay, this is how it should be," and I don't know the reality on the ground.
> And there is apathy, there is indifference, there are so many things going on right

now, it's crazy. And there has to be some semblance of sanity, or there has to be some kind of a balanced outlook. Then things have this ugliness that has seeped in, which we haven't really examined, or which we haven't really come to terms with. It has to play itself out. . . . People are very, very radicalized. Those who are very easily swayed by ideological propaganda, I think they're just getting brainwashed. They're getting swept by this wave. And those whose voices need to be heard, aren't being heard. Or they're just being crushed. So you see, it's becoming quite difficult for people to even voice their opinions. Even those who have the courage to stand up and say, "No," or think differently are not being allowed to express their feelings.

Rachna connected the dots to other leaders with authoritarian tendencies:

When you have a figurehead that awakens that racist in you, awakens those negative hatred and divisive kind of prejudices and biases, he [Modi] has done it and it's worked in India, [and] it is working in America. It was probably working with Trump. It's probably working with a lot of people.

The rising tide of ideological fervor in India can be ascribed in part to the shift in the tone and goals of education in India: where once education was concerned with opening a person's mind, now it increasingly closes minds through a focus on conformity and compliance. Vedhika recalled her own education and the fact that higher education fees were more often than not subsidized by the government, which believed that a democracy needs an educated population:

India was so much of a more secular country when we were growing up, in spite of the fact that we were not so liberalized [Western], and we had a great world-view, because education had a lot of value in that sense. I think it was part of the socialist environment that we sort of grew up in.

Her higher education was almost fully funded. Since then, government financial support has declined—but government meddling has increased:

So when it comes to politics, they [the BJP government] are very hands on, but not when it comes to helping students out. So, politics has come into campus life a lot. Everything is so polarized now, and you have to be careful as to what you say [and] to whom you say to. Everybody's under this impression that Hinduism is under threat, it's under siege. And so that is leading to every religion is saying, "We are under siege." It's so stupid and, frankly, as a practicing atheist, it doesn't matter to me. So I have to keep shutting people down every so often. You know, for spreading fake news, for just taking shit, in that sense—pardon my French.

Her final comment brought us back full circle. I asked her whom she thought were the beneficiaries of the current policies, and her response was direct and clear: "It's the middle class." She repeated:

> It's the middle class because in the present situation in India, the middle class has most to lose. This new middle class, we have most to lose. The poor will go anywhere. They don't have the agency to say, "Oh, I'm going to take a stand, and I'm going to you know [go do something] so principled." We [the middle class] get shepherded to wherever they feel that they will get a better deal. And the 1 percent are in their own bubble. They have their investments, they've invested in property they've invested abroad.

She ends by shaking her head thinking of the escape hatch some people have access to. She herself wavered, going back and forth between "we" and "they," further illustrating her insecurity in that balancing act. The middle class is constantly navigating in an insecure environment, making it vulnerable to tough-talking ideologues. Economic security feels fragile, religious fundamentalism becomes a way for political figures to absorb and maintain power, and those who have been historically marginalized, women and minorities especially, are targeted to ensure the primacy of those who feel they have the most to lose. The politics of the moment are real and present, and women are paying attention to what is happening. But how will their loyalties, aspirations, and ideals—which in many cases are embattled, conflicted, or uncertain—shift in the coming years and decades? How will what they have been witnessing and processing in Modi's India shape the decisions they and their families will make in a city that once allowed them more freedom and promised a more secure future? What does the future look like, not just for a city as vibrant as Bangalore but for cities around the world that are vulnerable to right-wing forces?

Conclusion

Seeking a Critical Hope

At the end of the foreword in one of the definitive explorations of World War II, William L. Shirer, in his 1960 book, *The Rise and Fall of the Third Reich*, ominously predicts:

> In our new age of terrifying, lethal gadgets, which supplanted so swiftly, the old ones, the first great aggressive war, if it should come, will be launched by suicidal little madmen, pressing an electronic button. Such a war will not last long and none will ever follow it. There will be no conquerors, and no conquest, but only the charred bones of the dead on an uninhabited plant.[1]

It is indeed true that the next bloody world war has the potential to be catastrophic, but the growing presence of "suicidal little madmen" seems to include an ever-expanding list of nominees. The increasing insecurity, the rapid proliferation of social media as a tool to enhance misinformation, and the overall lack of a cohesive sense of unity are some of the reasons the women describe for the rise of authoritarianism, but underneath it all, there seems to be a sense that "past is prologue," especially as we look at world events that have taken place since I began these conversations with my former classmates in 2020.

In the midst of my interviews, while taking a break over the winter holidays and 2020 moved into 2021, the experiences of these women crystallized in ways I never could have fathomed. Sitting in my desk at home on a cold January day, alerts on my phone led me to switch on CNN to see a mob of human beings sweeping toward the U.S. Capitol Building, just twenty-five miles from where I lived. The images of the events of January 6, 2021, were both instantly and eerily reminiscent of the pictures that I remembered seeing of the mobs that descended upon Ayodhya in 1992. It was another terrifying moment, and watching with my son, who himself was just nineteen in 2021,

was to immediately wonder if this incident would also shape another generation, nearly thirty years after the women of my generation were shaped by the
swarming mad crowds that besieged Ayodhya.

In forthcoming months, reading more about the events of January 6, I
caught an excerpt from Jeffrey Toobin's book *Homegrown: Timothy McVeigh
and the Rise of Right-Wing Extremism*, where he too identifies another odd
coincidence. He connects the events on Capitol Hill in 2021 with the bombing of the Alfred P. Murrah Federal Building in Oklahoma City in 1992. He
says that nearly thirty years after the Oklahoma City bombing, "the country
took an extraordinary journey—from nearly universal horror at the action of
a right-wing extremist to wide embrace of a former president (also possibly a
future president) who reflected the bomber's values."[2] This led me to wonder,
would the events of January 2021 unleash their own trajectory of violence,
anger, and hate over the next thirty years? Is the Q-Anon movement, today
a fringe ideological element in US politics, no different from the BJP in
1992 with the potential to become the leading political party of the future?
This was not an idle question as I reviewed the recordings of the conversations with my former classmates and reread their words. As I sought to make
sense of the various topics embedded in this book, I was constantly aware that
yet another mob had changed the direction of a country, maybe in the same
ways the women of BGHS had suggested had happened in India.

So in the three years it has taken this book to evolve from a fragment of an
idea to putting words down for a concluding chapter, the overall meaning of
this book has shifted and evolved. As someone who studies women's issues,
the news from India over the past decade has been troubling, from the rape
of Jyoti Pandey to the death of Gauri Lankesh, spurring my commitment to
speak to women about how they were reacting to the different events. The
second landslide victory for the BJP in 2019 coming during the nascent
stages of Donald J. Trump's reelection campaign prompted a sense of anxiety that the global movement toward authoritarianism was expanding. The
thirtieth anniversary of the demolition of the Babri Masjid mosque seemed
like a tragic reminder of what was lost in the intervening years and a somber
reminder that it was an appropriate time to take stock. But in finally arriving
at this point, there also seems to be a need to understand what is hopeful,
leading to actionable ways to respond.

Misogyny. Patriotism. Nationalism. These are not often words that we use
in our everyday conversations. Yet these topics permeate our regular lives in
a multitude of ways on a daily basis. Often left for journalists to describe,
scholars to interpret, and policymakers to enact, we ignore how people talk
about the influence of these three movements on their own lives. Hearing
from the women in this book, these issues are exhibited with palpable authen-
ticity, not as merely esoteric or incipient archetypes that exist in textbooks.

For me, one of the unique facets of this book remains the comprehensive and expansive analysis the women provide us when it comes to the rise of the BJP, in that they are not just exploring the attacks on secularism, intellectualism, science, or policy but can see the whole tapestry of issues interlaced in a systematic destruction of progressivism. In addition, while the Hindutva agenda has been designed to create a Hindu nation, the outcomes of that agenda have had extensive influence over diverse groups of people, including the premise for this book, that this ideology affects women in ways that are dangerous and often disregarded. Much of this has to do with how patriarchy and misogyny are deeply embedded all over the world, and so we tend to ignore how women understand and experience these structures.

Walking with these women through the course of this book, in their honesty and forthrightness, we have come to deeply understand the rot that percolates both under and over the surface of political authoritarianism. It can leave us feeling frustrated, angry, and powerless, but we also might want to consider what it means to engage in critical hope, as I felt most of the women tried to do despite their frank assessment of the current situation.

Critical hope can be defined as an "an action-oriented response to contemporary despair."[3] Derived from ideas of Paolo Freire who argues that "the dehumanization resulting from an unjust order is not a cause for despair but for hope, leading to the incessant pursuit of the humanity denied by injustice," he also includes the caveat that "hope, however, does not consist in crossing one's arms and waiting. As long as I fight, I am moved by hope."[4]

I share this because as I think about this book, the driving question for me has always been: Can what happened to Bangalore happen to other cities? Can the rising tide of nationalism, religious fundamentalism, and misogyny change the culture and personality of other cities? Does our tolerance for authoritarian leaders open the door to the dismantling of progressive, open, and inclusive ideas? How do mounting concerns about male supremacy intersect with a desire to return to "easier" times where nation and religion ensured the primacy of patriarchal systems and structures, and what can we do to counter that? These are not easy questions to consider, let alone answer, and this book is not an attempt to do that. Yet in listening to the conversations and reading the interviews again, I was struck by snippets of optimism that were articulated by the women in their insights and opinions and through their emotions. As such, I conclude this book by trying to frame a few of the ideas that stood out to me about the ways in which the women voiced that sense of critical hope in an effort to not sit complacently by as mobs of people are used to elevate and entrench authoritarian leaders in these times.

BREAKING THE GRIP OF AUTHORITARIAN LEADERS

While the women did not particularly talk about elections, they talked about the importance of voting. In all fairness, some had even opted to vote for the BJP in 2014, in an effort to try to jolt change in a country where politicians of all parties are considered to be cut from the same disappointing cloth. For those who did vote for the BJP in 2014, they did so assuming that the Hindutva ideology was just a political ploy. Seeing that it was not, by 2020, some voiced clear regret on those votes. Others raised the point that they tried to get to know local candidates, trying to avoid being overly influenced by party platforms. After the BJP landslide in 2019, most were not even thinking ahead to the next election cycle. Yet in May 2023, the Karnataka state elections, coming about a year before the national elections, were seen as a bellwether to determine the national mood. Political watchers kept a close eye on Karnataka, and there was a sense of anxiety and apprehension as the BJP and the Indian National Congress (INC), today helmed by Rahul Gandhi, the son and grandson of Rajiv Gandhi and Indira Gandhi, fought each other in this critical election. Amit Shah, the future hope for the BJP, in Trumpian fashion, made incendiary claims a few weeks before the election, claiming that if the INC won, the state of Karnataka would be "afflicted with communal riots."[5] Despite the subversive efforts to engage in politics of fear, in a staggering success, the INC won both the vote share and secured nearly fifty-five more seats in the state legislature. The BJP lost thirty-eight seats, from its previous high of 104.[6] High voter engagement and interest led to a turnout of just over 73 percent, the highest in the history of Karnataka elections.[7] Focusing on local issues, the INC sought to disengage with the "Modi Myth" to avoid focusing on him as a person. As a result, the party scored a decisive victory, potentially issuing a blow to the ten-year ascendancy of the BJP. Disappointingly, however, the city of Bangalore itself by a narrow margin still supported the BJP, which raises questions about the ways in which the middle class particularly is engaged in the politics of the Hindutva movement. This reminds me of what Vedhika said when asked point blank about who supports the BJP. She answered:

> I feel it's the middle class because in the present situation in India, this new middle class, we have most to lose. The poor will go anywhere. They don't have the agency to say, "Oh, I'm going to take a stand, and I'm going to [follow this political party alone]" and principled things like that. They get shepherded, wherever they feel that they will get a better deal. And the 1 percent [wealthy] are in their own bubble. They have their investments, they've invested in property they've invested abroad.

The narrative middle-class families are hearing from Brazil to France and from India to the United States is that that they are under threat and are vulnerable to the pressures that are coming from everywhere and a right-wing government is the only hope they have to hold out against the hordes of "others." In a new book, *The Autocratic Middle Class: How State Dependency Reduces the Demand for Democracy*, Bryn Rosenfield argues that the middle class, while a force of stability, is also a conservative entity that often depends on state employment (as public employees) to ensure their long-term viability as a member of the middle class. This vulnerability makes them more susceptible to autocratic tendencies, and as rising numbers of middle-class families reside in nondemocratic states, there is a predisposition to be more supportive of authoritarian leaders.[8] In India, the sheer numbers of voters can assuage this trend to some extent, but the reality is the middle class remains an undecided bank of votes, and that indecision can result in greater allegiances to autocrats.

Yet for critical hope to exist, there must be a recognition that change can come. In other surprising elections around the world, there have been readjustments as people have taken a more serious look at their prior flirtations with authoritarianism. Often choosing to reject those trends, we have seen some hopeful election results. In Brazil, Jair Bolsonaro's loss and the subsequent investigations into his actions have loosened the right-wing grip on Brazil's politics.[9] In Poland, after eight years of right-wing government, voters chose a new prime minister from the liberal opposition party.[10] After her loss to Emmanuel Macron in the 2022 French elections, Marine Le Pen is under investigation for embezzlement.[11] These signs of change offer critical hope, and if voting in elections can make a difference, 2024 will be another memorable year as both India and the United States head back to the polls to cast votes in monumentally important national elections.

COLLECTIVE ACTION FOR COLLECTIVE CHANGE

Critical hope was also evident in the women's conversations about the importance of collective action and the significance of protest. Most of the women from BGHS admired the efforts of the women of Shaheen Bagh. The Shaheen Bagh protest, as discussed earlier, was organized by Muslim women and allies to protest the Citizenship Amendment Act (CAA). The peaceful sit-in at a park in New Delhi called Shaheen Bagh illustrated how women coming out and acting on principle using peaceful methods of resistance captured my classmates' imaginations. In addition, the women from BGHS were also excited about the optimism and dynamism of the next generation of women. Chaya was one of the first few women I spoke with at the start of this project.

Her thoughtfulness, attention to politics, and willingness to speak frankly was something I treasured. It was an example of what I hoped would emerge (and did) from the other women because she energized me right from the start and validated the importance of bringing these ideas to a larger audience. While she was not the only one who discussed the ways in which protest movements were being successful, she was the first one who clearly pointed out that college students are not willing to sit back and be still. She said:

> If you had asked me a while back, I would have just said "That's it. There is no hope," but I feel that with the protests that are going on, I do feel that maybe there is something that's to be better. We needed a trigger and now we're coming out on the streets and saying "This is not okay." And there are a lot of people saying, this is not okay. So that is like some kind of hope, but I don't know if it's like a cycle and it's going to take a while for this. Is this like we're at the bottom now? It's going to take a while. I do think that the younger kids are cool. I think they're the ones, the college students. I met this girl [and] we were having this protest meeting kind of thing. And she came and she was [saying] "How can we move it forward? What do we need to do?" And then she said that Mounts [the college] has always been really apolitical, but what really triggered them was all those students being assaulted in Delhi. So that's why they were galvanizing and there are lots of student protests. But I think that, it seems to me, that the age is a little bit more involved and concerned about these things. I don't know if this is for the millennials, I don't know. I'm not so sure about that. But I think the younger they are, the Gen Z is [motivated]. I think so.

While Chaya was referencing the protests at Jawaharlal Nehru University (JNU), she could not imagine that just a year later, Disha Ravi would be arrested in Bangalore on a variety of charges. Nor could she imagine that the government would freeze assets of the international human rights organization Amnesty International and increase their restrictions on anything critical of the government. The most notable of those efforts was the banning of any public screening of the BBC film *India: The Modi Question*, a film critical of Modi's leadership. Coming among other stringent restrictions on free speech and protest, these forms of political harassment and prohibitions create an environment of fear and silence, both of which authoritarian governments require to be able to thrive. Yet Chaya's words reminded me again in 2023, when the Karnakata election was lost by the BJP, to wonder if these draconian measures were missteps on the part of the BJP. As the public became more aware of the attacks and were particularly offended by the arrest of a young woman, it offered a chance for other people to step into that space, recognizing that the government could go after anybody. If anything, it reiterates Yashika's words as she tried to be more transparent with her children. She said:

We do talk about it openly. So, we have dinnertime conversations about what's happening. And then my elder one has her own point of view and my younger two, sometimes they get a little more worried than they should be. And then we kind of tell them, "Know the issue, then it will be okay."

Chanchal shares the same hope:

I've really felt quite helpless. Growing up, as a child, in this kind of very strict, rigid environments, I've always had this irreverence for authority figures. Just this morning I was thinking, I don't care who comes and stands in before me, I just wish I had the courage to say things back then, that really were important to me. And I couldn't do that. And so, this is something that I would like to inculcate in the children of today. And I think a lot of them are doing it, from what I see around me, and from the children I've met, or the young adults that I've met. And I'm not talking about obnoxious millennials. I'm just talking about people who have really figured out who they are, and their place in the scheme of things. They don't need any system. They don't need any setup. It's allowed them to explore it on their own and given the space and the kind of stimuli to do these things, they're just growing on their own. That is something that I would like to really see as things evolve.

Darika was also very admiring of the next generation:

I've been through my own journey of trying to accept these different diversity things. I mean, it really is a mindset. I think I'm better than most, but you have to stop yourself sometimes and say, "You know what, I'm putting such a bias on this because that's how I've been brought up" and I don't see that with the younger generation. I think they're so welcoming and just so inclusive in the way they think and are towards each other. And I think that's fantastic.

She ends by saying, "They've got a lot of cleaning up to do, which we left them, I'm sorry to say." Taking responsibility for the problems while also hoping the next generation will get it right was quite evident in many of these conversations. There was also no sense that these young adults needed to follow any traditional path, but that was very reminiscent of how the women themselves found their own voices in the progressive streets, cafés, and bookstores of Bangalore during their own young adult years.

THE TRANSFORMATIVE POWER OF EDUCATION

To engage in critical hope, there must also be a desire to shift education from the historic "banking model," which limits the ability for people to engage in critical consciousness and transformative learning. The banking model holds the teacher as the central "depositor" of knowledge and the students as the receptacles or vessels within which that knowledge must be stored. Drawing again from the influential work of Paolo Freire, he argues that the "more students work at storing the deposits entrusted to them, the less they develop the critical consciousness which would result from their intervention in the world as transformers of that world." Further, he expands to say that "the more completely they accept the passive role imposed on them, the more they tend simply to adapt to the world as it is and to the fragmented view of reality deposited in them."[12] Part of the willingness for people to move toward a nationalist ideology comes from the ways in which education is structured. As governments work to convince people that education is a purely economic endeavor, educational institutions evolve to focus on monetization and credentialing for their "customers," leading to a focus on conformity and compliance. Conformity is expressed in how we structure our curriculum as well as the evolution of expectations of what learning *must* constitute. Congruent with that is how we then assess what has been learned, whether the learner is barely in kindergarten or seeking the most advanced degrees. Conforming to a particular outcome and output helps an individual become that much more vulnerable to the rhetoric of nationalism and ideological rigidity. Similarly, compliance ensures that we create a structure of education that seeks to align systems, structures, policies, people, and organizations into a state of acquiescence. Compliance infused into educational systems also weakens the fabric of society, allowing for authoritarianism to take root.[13] Almost all the women I spoke with were at the same time convinced of the power of education while also concerned that the educational models that they had been exposed to and that are currently in place are too restrictive for true liberatory thinking.

I think it was because the influence of BGHS was so strong with so many of us that there continues to be a strong connection to the power of education, as well as the idealistic belief that it can truly make a difference. The women spent a fair amount of time pondering, debating, analyzing, critiquing, and complimenting the ways in which structures of education, the curriculum, as well as the ways in which the culture of school could help or hinder individuals. This level of engagement meant that they were active on boards, present in the schools their children attended, or involved in advocating for changes in their local communities. Taking a hands-off approach to education leaves a void that allows for political actors and entities to increase their control over education. For these women, there was little that got past them, and as such, they were themselves vocal about what they wanted to see and oftentimes active in trying to make sure it happened.

Juhi's quote here gives us a sense of that perception of the power of education. She shared the story of her father's friend asking him why he was paying so much money to send both his daughters to medical school. She said: "I remember dad's friend asking, 'Two girls, why do you want to spend so much money for girls?' He said, 'I might have money today. In another one minute or 10 more, I might not have the same amount of money. But once I give them education, no one can take that education away from their hand.'" This was a common understanding for the girls. Early in this book, I talked about the sacrifices parents made to send their daughters to BGHS and that the value of that education was appreciated by the women in their later years.

While the women discussed many of the challenges that students faced in education today, from the high levels of pressure of exams to the relatively sorry state of government schools, there was some hope. Lipika spoke of the wide array of topics students were exposed to, and Parul spoke to me about how she was much happier that schools today would encourage everyone to participate in extracurricular activities. She remembered how at BGHS, there were a few favorites who had access to more of the extracurricular activities. She commented on how different that was for her children. She talked about how "every child needs to participate, irrespective of how they study well or not, everyone needs to take part . . . participation is very important."

Participation—in elections, in movements, and in education—has the power to offer critical hope. The women in this book have continued to express hope despite their frank assessment of the fears and concerns of the future.

SOME LAST WORDS

In January 2024, in a glitzy and glamourous ceremony, Narendra Modi opened the newly remodeled Ayodhya temple using a finely tuned, coordinated media blitz that was not lost on many that the timing of the event was tied to the national elections coming up in May 2024. To many, it felt that after thirty years, the BJP has finally accomplished what it set out to do when it initiated the destruction of the Babri Masjid. If this was the central accomplishment of the BJP, people will have to assess if this was worth the sacrifice of values such as secularism, safety, and progressivism. Others will have to determine if a political party's primary aim should be the creation of a religious monument while continuing to oversee inequitable economic progress, educational access, and the devaluing of human rights. Finally, one will have to see if the party will continue to foment forms of manufactured victimization to continue to stoke the flames of Hindu nationalism. The period that led to the creation of the temple is over, but now moving forward, one has to see how this will all unfold.

Yet for a city like Bangalore, evolving over five hundred years from a small fort complex to a bustling megacity that has a global footprint, the future is still unclear. It feels for the most part still like a small town. During the summer of 2023, my sons returned with me for a trip that marked thirty years since I had left Bangalore to study in the United States. This was not their first trip, as we have spent significant time there over the intervening years, but it was a milestone year in many ways. Casa Piccola was now closed. Premier Bookshop was also closed. The original Corner House was remodeled (and not to its advantage), and there were now branches all over the city. Koshy's, the place where real Bangaloreans went, still looked the same. It was still a place where you could meet a former teacher for a cup of tea or sit with a friend having a drink, see another person walk by, do a double-take, and come and join you even if they hadn't seen you in fifteen years. Yet there was a sense of anxiety and uncertainty. A city cannot turn its back on murdered journalists, arrested teenagers, and other daily forms of authoritarian creep without some impact.

For the women in this book, the larger challenges that have emerged in the city over the past thirty years are the true story of what happens when religious fundamentalism, misogyny, and nationalism intersect. The daily worries, from ensuring a young Christian daughter is not targeted for the lunch she brought to school to being confident that a non-Indian will not risk being harmed if they do not stand for the national anthem, are the real concerns. The expense of the temple, though paid for by private funds, is still galling to women who would prefer to see that money used to ensure better education, safer schools, and opportunities for those who need it the most. Looking over their shoulders before they say something negative about the BJP, wondering if their children will be arrested for something they have written on a social media post, or looking too educated, or Western, or independent, have changed how they think about their daily life in the city that had been more open, more liberal, and more empowering for a whole generation of women during their own adolescence. This is what authoritarianism has wrought over thirty years in the city that was our home.

And yes, Bangalore is still our home. It is a city that we are viscerally connected to, which would be no different for any young person whose adolescence is defined by where they hang out with friends and first loves and concoct big dreams. In sharing the story of a generation of women who called Bangalore home, there are lessons to be learned when we see the commonplace impact of what nativism, authoritarianism, and nationalism can do when it rears its ugly head. The ramifications of those ideologies are manifested in the day-to-day lives of people who are trying to balance their everyday responsibilities with the least amount of strain and stress.

When I started to write this book, I was not sure what the women I grew up with would say about the current political situation in India. I was confident they would have opinions, BGHS had taught us that much at least, but did they have time, energy, or the bandwidth to think about what was happening? Would these conversations be succinct and void of detail? That was not the case. Not only did they have the time, energy, and bandwidth, not only were they deeply attentive, but the effect of the political rhetoric and actions, in many cases, was personally affecting to them. In being observant, engaged, and analytic, I believe we can see the insidious consequences of nationalist ideologies. By sharing from their vantage point and uncovering how, step by step, the BJP has splintered and shredded the progressive fabric of a vibrant city, we can better understand the larger picture that is central to how authoritarians seek to gain, control, and maintain power. The courage and forthrightness of women, to tell their stories, share their experiences, and make frank assessments, gives us a clearer sense of how to counter the systematic approaches at play by those actors. It is now our time to be aware, act, and stay engaged, for if we are not—we risk going home and finding out we just don't recognize it anymore.

Epilogue

While much of this book was written between 2020 and 2023, the publication process was well underway during the spring and summer of 2024 when the Indian people went to the polls. Expectations were high that the Modi government, and the BJP, would win their third decisive electoral victory. The overwhelming opinion of pundits, scholars, and regular people, as well as the BJP party members themselves, was that they would triumph in a landslide, cementing the Hindutva agenda in India. When I talked to family in Bangalore in April and May, they would always tell me about the never-ending barrage of pro-BJP news that dominated airwaves and that, driving through the streets of the city, they were overcome by the sheer multitudes of billboards with images of Modi, larger than life. The election was expected to be the culmination of the BJP ambitions, launching its next phase, coming after the opening of the Ram temple in Ayodhya in February 2024.

The Indian elections are phased elections, where people across the country vote in seven stages. For the first time in my life, I saw people proudly sharing selfies on social media with the distinctive black ink spot on their nails, the evidence that they had cast their votes. With a turnout of just over 65%, the results would not be immediately available. Yet, in June 2024, many of us woke up to heartening news. The BJP had not won in a landslide, and though they still won, they were hobbled by strong losses, and needed the support of two other regional parties to be able to form a government. These two parties are not considered hardline factions, and in fact, are expected to have a moderating effect on the BJP agenda. Only time will tell if that is true, but in the meantime, these election results are being seen as a clear referendum on the discomfort of the Indian voter with the conservative, insular, and oppressive mandates of the BJP.

Does that mean that the stories and concerns the women have shared in this book hold less value because, by voting, the BJP is less powerful today than they were five or ten years ago? Absolutely not! What the women have outlined in this book is the story of thirty years of marginalization, manipulation, and misogyny that has permeated politics in India. The systematic policies of banning what people eat, what they write about, where they live, what they learn, and whom they fall in love with comes directly from the playbook of authoritarian leaders around the world. The women I grew up with have shared how their values of secularism, freedom, and independence have been curtailed by the actions of government leaders who seek to engage in the politics of control. These are not stories that will disappear with one political setback. The right-wing fundamentalists will return, and it is only through awareness, vigilance, and action that citizens can attempt to return to some semblance of secularism and openness. As I write this in July 2024, Prime Minister Narendra Modi is in the news, having just arrived in Moscow to embrace, both physically and metaphorically, another authoritarian leader, Vladimir Putin, who is currently engaged in a brutal cross-border conflict in Ukraine. It is unclear if the message from the voters was clearly heard, discounted, devalued, or ignored. What is clear is that authoritarian leaders find and support each other as well.

So, this book was never meant to be just the tale of a group of girls who became friends, grew up, and moved away, to return to tell me their stories. This book is meant to be a cautionary account that the slide towards authoritarianism can happen in any city, in any town, in any community, despite the best foundations that education, equality, and secularism can offer. But as I review these chapters, and return to the stories the women who were once my classmates shared with me, I am struck again, by the power of critical hope, and how accurate they were in predicting the importance of voting, the power of young people, and the transformative influence of education. These are lessons that I hope can be transferred to other communities that are seeing the steady creep of absolutism and repression. And I hope that we continue to seek out a deeper understanding of how people, in their day to day lives, understand, navigate, negotiate, counter, resist, or abdicate their responsibilities under these circumstances.

Notes

INTRODUCTION

1. Today, the city is officially called Bengaluru. The name was changed from Bangalore on November 1, 2014, as most cities in India returned to their pre-Anglicized names. For the women I spoke with, Bangalore was the city they grew up in, and for that reason, for this book, I will continue to use Bangalore rather than switching back and forth. While the official name of the city changed, the name Bangalore is still in use and remains popular with longtime residents of the city. Other cities in India have also changed names in recent years, and in such cases, I will use the name that was assigned during the time period I am discussing.

2. "High school" is a misnomer, at least from an American perspective. At the time, the school admitted girls aged from four to fifteen.

3. Banerjee, B., & Sharma, A. (2020, August 3). Hindus in India set to build temple at razed mosque site. *The Washington Post*. https://www.washingtonpost.com/world /asia_pacific/hindus-in-india-set-to-build-temple-at-razed-mosque-site/2020/08/03/ f6e6d4de-d5f7-11ea-a788-2ce86ce81129_story.html.

4. Slater, J., & Masih, N. (2020, September 30). Indian court acquits Hindu nationalist leaders accused of demolishing 16th-century mosque. *The Washington Post*. https://www.washingtonpost.com/world/asia_pacific/india-ayodhya-mosque -acquitted-hindu/2020/09/30/52da5ff8-02f4-11eb-b92e-029676f9ebec_story.html.

5. Thakur, R. (1993). Ayodhya and the politics of India's secularism: A double-standards discourse. *Asian Survey, 33*(7), 645–64. https://doi.org/10 .2307/2645353.

6. The Wire Staff. (2021, December 6). Babri masjid: The timeline of a demolition. The Wire. Retrieved September 16, 2022, from https://thewire.in/communalism/babri -masjid-the-timeline-of-a-demolitio.

7. Awasthi, D. (1992, December 31). Babri Masjid demolition: A detailed report. *India Today*. https://www.indiatoday.in/magazine/india-today-archives/story /19921231-a-detailed-report-on-the-demolition-of-babri-masjid-767304-1999-11-30.

8. Awasthi, D. (1992, December 31). Babri Masjid demolition: A detailed report. *India Today*. https://www.indiatoday.in/magazine/india-today-archives/story /19921231-a-detailed-report-on-the-demolition-of-babri-masjid-767304-1999-11-30.

9. Awasthi, D. (1992, December 31). Babri Masjid demolition: A detailed report. *India Today*. https://www.indiatoday.in/magazine/india-today-archives/story /19921231-a-detailed-report-on-the-demolition-of-babri-masjid-767304-1999-11-30.

10. Awasthi, D. (1992, December 31). Babri Masjid demolition: A detailed report. *India Today*. https://www.indiatoday.in/magazine/india-today-archives/story /19921231-a-detailed-report-on-the-demolition-of-babri-masjid-767304-1999-11-30.

11. Awasthi, D. (1992, December 31). Babri Masjid demolition: A detailed report. *India Today*. https://www.indiatoday.in/magazine/india-today-archives/story /19921231-a-detailed-report-on-the-demolition-of-babri-masjid-767304-1999-11-30.

12. Times of India. (1992, December 10). 24 burnt alive in Surat. *Times of India*, 1, 9.

13. State Bureau Reports. (2011, December 5). Bloody aftermath of Babri Masjid demolition across India. *India Today*. https://www.indiatoday.in/india/story/babri -masjid-bloody-aftermath-across-india-147823-2011-12-05.

14. Chakravarti, S. (2012, December 21). Babri Masjid demolition engulfs common Muslim's freedom. *India Today*. https://www.indiatoday.in/magazine/cover -story/story/19921231-babri-masjid-demolition-engulfs-common-muslims-freedom -767309-2012-12-21.

15. Non-BJP opposition blames Centre. (1992, December 7). *Deccan Herald*, 1, 9.

16. The Times of India News Service. (1992, December 9). Anger in Bihar shifts to PM. *The* Times of India, 7.

17. Non-BJP opposition blames Centre. (1992, December 7). *Deccan Herald*, 1, 9.

18. The Times of India News Service. (1992, December 9). BJP a traitor, says Scindia. *The Times of India*, 10.

19. Vaishnav, M. (Ed.). (2019). *The BJP in power: Indian democracy and religious nationalism*. Carnegie Endowment for International Peace. https://carnegieendowment .org/files/BJP_In_Power_final.pdf.

20. Varshney, A. (2002). *Ethnic conflict and civic life: Hindus and Muslims in India*. Yale University Press.

21. Metcalf, B. D., & Metcalf, T. R. (2012). *A* concise history of modern India (3rd ed.). Cambridge University Press.

22. Baily, S. (2009). Can you eat peace: Addressing development needs and peace education in Gujarat, India. In E. Ndura-Ouédraogo & R. Amster (Eds.), *Building cultures of peace: Transdisciplinary voices of hope and action*. (pp. 227–40). Cambridge Scholars Publishing.

23. Baily, S. (2009). Can you eat peace: Addressing development needs and peace education in Gujarat, India. In E. Ndura-Ouédraogo & R. Amster (Eds.), *Building cultures of peace: Transdisciplinary voices of hope and action*. (pp. 227–40). Cambridge Scholars Publishing.

24. Vaishnav, M. (Ed.). (2019). *The BJP in power: Indian democracy and religious nationalism*. Carnegie Endowment for International Peace. https://carnegieendowment .org/files/BJP_In_Power_final.pdf.

25. Goldsmith, B., & Beresford, M. (2018, June 26). Exclusive—India most dangerous country for women with sexual violence rife—global poll. *Thomson Reuters Foundation*. https://news.trust.org//item/20180612134519-cxz54/.

26. Huston, R., & Dastrup, A. (2020). *People, places, and cultures*. Tulsa Community College. https://open.library.okstate.edu/culturalgeography/chapter/6-1/.

27. This is particularly evident in the Facebook group "Bangalore—Photos from a Bygone Era," where a posting of an evocative photograph can generate a tidal wave of nostalgia among the more than 41,000 members.

28. TNM Staff. (2021, May 6). TS Shanbhag of Bengaluru's Premier Book Shop passes away, tributes pour in. The News Minute. https://www.thenewsminute .com/article/ts-shanbhag-bengaluru-s-premier-book-shop-passes-away-tributes-pour -148394.

29. Dhamija, A. (2012, April 5). Casa's gone too. *Times of India*. https://timesofindia .indiatimes.com/city/bengaluru/casas-gone-too/articleshow/12539488.cms.

30. Aravamudan, G. (2019, July 26). Evolution of Bangalore: From Garden City to Silicon Valley, how immigrants made the city their own. *Firstpost*. https://www .firstpost.com/living/evolution-of-bangalore-from-garden-city-to-silicon-valley-how -immigrants-made-the-city-their-own-7050821.html.

31. Central Square Foundation & Omidyar Network India. (2020). *State of the sector report on private schools in India*. https://centralsquarefoundation.org/State-of-the -Sector-Report-on-Private-Schools-in-India.pdf.

32. Pandey, S. (2019). *Identity issues of girls from single-sex convent schools in India*. Publication no. 28266992. Master's thesis, McGill University. ProQuest Dissertations Publishing.

33. In 1989 when the girls in this book graduated, they had just completed grade 10. Today, BGHS goes straight through to grade 12, but the expansion to grade 12 had just begun in 1988 and not all the students continued on.

34. Pandey, S. (2019). *Identity issues of girls from single-sex convent schools in India*. Publication no. 28266992. Master's thesis, McGill University. ProQuest Dissertations Publishing.

35. Pandey, S. (2019). *Identity issues of girls from single-sex convent schools in India*. Publication no. 28266992. Master's thesis, McGill University. ProQuest Dissertations Publishing.

36. Baldwin Girls High School. (1985). [Yearbook]. Baldwin Girls High School annual yearbook. BGHS, Bangalore, India.

37. Baily, S., Wang, G., & Scotto-Lavino, E. (2020). The inheritance of activism: Does social capital shape women's lives? *Girlhood Studies, 13*(2), 86–102. https: //doi.org/10.3167/ghs.2020.130208.

38. Deccan Chronicle. (2015, February 14). Bengaluru police assures people security on Valentine's Day. Retrieved September 16, 2022, from https://www .deccanchronicle.com/150214/nation-current-affairs/article/bengaluru-police-assures -people-security-valentine's-day.

39. Joy, S. (2021, February 14). 21-year-old activist Disha Ravi arrested in Bengaluru in "toolkit" case. *Deccan* Herald. https://www.deccanherald.com/state/ top-karnataka-stories/21-year-old-activist-disha-ravi-arrested-in-bengaluru-in-toolkit -case-951069.html.

40. Fivush, R. (2019). Integration and differentiation of self through reminiscing and narrative. *Social Development, 28*(4), 835–39. https://doi.org/10.1111/sode .12399.

41. Fivush, R. (2019). Integration and differentiation of self through reminiscing and narrative. *Social Development, 28*(4), 835–39. https://doi.org/10.1111/sode .12399.

42. Friedman, T. (2005, April 2). It's a flat world, after all. *The New York Times.* https://www.nytimes.com/2005/04/03/magazine/its-a-flat-world-after-all.html?smid =url-share.

43. The Federal. (2021, June 19). Most livable capital cities' survey: Bangalore tops, Delhi the worst. *The Federal.* https://thefederal.com/news/most-livable-capital -cities-survey-bangalore-tops-delhi-the-worst/.

44. Bureau, A. (2021, January 13). Tesla sets up India subsidiary in Bengaluru. *The Economic Times.* https://economictimes.indiatimes.com/industry/auto/auto-news /tesla-opens-india-subsidiary-in-bengaluru-ahead-of-rd-factory-plans/articleshow /80235735.cms.

45. Central Square Foundation and Omidyar Network India. (2020). *State of the sector report on private schools in India.* https://centralsquarefoundation.org/State-of -the-Sector-Report-on-Private-Schools-in-India.pdf.

CHAPTER 1

1. For readers interested in exploring the history of the city and the surrounding region in more depth, see Nagendra, H. (2016). *Nature in the city: Bengaluru in the past, present, and future.* Oxford University Press. https://oxford.universitypressscholarship .com/view/10.1093/acprof:oso/9780199465927.001.0001/acprof-9780199465927.

2. Ramanathan, S. (2015, August 14). Why is Bengaluru's weather so crazy good? We decode meteorology. *The News Minute.* https://www.thenewsminute.com/article/ why-bengaluru-s-weather-so-crazy-good-we-decode-meteorology-33242.

3. Nagendra, H. (2016). *Nature in the city: Bengaluru in the past, present, and future.* Oxford University Press. https://oxford.universitypressscholarship.com/view /10.1093/acprof:oso/9780199465927.001.0001/acprof-9780199465927.

4. Bengaluru Urban District. (n.d.). *History.* https://bengaluruurban.nic.in/en/ history/#.

5. Encyclopedia Britannica, E. (2010, August 12). *Hoysala dynasty: Indian dynasty.* Encyclopedia Britannica. https://www.britannica.com/topic/Hoysala-dynasty.

6. UNESCO. (2014, April 15). *Sacred ensembles of the Hoysala.* https://whc .unesco.org/en/tentativelists/5898.

7. Deyell, J. S. (2019). Indian Kingdoms 1200–1500 and the maritime trade in monetary commodities. *Currencies of the Indian Ocean World*, 49–69.

8. Saraswathi, N. (2003, January). The economic status of women during Hoyasala period. In *Proceedings of the Indian History Congress* (Vol. 64, pp. 185–87). Indian History Congress.

9. New World Encyclopedia. (n.d.). *Hoysala empire*. https://www.newworldencyclopedia.org/entry/Hoysala_Empire.

10. Shashidhar, H. (2003). A history of migration to Bangalore. *Artha Journal of Social Sciences*. https://journals.christuniversity.in/index.php/artha/article/view/751.

11. Encyclopedia Britannica, E. (2021, April 30). *Tippu Sultan: Sultan of Mysore*. Encyclopedia Britannica. https://www.britannica.com/biography/Tippu-Sultan.

12. Keay, J. (2000). *India: A history*. Grove Press.

13. Keay, J. (2000). *India: A history*. Grove Press.

14. Keay, J. (2000). *India: A history*. Grove Press.

15. Rajendran, D. (2017). Why is BJP against Tipu Sultan, and was this always the case? *The News Minute*. https://www.thenewsminute.com/article/why-bjp-against -tipu-sultan-and-was-always-case-71211.

16. While I will cite *The Hindu* as an influential national newspaper at various stages in this book, it is neither affiliated with nor controlled by Hindu political leaders. The paper is a daily independent English paper that was launched in 1878.

17. Gowda, C. (2016, November 9). All about Tipu Sultan. *The Hindu*. https://www.thehindu.com/opinion/op-ed/All-about-Tipu-Sultan/article16229407.ece?homepage =true.

18. Bengaluru Urban District. (n.d.). *History*. https://bengaluruurban.nic.in/en/history/#.

19. Raman, A. (1994). *Bangalore—mysore*. Disha Books.

20. Moorchung, N., & Moorchung, S. (2017, December 10). St Marks' cathedral: The church that kept rising from the ashes. *Bangalore Mirror*. https://bangaloremirror.indiatimes.com/bangalore/others/st-marks-cathedral-the-church-that -kept-rising-from-the-ashes/articleshow/62001638.cms.

21. Moorchung, S., & Moorchung, N. (2018, June 25). State central library: There's one for the books. *Bangalore Mirror*. https://bangaloremirror.indiatimes.com /bangalore/others/state-central-library-theres-one-for-the-books/articleshow /64723727.cms.

22. Roshini_m12. (2016, August 29). The colonial bungalows of Bengaluru. *Make Heritage Fun!* https://www.makeheritagefun.com/colonial-bungalows-bengaluru/.

23. Castán Broto, V., & Sudhira, H. S. (2019). Engineering modernity: Water, electricity and the infrastructure landscapes of Bangalore, India. *Urban Studies, 56*(11), 2261–79. ps://doi.org/10.1177/0042098018815600.

24. Castán Broto, V., & Sudhira, H. S. (2019). Engineering modernity: Water, electricity and the infrastructure landscapes of Bangalore, India. *Urban Studies, 56*(11), 2261–79. ps://doi.org/10.1177/0042098018815600.

25. Castán Broto, V., & Sudhira, H. S. (2019). Engineering modernity: Water, electricity and the infrastructure landscapes of Bangalore, India. *Urban Studies, 56*(11), 2261–79. ps://doi.org/10.1177/0042098018815600.

26. Sood, A. (2016). Emerging megacities: Hyderabad and Bangalore. *Sociology of Urban Transformations*. Also at E-PGPathshala. http://epgp.inflibnet.ac.in/epgpdata /uploads/epgp_content/S000033SO/P000293/M017900 /ET/1478673995Module8.3_ EmergingMegacities.pdf.

27. Sood, A. (2016). Emerging megacities: Hyderabad and Bangalore. *Sociology of Urban Transformations*. Also at E-PGPathshala. http://epgp.inflibnet.ac.in/epgpdata /uploads/epgp_content/S000033SO/P000293/M017900 /ET/1478673995Module8.3_ EmergingMegacities.pdf.

28. Keay, J. (2000). *India: A history*. Grove Press.

29. Bharadwaj, P., Khwaja, A. I., & Mian, A. R. (2009). The partition of India: Demographic consequences. *SSRN*. https://dx.doi.org/10.2139/ssrn.1294846.

30. Dalrymple, W. (2015). The great divide. *The New Yorker*. https://www .newyorker.com/magazine/2015/06/29/the-great-divide-books-dalrymple.

31. Singh, A., Iyer, N., & Gairola, K. R. (Eds.). (2016). *Revisiting India's partition: New essays on memory, culture, and politics*. Lexington Books.

32. Sudhira, H. S., Ramachandra, T. V., & Subrahmanya, M. B. (2007). Bangalore. *Cities, 24*(5), 379–90. https://doi.org/10.1016/j.cities.2007.04.003.

33. Benjamin, S. (2000). Governance, economic settings and poverty in Bangalore. *Environment and Urbanization, 12*(1), 35–56. https://doi.org/10.1177 /095624780001200104.

34. Moorchung, S., & Moorchung, N. (2018, March 12). Vidhana Soudha: Bengaluru's building art is a great living tradition. *Bangalore Mirror*. https://bangaloremirror .indiatimes.com/bangalore/others/vidhana-soudha-bengalurus-building-art-is-a-great -living-tradition/articleshow/63260067.cms.

35. Karnataka Legislature. *Vidhana Soudha*. https://kla.kar.nic.in/vds.htm.

36. Karnataka Legislature. (n.d.). *Vidhana Soudha*. https://kla.kar.nic.in/vds.htm.

37. Ramachandran, V., & Jandhyala, K. (Eds.). (2014). *Cartographies of empowerment: The Mahila Samakhya story*. Zubaan.

38. Ramachandran, V., & Jandhyala, K. (Eds.). (2014). *Cartographies of empowerment: The Mahila Samakhya story*. Zubaan.

39. Census of India. (1991). *Attending school or college by completed level of education—urban* [Data set]. Office of the Registrar General & Census Commissioner India. https://tn.data.gov.in/catalog/population-attending-school-or-college -completed-level-education-census-1991-india-and#web_catalog_tabs_block_10.

40. Guardian Weekly. (January 14, 1990). Yuppies gather down at the Pub. https:// advance.lexis.com/api/document?collection=news&id=urn:contentItem:3SPF-1NP0 -0010-N2H0-00000-00&context=1516831.

41. PricewaterhouseCoopers. (2007). *Bangalore: Citizen perceptions on democratic capital: Cities of the future*. https://www.pwc.in/assets/pdfs/citizens-perception -on-democratic-capital.pdf.

42. PricewaterhouseCoopers. (2007). *Bangalore: Citizen perceptions on democratic capital: Cities of the future*. https://www.pwc.in/assets/pdfs/citizens-perception -on-democratic-capital.pdf.

43. Sudhira, H. S., Ramachandra, T. V., & Subrahmanya, M. B. (2007). Bangalore. *Cities, 24*(5), 379–90. https://doi.org/10.1016/j.cities.2007.04.003.

44. Sorkin, A. (Writer), Goffman, M. (Writer), Booth, C. (Writer), & Busfield, T. (Director). The West Coast delay (2006, October 9) (Season 1, Episode 4) [TV series episode]. In T. Schlamme & A. Sorkin (Executive Producers), *Studio 60 on the Sunset Strip*. Shoe Money Productions; Warner Bros. Television.

45. CNN. (2000, December 2). Grooming, Indian mystique behind pageant crowns. https://www.cnn.com/2000/ASIANOW/south/12/01/people.world.india.reut /index.html.

46. Saldanha, A. (2002). Music, space, identity: Geographies of youth culture in Bangalore. *Cultural Studies, 16*(3), 337–50. https://doi.org/10.1080/09502380210128289.

47. Goldman, M. (2011). Speculative urbanism and the making of the next world city. *International Journal of Urban and Regional Research, 35*(3), 555–81. https://doi.org/10.1111/j.1468-2427.2010.01001.x.

48. Dittrich, C. (2007). Bangalore: Globalisation and fragmentation in India's hightech-capital. *Asien, 103*(3), 45–58. http://asien.asienforschung.de/wp-content/uploads/sites/6/2018/05/ASIEN_103_Dittrich.pdf.

49. Ogburn, J. (2018, August 29). Research on Bengaluru slums receiving national attention in India. *Duke Stanford School of Public Policy.* https://sanford.duke.edu/story/research-bengaluru-slums-receiving-national-attention-india/.

50. Frazier, C. (2019). Urban heat: Rising temperatures as critique in India's airconditioned city. *City & Society, 31*(3), 441–61. https://doi.org/10.1111/ciso.12228.

51. Reddy, L. S., & Ramasamy, K. (2020). The significant challenges in Bangalore—An introspection. *Adalya Journal, 9*(4). https://doi.org/10.37896/aj9.4/026.

52. Reddy, L. S., & Ramasamy, K. (2020). The significant challenges in Bangalore—An introspection. *Adalya Journal, 9*(4). https://doi.org/10.37896/aj9.4/026.

53. Mahadevan, J. (2011). Power/knowledge in postcolonial settings: The case of IT Bangalore. *Interculture Journal: Online-Zeitschrift für interkulturelle Studien, 10*(13), 61–82. https://nbn-resolving.org/urn:nbn:de:0168-ssoar-452856.

54. Castán Broto, V., & Sudhira, H. S. (2019). Engineering modernity: Water, electricity and the infrastructure landscapes of Bangalore, India. *Urban Studies, 56*(11), 2261–79. https://doi.org/10.1177/0042098018815600.

55. Castán Broto, V., & Sudhira, H. S. (2019). Engineering modernity: Water, electricity and the infrastructure landscapes of Bangalore, India. *Urban Studies, 56*(11), 2261–79. https://doi.org/10.1177/0042098018815600.

56. PricewaterhouseCoopers. (2007). *Bangalore: Citizen perceptions on democratic capital: Cities of the future.* https://www.pwc.in/assets/pdfs/citizens-perception -on-democratic-capital.pdf.

57. Pullanoor, H. (2017, August 9). Bangalore, before the dystopia: The birth, life, and death of India's most liveable city. *Quartz India.* https://qz.com/india/1047419 /bangalore-turns-bengaluru-the-birth-life-and-descent-into-dystopia-of-indias-most -liveable-metro/.

58. Dezan Shira & Associates. (2019, March 22). Bengaluru: Economy, industries, and infrastructure. *India Briefing.* https://www.india-briefing.com/news/city -spotlight-bangalore-6371.html/.

59. Philip, C. M. (2021, January 15). Bengaluru: Namma Metro took 7 years to complete 6 km line, rue activists. *The Times of India.* https://timesofindia.indiatimes .com/city/bengaluru/took-7-yrs-to-complete-6km-line-rue-activists/articleshow /80274002.cms.

60. Chatterjee, S. (2021, November 12). Bengaluru metro is turning into a white elephant—thanks to delays and bad planning. *The News Minute.* https://www

.thenewsminute.com/article/bengaluru-metro-turning-white-elephant-thanks-delays
-and-bad-planning-157534.

61. Jayadeva, S. (2019). English-medium: Schooling, social mobility, and inequality in Bangalore, India. *Anthropology & Education Quarterly, 50*(2), 151–69. https://doi.org/10.1111/aeq.12287.

CHAPTER 2

1. Madanipour, A. (2003). *Public and private spaces of the city*. Routledge.

2. Nisbett, N. (2007). Friendship, consumption, morality: Practising identity, negotiating hierarchy in middle-class Bangalore. *Journal of the Royal Anthropological Institute, 13*(4), 935–50. https://doi.org/10.1111/j.1467-9655.2007.00465.x.

3. Embong, A. R. (2007). New middle classes in Asia. *The Blackwell encyclopedia of sociology*, 1–5. https://doi.org/10.1002/9781405165518.wbeosn019.

4. Ramanathan, S., & Ramanathan, R. (2019, April 16). Many layers within India's middle class. *Hindustan Times*. https://www.hindustantimes.com/india-news/many-layers-within-india-s-middle-class/story-18h8YO4jgMpeivUgdKyAkO.html.

5. Upadhya, C. (2009). India's "new middle class" and the globalising city: Software professionals in Bangalore, India. In *The new middle classes* (pp. 253–68). Springer, Dordrecht.

6. Indiparambil, J. J. (2018). Indian economic sectors and new working class: A socio-cultural review. *International Journal of Innovative Science and Research Technology, 3*(4): 386, 392.

7. Jodhka, S. S. (2007). The other side of development: Poverty, bondage and marginalisation of the rural underclass.

8. Saldanha, A. (2002). Music, space, identity: Geographies of youth culture in Bangalore. *Cultural Studies, 16*(3), 337–50. https://doi.org/10.1080/09502380210128289.

9. *The Independent*. (1989, March 11). Amid the stately: Bruce Palling extols the untrammelled charm of southern India, with its simple beauty and splendid pavilions.

10. Dhamija, A. (2012, April 5). Casa's gone too. *The Times of India*. https://timesofindia.indiatimes.com/city/bengaluru/casas-gone-too/articleshow/12539488.cms?utm_source=contentofinterest&utm_medium=text&utm_campaign=cppst.

11. Lexico. (n.d.). Elocution. Retrieved June 2, 2022, from https://www.lexico.com/en/definition/elocution.

12. Phillipson, R. (2001). English for globalisation or for the world's people? *International Review of Education, 47*, 185–200. https://doi.org/10.1023/A:1017937322957.

13. In the design of the city, "extensions" were new tracts of land that were absorbed into the city limits. The original city limits could not meet the needs of the growing population, so as Bangalore grew, city leaders would authorize new "extensions" that would then be developed to meet the housing needs of city residents. The extensions would often immediately draw middle-class families to purchase sites of land to construct homes in these organized and planned communities.

14. *The Independent.* (1989, March 11). Amid the stately: Bruce Palling extols the untrammelled charm of southern India, with its simple beauty and splendid pavilions.

CHAPTER 3

1. Madanipour, A. (2003). *Public and private spaces of the city.* Routledge.

2. Nair, S. (2020). Metropolitan feminisms of middle-class India: Multiple sites, conflicted voices. *Indian Journal of Gender Studies, 27*(1), 127–40. https://doi.org/10.1177/0971521519891483.

3. Italics added.

4. Stacki, S. L., & Baily, S. (Eds.). (2015). *Educating adolescent girls around the globe: Challenges and opportunities.* Routledge.

5. Karam, A. (n.d.). *Education as the pathway towards gender equality.* United Nations. https://www.un.org/en/chronicle/article/education-pathway-towards-gender-equality.

6. Stacki, S. L., & Baily, S. (Eds.). (2015). *Educating adolescent girls around the globe: Challenges and opportunities.* Routledge.

7. In part due to the increase in funding in the early 1990s, the number of organizations—whether local nongovernmental organizations or transnational entities such as UNESCO—that support the empowerment of girls has been growing.

8. Stacki, S. L., & Baily, S. (Eds.). (2015). *Educating adolescent girls around the globe: Challenges and opportunities.* Routledge.

9. Nike News. (2012, December 11). Nike foundation launches new girleffect.org. *Nike.* https://news.nike.com/news/nike-foundation-launches-new-girleffectorg.

10. Girl Effect. (2014). *The girl effect fact sheet* [Infographic]. Globalgiving.org. https://www.globalgiving.org/pfil/3903/projdoc.pdf.

11. Girl Effect. (2014). *The girl effect fact sheet* [Infographic]. Globalgiving.org. https://www.globalgiving.org/pfil/3903/projdoc.pdf.

12. Luhr, S. (2018). How social class shapes adolescent financial socialization: Understanding differences in the transition to adulthood. *Journal of Family and Economic Issues, 39*(3), 457–73. https://doi.org/10.1007/s10834-018-9573-8

13. Best, A. L., & Lynn, R. (2007). Consumption, girls' culture and. *The Blackwell encyclopedia of sociology.* https://doi.org/10.1002/9781405165518.wbeosc110.

14. Chadda, R. K., & Deb, K. S. (2013). Indian family systems, collectivistic society and psychotherapy. *Indian Journal of Psychiatry, 55*(2), S299–S309. https://doi.org/10.4103/0019-5545.105555.

15. Crosnoe, R. (2007). Friendships of adolescence. *The Blackwell encyclopedia of sociology.* https://doi.org/10.1002/9781405165518.wbeosf073.

16. Magazines that used photographs in a comic book style to tell a romantic story. For more information, see https://mitpress.mit.edu/books/photoromance.

17. Baldwin Boys High School (BBHS) was the brother school associated with the same Methodist Church that ran BGHS and was located about a half mile away.

18. Zietz, S., & Das, M. (2018). "Nobody teases good girls": A qualitative study on perceptions of sexual harassment among young men in a slum of Mumbai. *Global public health, 13*(9), 1229–240. https://doi.org/10.1080/17441692.2017.1335337.

19. Anti-Defamation League. (2017, May 30). *Myths and facts about Muslim people and Islam.* https://www.adl.org/resources/tools-and-strategies/myths-and-facts-about-muslim-people-and-islam.

20. Room where the family gods would be housed.

CHAPTER 4

1. No relation to M. K. Gandhi, or Mahatma Gandhi, with whom many are familiar.

2. Jeet Singh, S. (2014, October 31). It's time India accept responsibility for its 1984 Sikh genocide. *Time.* https://time.com/3545867/india-1984-sikh-genocide-anniversary/.

3. Ranganna, S. S. S. (2009, October 31). Bangaloreans recall a cataclysmic day. *The Hindu.* Retrieved June 8, 2022, from https://www.thehindu.com/news/cities/bangalore/Bangaloreans-recall-a-cataclysmic-day/article16890004.ece.

4. Chatterji, J. (2013). Nationalisms in India, 1857–1947. In J. Breuilly (Ed.), *The Oxford handbook of the history of nationalism.* University of Chicago Press and Manchester University Press. DOI:10.1093/oxfordhb/9780199209194.001.0001.

5. Chatterji, J. (2013). Nationalisms in India, 1857–1947. In J. Breuilly (Ed.), *The Oxford handbook of the history of nationalism.* University of Chicago Press and Manchester University Press. DOI:10.1093/oxfordhb/9780199209194.001.0001.

6. Verghese, A. (2018, August 23). British rule and Hindu-Muslim riots in India: A reassessment. Berkeley Center. https://berkleycenter.georgetown.edu/responses/british-rule-and-hindu-muslim-riots-in-india-a-reassessment.

7. Jahn, E. (2020). *War and compromise between nations and states* (first ed., Vol. 4). (A. Güttel-Bellert, Trans.). Springer. https://link.springer.com/chapter/10.1007/978-3-030-34131-2_5.

8. Van Der Veer, P. (2013). Nationalism and religion. In J. Breuilly (Ed.), *The Oxford handbook of the history of nationalism.* University of Chicago Press and Manchester University Press. DOI:10.1093/oxfordhb/9780199209194.001.0001.

9. No relation to Indira or Rajiv Gandhi.

10. Biswas, S. (2022, January 14). Nathuram Godse: The mystery surrounding Mahatma Gandhi's killer. *BBC.* https://www.bbc.com/news/world-asia-india-60013807.

11. Nussbaum, M. C. (2008). The clash within: Democracy and the Hindu right. *Journal of Human Development, 9*(3), 357–75. https://doi.org/10.1080/14649880802236565.

12. Biswas, S. (2022, January 14). Nathuram Godse: The mystery surrounding Mahatma Gandhi's killer. *BBC.* https://www.bbc.com/news/world-asia-india-60013807.

13. Palshikar, S. (2015). The BJP and Hindu nationalism: Centrist politics and majoritarian impulses. *South Asia: Journal of South Asian Studies, 38*(4), 719–35. https://doi.org/10.1080/00856401.2015.1089460.

14. Palshikar, S. (2015). The BJP and Hindu nationalism: Centrist politics and majoritarian impulses. *South Asia: Journal of South Asian Studies, 38*(4), 719–35. https://doi.org/10.1080/00856401.2015.1089460.

15. The publication *The BJP in Power: Indian Democracy and Religious National-ism*, from the Carnegie Endowment for International Peace, traces the overall trajectory of the BJP since Independence to 2019.

16. Rhude, K. (2018). Destruction of Ayodhya mosque. Religion and Public Life at Harvard Divinity School. https://rpl.hds.harvard.edu/religion-context/case-studies/violence-peace/destruction-ayodhya-mosque.

17. Verma, R. (2019). The emergence, stagnation, and ascendance of the BJP. In M. Vaishnav (Ed.), *The BJP in power: Indian democracy and religious nationalism* (pp. 23–36). Carnegie Endowment for International Peace. https://carnegieendowment.org/files/BJP_In_Power_final.pdf.

18. Ramani, S. (2019, May 24). Analysis: Highest-ever national vote for the BJP. *The Hindu.* https://www.thehindu.com/elections/lok-sabha-2019/analysis-highest-ever-national-vote-share-for-the-bjp/article27218550.ece.

19. Gokhale, P. (2020). *Classical Buddhism, neo-Buddhism and the question of caste*. Routledge India.

20. Mukherjee, P. (1983). The image of women in Hinduism. *Women's Studies International Forum, 6*(4), 375–81. https://doi.org/10.1016/0277-5395(83)90030-4.

21. Gokhale, P. (2020). *Classical Buddhism, neo-Buddhism and the question of caste*. Routledge India.

22. Guest Writer. (2018, January 11). Manusmriti: The ultimate guide to becoming a "good woman." *Feminism in India.* https://feminisminindia.com/2018/01/11/manusmriti-ultimate-guide-good-woman/.

23. Banerjee, S. (2019, December 16). The new age politics of gender in the Hindutva movement and faith-based identity contestation. *Open Democracy.* https://www.opendemocracy.net/en/rethinking-populism/new-age-politics-gender-hindutva-movement-and-faith-based-identity-contestation/.

24. Mukherjee, R., & Malone, D. M. (2011). Indian foreign policy and contemporary security challenges. *International Affairs, 87*(1), 87–104. https://doi.org/10.1111/j.1468-2346.2011.00961.x.

25. Singh Devi, A. (2010, June 27). All we need is love, say cascade 2010 participants. *Citizen* Matters. https://bengaluru.citizenmatters.in/2131-nehru-bal-sangh-cultural-fest-cascade-2131.

26. Chandra, N. (2010). The Amar Chitra Katha Shakuntala: Pin-up or role model? *South Asia Multidisciplinary Academic Journal* (4). https://doi.org/10.4000/samaj.3050.

27. Chandra, N. (2010). The Amar Chitra Katha Shakuntala: Pin-up or role model? *South Asia Multidisciplinary Academic Journal* (4). https://doi.org/10.4000/samaj.3050.

28. L.A. Times Archives. (1987). Kin killed widow, India court told. Los Angeles Times. https://www.latimes.com/archives/la-xpm-1987-11-23-mn-15923-story.html.

29. Bumiller, E. (1991). *May you be the mother of a hundred sons: A journey among the women of India*. Ballantine Books.

30. TTN. (2019, September 5). In Rajasthan's sati village, Roop Kanwar still burns bright. *The Times of India*. https://timesofindia.indiatimes.com/city/jaipur/in-sati -village-roop-kanwar-still-burns-bright/articleshow/70984735.cms.

31. BGHS had just launched a grade 11–12 program, and while a few girls contin-ued there, most would move to the junior colleges that peppered the city.

CHAPTER 5

1. Abi-Habib, M. (2018, April 16). "Men treat us like we aren't human." Indian girls learn to fight back. *The New York Times*. https://www.nytimes.com/2018/04/16/ world/asia/india-girls-self-defense.html.

2. Shandilya, K. (2015). Nirbhaya's body: The politics of protest in the aftermath of the 2012 Delhi gang rape. *Gender & History, 27*(2), 465–86. https://doi.org/10.1111 /1468-0424.12134.

3. Dutta, D., & Sircar, O. (2013). India's winter of discontent: Some feminist dilemmas in the wake of a rape. *Feminist Studies, 39*(1), 293–306. https://www.jstor .org/stable/23719318.

4. Das, K., & Mohanty, B. (2020, November 25). *The growing concern around violence against women in India—Where do we stand?* International Growth Centre. https://www.theigc.org/blog/the-growing-concern-around-violence-against-women -in-india-where-do-we-stand/.

5. Das, K., & Mohanty, B. (2020, November 25). *The growing concern around violence against women in India—Where do we stand?* International Growth Centre. https://www.theigc.org/blog/the-growing-concern-around-violence-against-women -in-india-where-do-we-stand/.

6. Pandey, G. (2022, September 13). *Rising crime against Indian women in five charts*. British Broadcasting Corporation. https://www.bbc.com/news/world-asia -india-62830634.

7. Pandey, G. (2022, September 13). *Rising crime against Indian women in five charts*. British Broadcasting Corporation. https://www.bbc.com/news/world-asia -india-62830634.

8. Harbishettar, V., & Math, S. B. (2014). Violence against women in India: Com-prehensive care for survivors. *The Indian Journal of Medical Research, 140*(2), 157–59. https://www.ncbi.nlm.nih.gov/pmc/articles/PMC4216486/.

9. Kaul, N. (2021). The misogyny of authoritarians in contemporary democra-cies. *International Studies Review, 23*(4), 1619–45.

10. Gökarıksel, B., Neubert, C., & Smith, S. (2019). Demographic fever dreams: Fragile masculinity and population politics in the rise of the global right. *Signs: Journal of Women in Culture and Society, 44*(3), 561–87.

11. Banerjee, S. (2012). Muscular *nationalism: Gender, violence, and empire in India and Ireland, 1914–2004*. Vol. 2. NYU Press.

12. Rubio-Marín, R. (2020). Gendered nationalism and constitutionalism. *International Journal of Constitutional Law, 18*(2), 441–46.

13. Derichs, C., & Fleschenberg, A., (Eds.). (2010). *Religious fundamentalisms and their gendered impacts in Asia*. Friedrich-Ebert-Stiftung. https://library.fes.de/pdf-files/iez/07061.pdf.

14. Chacko, P. (2020). Gender and authoritarian populism: Empowerment, protection, and the politics of resentful aspiration in India. *Critical Asian Studies, 52*(2), 204–25.

15. Evans, J., Sahgal, N., Salazar, A., Starr, K., & Corichi, M. (2022) *How Indians view gender roles in families*. Pew Research Center's Religion & Public Life Project. Pew Research Center. Available at https://www.pewresearch.org/religion/2022/03/02/gender-roles-in-the-family/. Accessed April 24, 2023.

16. Chacko, P. (2020). Gender and authoritarian populism: Empowerment, protection, and the politics of resentful aspiration in India. *Critical Asian Studies, 52*(2), 204–25.

17. Many new extensions of Bangalore would be anchored by one long "Hundred Feet" road around which local businesses would cluster. A city could have multiple "Hundred Feet Roads."

18. Statista Research Department. (2021, September 18). *Total number of rape cases reported in India from 2005 to 2020* [Data set]. https://www.statista.com/statistics/632493/reported-rape-cases-india/.

19. *Times of India*. (2019, December 19). How Nirbhaya case changed rape laws in India. https://timesofindia.indiatimes.com/india/how-nirbhaya-case-changed-rape-laws-in-india/articleshow/72868366.cms.

20. Thiagarajan, K. (2018, May 4). India reforms its anti-rape laws—To mixed reaction. NPR. https://www.npr.org/sections/goatsandsoda/2018/05/04/608516694/india-reforms-its-anti-rape-laws-to-mixed-reaction.

21. Statista Research Department. (2021, September 18). *Total number of rape cases reported in India from 2005 to 2020* [Graph]. https://www.statista.com/statistics/632493/reported-rape-cases-india/.

22. Thiagarajan, K. (2018, May 4). India reforms its anti-rape laws—To mixed reaction. NPR. https://www.npr.org/sections/goatsandsoda/2018/05/04/608516694/india-reforms-its-anti-rape-laws-to-mixed-reaction.

23. Another local school for girls, similar to BGHS.

24. Express News Service. (2022, February 9). Karnataka BJP MLA blames clothes worn by women for rise in cases of sexual assault. https://indianexpress.com/article/cities/bangalore/karnataka-bjp-mla-blames-clothes-worn-by-women-for-rise-in-cases-of-sexual-assault-7764438/.

25. Sanjiv, D. (2022, December 18). Oppn: Moral policing is BJP's election agenda. *Times of India*. http://timesofindia.indiatimes.com/articleshow/96313290.cms?utm_source=contentofinterest&utm_medium=text&utm_campaign=cppst.

26. Goldsmith, B., & Beresford, M. (2018, June 26). India most dangerous country for women with sexual violence rife—global poll. Reuters. https://www.reuters.com/article/women-dangerous-poll-idINKBN1JM076.

27. Thomson Reuters Foundation. (2018, June 26). Factbox: Which are the world's 10 most dangerous countries for women? Reuters. https://www.reuters.com/article/us-women-dangerous-poll-factbox/factbox-which-are-the-worlds-10-most-dangerous-countries-for-women-idUSKBN1JM01Z.

28. Chandran, R. (2009, February 14). Indian police arrest hundreds in Valentine protests. Reuters. https://www.reuters.com/article/idINIndia-38015720090214.

29. Bhandari, A. (2021). *Indian media narratives in gang rape*. Doctoral dissertation, Old Dominion University.

30. De Sarkar, D. (2017, February 17). How Saffron lost the war against Valentine's Day in India. Mint. https://www.livemint.com/Opinion/dCMfdAAVnmVMEnR4XpmhuM/How-Saffron-lost-the-war-against-Valentines-Day-in-India.html.

31. Harriss, J., Corbridge, S., & Jeffrey, C. (2017). Is India becoming the "Hindu Rashtra" sought by Hindu nationalists? *Simons* Papers in Security and Development, *60*. http://summit.sfu.ca/item/17627.

32. Jain, N. (2022, July 8). *The gradual normalization of violence against Indian Muslim women*. https://womensmediacenter.com/women-under-siege/the-gradual-normalization-of-violence-against-indian-muslim-women.

33. Dossani, R. (2018, June 19). *Politics in India—Not business as usual*. Rand Cooperation. https://www.rand.org/blog/2018/06/politics-in-india-not-business-as-usual.html; and Sonkar, S. (2022). Policing interfaith marriages: Constitutional infidelity of the love jihad ordinance. *Journal of Law and Religion, 37*(3), 432–45. doi:10.1017/jlr.2022.37; and Outlook Web Bureau. (2018, April 20). PM Modi should pay more attention to women safety, IMF Chief Christine LaGarde. *Outlook*. https://www.outlookindia.com/website/story/pm-modi-should-pay-more-attention-to-women-safety-imf-chief-christine-lagarde/311189.

34. Ela has lived outside India for the past decade but travels back frequently to see family.

35. Sundari, S. (2020). Structural changes and quality of women's labour in India. *The Indian Journal of Labour Economics, 63*, 689–717.

36. World Bank. (2022). World Bank data. https://data.worldbank.org/indicator/SP.POP.1564.FE.IN?locations=IN.

37. Baily, B. (2008). *Sharing power: How nonformal education for women shapes the perceptions and attitudes of community leaders—A case study in India*. Publication No. 3321162. Doctoral dissertation, George Mason University. ProQuest Dissertation and Theses Global.

38. A colloquial reference to any girl/woman.

39. Leavitt, C. E., Allsop, D. B., Price, A. A., Marks, L. D., & Dollahite, D. C. (2021). Exploring gender roles in highly religious families. *Review of Religious Research, 63*, 511–33.

40. Derichs, C., & Fleschenberg, A., (Eds.). (2010). *Religious fundamentalisms and their gendered impacts in Asia*. Friedrich-Ebert-Stiftung. https://library.fes.de/pdf-files/iez/07061.pdf.

41. Evans, J., Sahgal, N., Salazar, A., Starr, K., & Corichi, M. (2022) *How Indians view gender roles in families.* Pew Research Center's Religion & Public Life Project. Pew Research Center. Available at https://www.pewresearch.org/religion/2022/03/02 /gender-roles-in-the-family/. Accessed April 24, 2023.

CHAPTER 6

1. Shiksha. (2022). *NIRF rankings 2022—Top 100 colleges/universities in India.* https://www.shiksha.com/humanities-social-sciences/articles/nirf-college-rankings -2021-top-100-colleges-in-india-blogId-17637.
2. Chettri, S., & Ibrar, M. (2022, October 11). DU on a new high: Lady Shri Ram College pegs cutoff at 100% for 3 courses. *Times of India.* https://timesofindia .indiatimes.com/city/delhi/du-on-a-new-high-lady-shri-ram-college-pegs-cutoff-at -100-for-3-courses/articleshow/78598090.cms.
3. Lady Shri Ram College for Women. (n.d.) *Our mission.* https://lsr.edu.in/about -lsr/our-mission/.
4. Hamid, R. D., & Orakwue, N. L. (2022, April 1). Harvard College accepts record-low 3.19% of applicants to class of 2026. *The Harvard Crimson.* https://www .thecrimson.com/article/2022/4/1/admissions-class-of-2026/.
5. Redding, G., Drew, A., & Crump, S. (Eds.). (2019). *The Oxford handbook of higher education systems and university management.* Oxford University Press.
6. Kaur, R. (2022). Gendered parenting and returns from children in contemporary India: A study of IIT students and their parents. *Current Sociology, 70*(4), 578–97.
7. Punjabi, S. (2022). Chasing elite higher education: Shadow education and middle-class strategies of credentialism around the Indian Institute of Technology Joint Entrance Exam. *Sociological Bulletin, 71*(2), 193–209.
8. https://www.pewresearch.org/fact-tank/2023/02/09/key-facts-as-india-surpasses -china-as-the-worlds-most-populous-country/
9. *India: Overview of the education system.* (2022). Education GPS, Organization for Economic Co-operation and Development. Retrieved March 1, 2023, from https: //gpseducation.oecd.org/CountryProfile?primaryCountry=IND&treshold=5&topic =EO.
10. Indian schools must comply and be accredited to follow a prescribed curriculum. For most of India's history these boards included state boards for schools under state control; the ICSE, or the Indian School Certificate Examination, for most private schools; and the CBSE, or the Central Board of Secondary Education, under which schools controlled by the central government operate.
11. Chalam, K. S. (2007). *Caste-based reservations and human development in India.* Sage Publication.
12. Ghosh, J. (2006). Case for caste-based quotas in higher education. *Economic and Political Weekly*, 2428–32. https://www.jstor.org/stable/4418343.
13. Medical, engineering, architecture, and other schools where students complete a professional degree.

14. Kumar, S. (2020). Verdict 2019: The expanded support base of the Bharatiya Janata party. *Asian Journal of Comparative Politics, 5*(1), 6–22.

15. The Conversation. (2019, May 9). India: how some Hindu nationalists are rewriting caste history in the name of decolonisation. https://theconversation .com/india-how-some-hindu-nationalists-are-rewriting-caste-history-in-the-name-of -decolonisation-114133.

16. Chhibber, P., & Verma, R. (2019). The rise of the second dominant party system in India: BJP's new social coalition in 2019. *Studies in Indian Politics, 7*(2), 131–48. https://doi.org/10.1177/2321023019874628.

17. Chhibber, P., & Verma, R. (2019). The rise of the second dominant party system in India: BJP's new social coalition in 2019. *Studies in Indian Politics, 7*(2), 131–48. https://doi.org/10.1177/2321023019874628.

18. Flåten, L. T. (2017). Spreading Hindutva through education: Still a priority for the BJP? *India Review, 16*(4), 377–400. https://doi.org/10.1080/14736489.2017 .1378481.

19. Sengupta, S. (2002, May 13). Hindu right goes to school to build a nation. *The New York Times.* https://www.nytimes.com/2002/05/13/world/hindu-right-goes-to -school-to-build-a-nation.html.

20. Dhankar, R. (2021, December 4). Indoctrination in the guise of education. *The Hindu.* Retrieved August 7, 2022, from https://www.thehindu.com/opinion/op-ed/ Indoctrination-in-the-guise-of-education/article62119869.ece.

21. Gohain, H. (2002). On saffronisation of education. *Economic and Political Weekly,* 4597–99. https://www.jstor.org/stable/4412835.

22. Sutoris, P. (2018). Elitism and its challengers: Educational development ideol- ogy in postcolonial India through the prism of film, 1950–1970. *International Journal of Educational Development, 60*, 1–9. https://doi.org/10.1016/j.ijedudev.2017.10.017.

23. Kanwal, S. (2021, November 24). Number of enrolled students in India 2017–2018, by school type. *statista.* https://www.statista.com/statistics/1175285/ india-number-of-enrolled-students-by-school-type/.

24. Gohain, M. P. (202, July 13). Private schools grooming about 50% of students in country. *The Times of India.* https://timesofindia.indiatimes.com/india/private -schools-grooming-about-50-of-students-in-country/articleshow/77118276.cms.

25. All Schools in India. (n.d.). *How many government and private schools in India?* https://allschoolsinindia.in/how-many-government-and-private-schools-in -india/.

26. Central Square Foundation. 2020. State of the sector report on private schools in India.

27. Vidya Bharati. (n.d.). *About Vidya Bharati.* https://vidyabharti.net/about-vidya -bharati.

28. Bhattacharya, S. (2021, August 24). From Hindu Ocean to Sindhu Sea: Here's what RSS-backed schools are teaching children about history. *newslaundry.* https:// www.newslaundry.com/2021/08/24/from-hindu-ocean-to-sindhu-sea-heres-what-rss -backed-schools-are-teaching-children-about-history.

29. Bhattacharya, S. (2021, August 24). From Hindu Ocean to Sindhu Sea: Here's what RSS-backed schools are teaching children about history. *newslaundry.* https://

www.newslaundry.com/2021/08/24/from-hindu-ocean-to-sindhu-sea-heres-what-rss
-backed-schools-are-teaching-children-about-history.

30. Tharoor, S. (2018). *Why I am a Hindu.* Scribe.

31. Not by her but by others who are pro-Hindutva, as they would not find that to be a concern.

32. Further details on the beef bans will be shared in chapter 7.

33. Sanghera, T. (2020). Modi's textbook manipulations [News]. *Foreign Policy.* Retrieved from https://foreignpolicy. com/2020/08/06/textbooks-modi-remove-chap-ters-democracy-secularism-citizenship.

34. Gahlot, M. (2015, March 19). India's new school textbooks favor Hindu nationalist themes, making minorities uneasy. *The Washington Post.* https://www .washingtonpost.com/national/religion/indias-new-school-textbooks-favor-hindu -nationalist-themes-making-minorities-uneasy/2015/03/19/30b5dad6-ce4a-11e4 -8730-4f473416e759_story.html.

35. Singh, S. (2022, May 8). The world ignored Russia's delusions. It shouldn't make the same mistake with India. *Foreign Policy.* https://foreignpolicy.com/2022/05 /08/india-akhand-bharat-hindu-nationalist-rss-bjp/.

36. DW. (n.d.). *India: Is the BJP altering school curriculum to promote Hindu nationalism?* https://www.dw.com/en/india-is-the-bjp-altering-school-curriculum-to -promote-hindu-nationalism/a-61932435.

37. Flåten, L. T. (2017). Spreading Hindutva through education: Still a priority for the BJP? *India Review, 16*(4), 377–400. https://doi.org/10.1080/14736489.2017 .1378481.

38. Carnegie Endowment for International Peace. (2019). *The BJP in power: Indian democracy and religious nationalism.* https://carnegieendowment.org/files/BJP_In _Power_final.pdf.

39. Carnegie Endowment for International Peace. (2019). *The BJP in power: Indian democracy and religious nationalism.* https://carnegieendowment.org/files/BJP_In _Power_final.pdf.

40. Sharma, B. (2017, September 19). In RSS schools, Muslim students are learn-ing to live with Hindutva. *HuffPost.* https://www.huffpost.com/archive/in/entry/in-rss -schools-muslims-students-are-learning-to-live-with-hindutva_a_23155028.

41. Reporter, S. (2020, January 15). BJP workers use saffron paint to cover graffiti outside Srishti Art Institute. *The Hindu.* Retrieved April 22, 2023, from https://www .thehindu.com/news/cities/bangalore/bjp-workers-use-saffron-paint-to-cover-graffiti -outside-srishti-art-institute/article30572181.ece.

42. Goswami, R. (2017, July 3). Rajasthan removes Indira Gandhi's name from schoolgirls' award scheme. *Hindustan Times.* https://www.hindustantimes.com/ india-news/rajasthan-removes-indira-gandhi-s-name-from-schoolgirls-award-scheme /story-2h3usl1JfvjXa7RCfFqXtM.html.

43. Goswami, R. (2017, July 3). Rajasthan removes Indira Gandhi's name from schoolgirls' award scheme. *Hindustan Times.* https://www.hindustantimes.com/ india-news/rajasthan-removes-indira-gandhi-s-name-from-schoolgirls-award-scheme /story-2h3usl1JfvjXa7RCfFqXtM.html.

44. Behrensen, M., & Stanoeva, E. (2019). *Hypochondriac identities: Gender and nationalism in Bulgaria and Germany*. Campus Verlag.

45. Jack, I. (2018, January 13). India has 600 million young people—and they're set to change our world. *The Guardian*. https://www.theguardian.com/commentisfree /2018/jan/13/india-600-million-young-people-world-cities-internet.

46. Virmani, P. (2014, April 8). Note to India's leaders: Your 150m young people are calling for change. *The Guardian*. https://www.theguardian.com/commentisfree /2014/apr/08/india-leaders-young-people-change-2014-elections.

47. Jack, I. (2018, January 13). India has 600 million young people—and they're set to change our world. *The Guardian*. https://www.theguardian.com/commentisfree /2018/jan/13/india-600-million-young-people-world-cities-internet.

48. Tomassini, M. (2019, March 8). How parents in India are keeping their girls in school, and away from early marriages. *UNICEF*. https://www.unicef.org/stories/how -parents-india-keeping-girls-in-school-away-from-early-marriages.

49. Fuller, C. J., & Narasimhan, H. (2008). Companionate marriage in India: The changing marriage system in a middle-class Brahman subcaste. *Journal of the Royal Anthropological Institute, 14*(4), 736–54. https://www.jstor.org/stable/20203738.

50. https://www.pewresearch.org/religion/2021/06/29/attitudes-about-caste/

51. Baily, S. (2020, December 9). Neo-nationalism: A 2020 Perspective. *International* Educator. https://www.nafsa.org/ie-magazine/2020/12/9/neo-nationalism-2020 -perspective.

CHAPTER 7

1. Arif, A. M. (2015, November). *Muslims of Bangalore under Narendra Modi's regime: Perspectives from South India*. Nori Research. https://noria-research.com/ muslims-of-bangalore-under-narendra-modis-regime-perspectives-from-south-india/.

2. Deshmukh, J. (2021). Terrorizing Muslims: Communal violence and emergence of Hindutva in India. *Journal of Muslim Minority Affairs, 41*(2), 317–36. https://doi .org/10.1080/13602004.2021.1943884.

3. Human Rights Watch. (1995, April 1). Playing the "communal card": Communal violence and human rights. https://www.hrw.org/legacy/reports/1995/communal/.

4. Public Policy Research Center. (n.d.). *A fact sheet on communal riots in India*. http://www.pprc.in/upload/Fact-Sheet%20of%20Communal%20riots%20in %20India.pdf.

5. Swamy, R. (2020, August 13). Bengaluru has seen 8 major riots since 1986—including two over Prophet Muhammad. *The Print*. https://theprint.in/ india/bengaluru-has-seen-8-major-riots-since-1986-including-two-over-prophet -muhammad/481085/.

6. Shastri, S. (2020). Communal violence in twenty-first century India: Moving beyond the Hindi heartland. *Studies in Indian Politics, 8*(2), 266–80.

7. Gupta, H., & Medappa, K. (2020). Nostalgia as affective landscape: Negotiating displacement in the "world city." *Antipode, 52*(6), 1688–709.

8. Dev, A. (2021, March 15). 3 waves of migrations that shaped Bengaluru. *Hindustan Times*. https://www.hindustantimes.com/cities/others/3-waves-of-migrations -that-shaped-bengaluru-101615660544003.html.

9. Mishra, M. (2020, January 31). Bangalore is now officially the world's most traffic congested city. *GoMechanic Blog*. https://gomechanic.in/blog/bangalore-is-the -worlds-most-traffic-congested-city/.

10. Bourah, M. (2021, December 29). Christians on edge in India's Karnataka ruled by Modi's BJP. *Aljazeera*. https://www.aljazeera.com/news/2021/12/29/christians -india-karnataka-anti-conversion-bill-bjp-hate-attacks.

11. Sahu, S. (2020, February 11). "Even in Bengaluru, even today, you could find it hard to rent a flat if you have a Muslim name." *Citizen Matters*. https://bengaluru .citizenmatters.in/even-bengaluru-today-muslim-name-hard-to-rent-apartment -religious-discrimination-in-housing-42520.

12. Sridhar, D. (2011, November 3). "We don't want Muslim tenants." *Bangalore Mirror*. https://bangaloremirror.indiatimes.com/bangalore/others/we-dont-want -muslim-tenants/articleshow/21487866.cms.

13. Thorat, S., Banerjee, A., Mishra, V. K., & Rizvi, F. (2015). Urban rental housing market: Caste and religion matters in access. *Economic and Political Weekly*, 47–53.

14. Monda, S. (2012, July 8). India's IT powerhouse is mired in social prejudice. *The Hindu*. Retrieved August 21, 2022, from https://www.thehindu.com/news/ national//article60454200.ece.

15. Mangaldas, L. (2017, June 5). India's got beef with beef: What you need to know about the country's controversial "beef ban." Forbes. https://www.forbes.com/ sites/leezamangaldas/2017/06/05/indias-got-beef-with-beef-what-you-need-to-know -about-the-countrys-controversial-beef-ban/?sh=6fd63ae853c2.

16. No author. (2022, December 20). The myth of the holy cow. *The Economist*. https://www.economist.com/christmas-specials/2022/12/20/indias-movement -to-protect-cows-is-rooted-in-politics-not-religion.

17. Saldanha, A. (2019, February 19). Incomes shrink as cow-related violence scuttles beef, leather exports: New report. *India Spend*. https://www.indiaspend.com /incomes-shrink-as-cow-related-violence-scuttles-beef-leather-exports-new-report/.

18. Parikh, A., & Miller, C. (2019). Holy cow! Beef ban, political technologies, and Brahmanical supremacy in Modi's India. *ACME: An International Journal for Critical Geographies, 18*(4), 835–74.

19. Saldanha, A. (2019, February 19). Incomes shrink as cow-related violence scuttles beef, leather exports: New report. *India Spend*. https://www.indiaspend.com /incomes-shrink-as-cow-related-violence-scuttles-beef-leather-exports-new-report/.

20. Human Rights Watch. (1995, April 1). *Playing the "communal card": Communal violence and human rights*. https://www.hrw.org/report/1995/04/01/playing -communal-card/communal-violence-and-human-rights.

21. Paliath, S. (2022, February 8). New anti-cattle slaughter law in Karnataka causing loss of livelihoods. *India Spend*. https://www.indiaspend.com/governance/new -anti-cattle-slaughter-law-in-karnataka-causing-loss-of-livelihoods-802323.

22. Deshmukh, J. (2021). Terrorizing Muslims: Communal violence and emergence of Hindutva in India. *Journal of Muslim Minority Affairs, 41*(2), 317–36. https://doi.org/10.1080/13602004.2021.1943884.

23. Ramachandran, S. (2020). Hindutva violence in India. *Counter Terrorist Trends and Analyses, 12*(4), 15–20. https://www.jstor.org/stable/10.2307/26918077.

24. Deshmukh, J. (2021). Terrorizing Muslims: Communal violence and emergence of Hindutva in India. *Journal of Muslim Minority Affairs, 41*(2), 317–36. https://doi.org/10.1080/13602004.2021.1943884.

25. Basu, A. (2018). Whither democracy, secularism, and minority rights in India? *The Review of Faith & International Affairs, 16*(4), 34–46. https://doi.org/10.1080/15570274.2018.1535035.

26. Basu, A. (2018). Whither democracy, secularism, and minority rights in India? *The Review of Faith & International Affairs, 16*(4), 34–46. https://doi.org/10.1080/15570274.2018.1535035.

27. Union ministers are equivalent to cabinet secretaries in the United States, appointed by the president; Basu, A. (2018). Whither democracy, secularism, and minority rights in India? *The Review of Faith & International Affairs, 16*(4), 34–46. https://doi.org/10.1080/15570274.2018.1535035.

28. Gallup. (n.d.). *Islamophobia: Understanding anti-Muslim sentiment in the West.* https://news.gallup.com/poll/157082/islamophobia-understanding-anti-muslim-sentiment-west.aspx.

29. Gowen, A. (2018, April 26). A Muslim and a Hindu thought they could be a couple. Then came the "love jihad" hit list. *The Washington Post.* https://www.washingtonpost.com/world/asia_pacific/a-muslim-and-a-hindu-thought-they-could-be-a-couple-then-came-the-love-jihad-hit-list/2018/04/26/257010be-2d1b-11e8-8dc9-3b51e028b845_story.html; TNN. (2020, November 3). Karnataka hints at law against "love jihad." *The Times of India.* https://timesofindia.indiatimes.com/city/bengaluru/karnataka-hints-at-law-against-love-jihad/articleshow/79010254.cms.

30. Ellis-Petersen, H., & Khan, A. (2022, January 21). "They cut him into pieces": India's "love jihad" conspiracy theory turns lethal. *The Guardian.* https://www.theguardian.com/world/2022/jan/21/they-cut-him-into-pieces-indias-love-jihad-conspiracy-theory-turns-lethal.

31. Arkal, R. A. (2020, December 1). Protests planned in Bengaluru as Karantaka mulls "love jihad" law. *The Indian Express.* https://indianexpress.com/article/cities/bangalore/protests-planned-in-bengaluru-to-oppose-karnatakas-proposed-love-jihad-law-7074294/.

32. Thapar, A., & Wahidi, Z. (2020, August 22). Bombay HC's tolerance lesson on tablighis. *Article 14.* https://www.article-14.com/post/bombay-high-court-s-tolerance-lesson-on-tablighi-jamaat.

33. Thapar, A., & Wahidi, Z. (2020, August 22). Bombay HC's tolerance lesson on tablighis. *Article 14.* https://www.article-14.com/post/bombay-high-court-s-tolerance-lesson-on-tablighi-jamaat; and Criminal Written Petition No. 548 of 2020. High Court of Judicature at Bombay, India. Retrieved March 1, 2023. https://www.livelaw.in/pdf_upload/pdf_upload-380282.pdf.

34. Criminal Written Petition No. 548 of 2020. High Court of Judicature at Bombay, India. Retrieved March 1, 2023. https://www.livelaw.in/pdf_upload/pdf_upload-380282.pdf.

35. Frayer, L. (2020, April 23). Blamed for coronavirus outbreak, Muslims in India come under attack. *NPR*. https://www.npr.org/2020/04/23/839980029/blamed-for-coronavirus-outbreak-muslims-in-india-come-under-attack; BBC. (2020, April 2). Tablighi Jamaat: The group blamed for new Covid-19 outbreak in India. https://www.bbc.com/news/world-asia-india-52131338; and Slater, J., & Masih, N. (2020, April 23). As the world looks for coronavirus scapegoats, Muslims are blamed in India. *The Washington Post*. https://www.washingtonpost.com/world/asia_pacific/as-world-looks-for-coronavirus-scapegoats-india-pins-blame-on-muslims/2020/04/22/3cb43430-7f3f-11ea-84c2-0792d8591911_story.html.

36. Dey, S. (2020, April 19). 30% of cases across India tied to Jamaat event: Govt. *The Times of India*. https://timesofindia.indiatimes.com/india/corona-cases-in-india-30-of-cases-across-india-tied-to-jamaat-event/articleshow/75227980.cms.

37. Yasir, S. (2020, April 22). India is scapegoating Muslims for the spread of the coronavirus. *Foreign Policy*. https://foreignpolicy.com/2020/04/22/india-muslims-coronavirus-scapegoat-modi-hindu-nationalism/#.

38. Yasir, S. (2020, April 22). India is scapegoating Muslims for the spread of the coronavirus. *Foreign Policy*. https://foreignpolicy.com/2020/04/22/india-muslims-coronavirus-scapegoat-modi-hindu-nationalism/#.

39. Indian slang term to mean "friend," "sir," or "man." Used colloquially.

CHAPTER 8

1. Nagaraj, P. (2017, September 6). Gauri Lankesh: A fierce tale of grit and determination. *National Herald*. https://www.nationalheraldindia.com/obituary/gauri-lankesh-a-fierce-tale-of-grit-and-determination.

2. The Times of India. (2017, September 6). Journalist-activist Gauri Lankesh gunned down outside her house. https://timesofindia.indiatimes.com/city/bengaluru/journalist-activist-gauri-lankesh-gunned-down-outside-her-house/articleshow/60385024.cms.

3. The Times of India. (2017, September 7). Gauri Lankesh's murder: Citizens rally for justice. https://timesofindia.indiatimes.com/city/hyderabad/gauri-lankeshs-murder-citizens-rally-for-justice/articleshow/60401272.cms.

4. Pinto, S. (2017, September 6). Gauri Lankesh death raises concerns about freedom of expression: Amnesty India. *The Times of India*. https://timesofindia.indiatimes.com/city/bengaluru/gauri-lankesh-death-raises-concerns-about-freedom-of-expression-amnesty-india/articleshow/60390308.cms.

5. Motta, M. (2018). The dynamics and political implications of anti-intellectualism in the United States. *American Politics Research, 46*(3), 465–98. https://doi.org/10.1177/1532673X17719507.

6. Motta, M. (2018). The dynamics and political implications of anti-intellectualism in the United States. *American Politics Research, 46*(3), 465–98. https://doi.org/10.1177/1532673X17719507.

7. Freckelton Qc I. (2020). COVID-19: Fear, quackery, false representations and the law. *International Journal of Law and Psychiatry, 72*, 101611. https://doi.org/10.1016/j.ijlp.2020.101611.

8. Peters, M. A. (2019). Anti-intellectualism is a virus. *Educational Philosophy and Theory, 51*(4), 357–63. https://doi.org/10.1080/00131857.2018.1462946; and Merkley, E., & Loewen, P. J. (2021). Anti-intellectualism and the mass public's response to the COVID-19 pandemic. *Nature Human Behaviour, 5*(6), 706–15. https://doi.org/10.1038/s41562-021-01112-w.

9. Menon, S. (2019, July 29). "The intellectual act today has no prestige whatsoever." *The Hindu.* https://www.thehindu.com/opinion/columns/the-intellectual-act-today-has-no-prestige-whatsoever/article28740158.ece.

10. Jenne, E. K., Hawkins, K. A., & Silva, B. C. (2021). Mapping populism and nationalism in leader rhetoric across North America and Europe. *Studies in Comparative International Development, 56*(2), 170–96. https://doi.org/10.1007/s12116-021-09334-9.

11. Schwartz, D. (2017, February 1). Why Trump supporters love calling people "snowflakes." *GQ.* https://www.gq.com/story/why-trump-supporters-love-calling-people-snowflakes.

12. Sundar. N. (2018). Academic freedom and Indian universities. *Economic & Political Weekly, 53*(24), 49. http://164.100.47.193/fileupload/current/111991.pdf.

13. Azizur Rahman, S. (2022, June 27). India arrests prominent rights activist, triggering outrage. Voice of America. https://www.voanews.com/a/india-arrests-prominent-rights-activist-triggering-outrage-/6635960.html/; and BBC. Why India activist arrests have kicked up a storm. https://www.bbc.com/news/world-asia-india-45294286.

14. *India: Authorities should stop targeting, prosecuting journalists and online critics.* (2022, May 3). Amnesty International. Retrieved September 23, 2022, from https://www.amnesty.org/en/latest/news/2022/05/india-authorities-should-stop-targeting-prosecuting-journalists-and-online-critics/.

15. *31 journalists and media workers killed in India* (n.d.). Committee to Project Journalists. Retrieved September 23, 2022, from https://cpj.org/data/killed/asia/India/murdered/?status=Killed&motiveConfirmed%5B%5D=Confirmed&motiveUnconfirmed%5B%5D=Unconfirmed&type%5B%5D=Journalist&type%5B%5D=Media%20Worker&cc_fips%5B%5D=IN&start_year=2014&end_year=2022&group_by=location.

16. Leidig, E. (2020). Hindutva as a variant of right-wing extremism. *Patterns of Prejudice, 54*(3), 215–37. https://doi.org/10.1080/0031322X.2020.1759861.

17. Johnson, T. A. (2019, May 26). Explained: Dabholkar-Lankesh murders— What the investigations into violent right-wing activism show. *The India Express.* https://indianexpress.com/article/explained/explained-dabholkar-lankesh-murders-investigations-right-wing-activism-cbi-sit-pansare-kalburgi-5749338/.

18. Deb, S. (2019). Killing press freedom in India. In T. Burrett & J. Kingston (Eds.), *Press freedom in contemporary Asia* (pp. 28–295). Routledge. https://doi.org /10.4324/9780429505690.

19. Deb, S. (2019). Killing press freedom in India. In T. Burrett & J. Kingston (Eds.), *Press freedom in contemporary Asia* (pp. 281–95). Routledge. https://doi.org /10.4324/9780429505690.

20. Deb, S. (2019). Killing press freedom in India. In T. Burrett & J. Kingston (Eds.), *Press freedom in contemporary Asia* (pp. 281–95). Routledge. https://doi.org /10.4324/9780429505690.

21. Jawaharlal Nehru University. (n.d.) *JNU* at a glance. https://www.jnu.ac.in/ jnuataglance.

22. Jawaharlal Nehru University. (n.d.) *JNU* at a glance. https://www.jnu.ac.in/ jnuataglance.

23. Chatterjee, S. (2022, April 12). JNU's tryst with on-campus violence: A complete timeline. *India Today*. https://www.indiatoday.in/india/story/jawaharlal-nehru -university-tryst-with-violence-a-complete-timeline-1936608-2022-04-12.

24. Martelli, J. T. (2018). *"JNU is not just where you go, it's what you become" Everyday political socialisation and left activism at Jawaharlal Nehru University (JNU), New Delhi*. Publication No. tel-01790491. Doctoral dissertation, King's College London. Hal Archives. https://hal.archives-ouvertes.fr/tel-01790491/document.

25. Martelli, J. T. (2018). *"JNU is not just where you go, it's what you become" Everyday political socialisation and left activism at Jawaharlal Nehru University (JNU), New Delhi*. Publication No. tel-01790491. Doctoral dissertation, King's College London. Hal Archives. https://hal.archives-ouvertes.fr/tel-01790491/document.

26. Martelli, J. T. (2018). *"JNU is not just where you go, it's what you become" Everyday political socialisation and left activism at Jawaharlal Nehru University (JNU), New Delhi*. Publication No. tel-01790491. Doctoral dissertation, King's College London. Hal Archives. https://hal.archives-ouvertes.fr/tel-01790491/document.

27. Kumar, N. (2016, February 25). The arrest of a student leader spotlights India's battle for free speech. *TIME*. https://time.com/4237319/the-arrest-of-a-student-leader -spotlights-indias-battle-for-free-speech/.

28. Kumar was subsequently released on bail at the time. After he completed his PhD he went on to run for political office, losing to a BJP candidate in 2019.

29. Outlook Web Bureau. (2017, September 6). Gauri Lankesh's "adopted children" Jignesh Mevani, Kanhaiya, Shehla Rashid, Umar Khalid express shock on social media. *Outlook*. https://www.outlookindia.com/website/story/gauri-lankeshs -adopted-children-jignesh-mevani-kanhaiya-shehla-rashid-umar-khali/301316.

30. Outlook Web Bureau. (2017, September 6). Gauri Lankesh's "adopted children" Jignesh Mevani, Kanhaiya, Shehla Rashid, Umar Khalid express shock on social media. *Outlook*. https://www.outlookindia.com/website/story/gauri-lankeshs -adopted-children-jignesh-mevani-kanhaiya-shehla-rashid-umar-khali/301316.

31. Rashtriya Swayamsevak Sangh, the political party that preceded the BJP.

32. Bhatty, K., & Sundar, N. (2020). Sliding from majoritarianism toward fascism: Educating India under the Modi regime. *International Sociology, 35*(6), 632–50.

33. Singh, M., & Dasgupta, R. (2019). Exceptionalising democratic dissent: A study of the JNU event and its representations. *Postcolonial Studies, 22*(1), 59–78. https://doi.org/10.1080/13688790.2019.1568169.

34. Rajghatta, C. (2018). *Illiberal India: Gauri Lankesh and the age of unreason.* Westland.

35. Goel, V. (2018, May 14). In India, Facebook's WhatsApp plays central role in elections. *The New York Times.* https://www.nytimes.com/2018/05/14/technology/whatsapp-india-elections.html.

36. Sharm, B., & Khan, A. (2021, July 3). Hindu vigilantes work with police to enforce "Love Jihad" law in North India. *The Intercept.* https://theintercept.com/2021/07/03/love-jihad-law-india/.

37. For more information see Banaji, S., Bhat, R., Agarwal, A., Passanha, N., & Sadhana Pravin, M. (2019) *WhatsApp vigilantes: An exploration of citizen reception and circulation of WhatsApp misinformation linked to mob violence in India.* Department of Media and Communications, London School of Economics and Political Science. http://eprints.lse.ac.uk/104316/1/Banaji_whatsapp_vigilantes_exploration_of_citizen_reception_published.pdf; Freitas Melo, P. D., Vieira, C. C., Garimella, K., Melo, P. O., & Benevenuto, F. (2019). Can WhatsApp counter misinformation by limiting message forwarding? In H. Cherifi, S. Gaito, H. Ferendo Mendes, E. Moro, & L. Mateus Rocha (Eds.), *Complex networks and their applications VIII* (pp. 372–84). Springer; and Gowen, A. (2018, July 2). As mob lynchings fueled by WhatsApp sweep India, authorities struggle to combat fake news. *The Washington Post.* https://www.washingtonpost.com/world/asia_pacific/as-mob-lynchings-fueled-by-whatsapp-sweep-india-authorities-struggle-to-combat-fake-news/2018/07/02/683a1578-7bba-11e8-ac4e-421ef7165923_story.html.

38. Banaji, S., Bhat, R., Agarwal, A., Passanha, N., & Sadhana Pravin, M. (2019). *WhatsApp vigilantes: An exploration of citizen reception and circulation of WhatsApp misinformation linked to mob violence in India.* Department of Media and Communications, London School of Economics and Political Science. http://eprints.lse.ac.uk/104316/1/Banaji_whatsapp_vigilantes_exploration_of_citizen_reception_published.pdf.

39. Banaji, S., Bhat, R., Agarwal, A., Passanha, N., & Sadhana Pravin, M. (2019). *WhatsApp vigilantes: An exploration of citizen reception and circulation of WhatsApp misinformation linked to mob violence in India.* Department of Media and Communications, London School of Economics and Political Science. http://eprints.lse.ac.uk/104316/1/Banaji_whatsapp_vigilantes_exploration_of_citizen_reception_published.pdf.

40. Times of India. (2017, November 22). "Ganesha's was world's first case of head transplant." *Times* of India. https://timesofindia.indiatimes.com/city/ajmer/ganeshas-was-worlds-first-case-of-head-transplant/articleshow/61745783.cms.

41. Amar Chitra Katha. (n.d.). *Gandhari.* Amar Chitra Katha.

42. Chauhan, B. (2021, February 14). 21-year-old climate activist "picked up" in Bengaluru for sharing Greta "toolkit." *The* New Indian Express. https://www.newindianexpress.com/cities/bengaluru/2021/feb/14/21-year-old-climate-activist-picked-up-in-bengaluru-for-sharing-greta-toolkit-2263830.html.

43. Fridays for Future. (n.d.). *Who we are*. https://fridaysforfuture.org/what-we-do/who-we-are/.

44. Saaliq, S. (2021, January 27). Explainer: Why India's farmers are revolting against PM Modi. *AP News*. https://apnews.com/article/india-farmers-protest-explained-1ccbf48d76a55a1061f40d9a1e951314.

45. The News Minute. (2021, February 14). Disha Ravi sent to 5-day police custody, she breaks down in court. https://www.thenewsminute.com/article/disha-ravi-sent-5-day-police-custody-cops-allege-she-edited-greta-toolkit-doc-143421.

46. The Economic Times. (2021, February 15). Paranoid govt should stop persecution of activists: CPI(M) on Disha Ravi's arrest in toolkit case. https://economictimes.indiatimes.com/news/politics-and-nation/paranoid-govt-should-stop-persecution-of-activists-cpim-on-disha-ravis-arrest-in-toolkit-case/articleshow/80924360.cms?from=mdr.

47. ANI. (2021, February 15). Disha's arrest reflects govt's frustration in trouncing independent thinking: Adhir Ranjan Chowdhury. *The New Indian Express*. https://www.newindianexpress.com/nation/2021/feb/15/dishas-arrest-reflects-govts-frustration-in-trouncing-independent-thinking-adhir-ranjan-chowdhury-2264354.html.

48. The Times of India. (2021, February 15). India on shaky foundations if 22-year-old a threat: PC. https://timesofindia.indiatimes.com/india/india-on-shaky-foundations-if-22-year-old-a-threat-pc/articleshow/80916183.cms.

CHAPTER 9

1. Cammaerts, B. (2020). The neo-fascist discourse and its normalisation through mediation. *Journal of Multicultural Discourses, 15*(3), 241–56.

2. Office of the Press Secretary. (2001, September 20). Address to the Joint Session of Congress and the American People. The White House Archives. https://georgewbush-whitehouse.archives.gov/news/releases/2001/09/20010920-8.html.

3. Tharoor, S. (2016, December 5). From Trump's America to Modi's India, Mandatory Patriotism is Dangerous. *Noema*. https://www.noemamag.com/from-trumps-america-to-modis-india-mandatory-patriotism-is-dangerous/.

4. Dasgupta, N., & Yogeeswaran, K. (2011). Obama-nation? Implicit beliefs about American nationality and the possibility of redefining who counts as "truly" American. *The Obamas and a (post) racial America*, 72–90.

5. Chen, A. K. (2003). Forced patriot acts. *Denv. UL Rev., 81*, 703.

6. India national anthem no longer compulsory in cinemas. (2018, January 9). BBC News. Retrieved September 30, 2022, from https://www.bbc.com/news/world-asia-india-42618830.

7. Kaul, V. (2017, August 30). Viewpoint: Why Modi's currency gamble was "epic failure." BBC News. https://www.bbc.com/news/world-asia-india-41100610.

8. Echeverri-Gent, J., Sinha, A., & Wyatt, A. (2021). Economic distress amidst political success: India's economic policy under Modi, 2014–2019. *India Review, 20*(4), 402–35. https://doi.org/10.1080/14736489.2021.1958582.

9. The Citizenship (Amendment) Bill, 2019, Bill No. 370. (2019). http://164.100.47.4/BillsTexts/LSBillTexts/Asintroduced/370_2019_LS_Eng.pdf.

10. The Citizenship (Amendment) Bill, 2019, Bill No. 370. (2019). http://164.100.47.4/BillsTexts/LSBillTexts/Asintroduced/370_2019_LS_Eng.pdf.

11. Why Rohingya, Ahmadiyya Muslims not covered under CAA? Karat asks. (2020, February 18). *The Economic Times*. Retrieved September 30, 2022, from https://economictimes.indiatimes.com/news/politics-and-nation/why-rohingya-ahmadiyya-muslims-not-covered-under-caa-karat-asks/articleshow/74186741.cms?from=mdr.

12. Yadav, J. P. (2019, October 12). With 2 bills Shah cements himself as Modi heir. *The Telegraph Online*. https://www.telegraphindia.com/india/with-2-bills-amit-shah-cements-himself-as-narendra-modi-heir/cid/1725795.

13. What is NRC: All you need to know about National Register of Citizens. (2019, December 18). *India Today*. Retrieved September 30, 2022, from https://www.indiatoday.in/india/story/what-is-nrc-all-you-need-to-know-about-national-register-of-citizens-1629195-2019-12-18.

14. Bhatia, K. V. & Gajjala, R. (2020). Examining anti-CAA protests at Shaheen Bagh: Muslim women and politics of the Hindu India. *International Journal of Communication, 14*, 6286–303.

15. Mirza, S. A. (2020, May 17). Remembering the women of Shaheen Bagh, who showed how poetry can overpower violence and hate. *Scroll.in*. https://scroll.in/article/960659/remembering-the-women-of-shaheen-bagh-who-showed-how-poetry-can-overpower-violence-and-hate.

16. Nigam, S. (2020). Many dimensions of Shaheen Bagh Movement in India. *Social Science Research Network*. https://doi.org/10.2139/ssrn.3543398.

17. Mueller, J. E. (2020). *Overblown: How politicians and the terrorism industry inflate national security threats, and why we believe them*. Simon and Schuster.

18. *Oxford Conference Series*. (2019, October). 8th Academic International Conference on Business, Economics and Management, AICBEM 2019 & 8th Annual International Conference on Law, Economics and Politics, AICLEP 2019. Retrieved September 30, 2022, from https://www.researchgate.net/profile/Asma-Khan-34/publication/340299181_Oxford_Conference_Series/links/5e832aa392851c2f526d9b2b/Oxford-Conference-Series.pdf#page=34.

19. Shan, K., & Shah, K. (2020). Kashmir Article 370: India's diplomatic challenge. *Observer Research Foundation*. Retrieved September 30, 2022, from https://policycommons.net/artifacts/1349555/kashmir-after-article-370/1961716/.

20. Pandow, B. A. (2021). Communication blackout and media gag: State-sponsored restrictions in conflict-hit region of Jammu and Kashmir. *Identities*. https://doi.org/10.1080/1070289X.2021.1920772.

21. Sodhi, J. (2021). The Article 370 amendments on Jammu and Kashmir: Explaining the global silence. *Observer Research Foundation, 318*.

22. Pandow, B. A. (2021). Communication blackout and media gag: State-sponsored restrictions in conflict-hit region of Jammu and Kashmir. *Identities*. https://doi.org/10.1080/1070289X.2021.1920772.

23. Twitter reels as Amit Shah announces scrapping of special powers to Kashmir. (2019, May 8). *The Telegraph Online*. Retrieved September 30, 2022, from https:

//www.telegraphindia.com/india/twitter-reels-as-amit-shah-announces-scrapping-of -article-370-in-kashmir/cid/1695882.

24. Meskell, L. (2021). Toilets first, temples second: Adopting heritage in neoliberal India. *International Journal of Heritage Studies, 27*(2), 151–69. https://doi.org /10.1080/13527258.2020.1780464.

25. Meskell, L. (2021). Toilets first, temples second: Adopting heritage in neoliberal India. *International Journal of Heritage Studies, 27*(2), 151–69. https://doi.org /10.1080/13527258.2020.1780464.

26. Pasricha, A. (2019, October 7). World's biggest toilet-building program in India gets mixed results. *Voice of America News.* https://www.voanews.com/a/ south-central-asia_worlds-biggest-toilet-building-program-india-gets-mixed-results /6177168.html.

27. Sinha, S. (2021). "Strong leaders," authoritarian populism and Indian developmentalism: The Model moment in historical context. *Geoforum, 124,* 320–33. https: //doi.org/10.1016/j.geoforum.2021.02.019.

28. Jangid, K. (2021, September 14). How the legend of Modi, Hindu hero and political messiah, is breaking India's politics [Editorial]. *Haaretz.* Retrieved September 30, 2022, from https://www.haaretz.com/world-news/2021-09-14/ty-article -opinion/.premium/the-legend-of-modi-hindu-hero-and-political-messiah-is-breaking -indias-politics/0000017f-da7a-d42c-afff-dffafe730000.

29. Jaffrelot, C. (2019). Class and caste in the 2019 Indian election—Why have so many poor started voting for Modi? *Studies in Indian Politics, 7*(2), 149–60. https:// doi.org/10.1177/2321023019874890.

30. Verma, R., & Barthwal, A. (2022, March 13). Why more women voted for the BJP in 2022 elections: Analysis. *India Today.* Retrieved September 30, 2022, from https://www.indiatoday.in/elections/story/why-more-women-voted-bjp-2022 -elections-analysis-1924821-2022-03-13.

31. Deshpande, R., Tillin, L., & Kailash, K. K. (2019). The BJP's welfare schemes: Did they make a difference in the 2019 elections? *Studies in Indian Politics, 7*(2), 219–33. https://doi.org/10.1177/2321023019874911.

32. Chatterjee, M. (2020). The nation and the hero, or the 56-inch paradox. In A. Ray & I. Banerjee-Dube (Eds.), *Nation, nationalism and the public sphere* (pp. 168–88). SAGE Publishing India.

33. Chatterjee, M. (2020). The nation and the hero, or the 56-inch paradox. In A. Ray & I. Banerjee-Dube (Eds.), *Nation, nationalism and the public sphere* (pp. 168–88). SAGE Publishing India.

34. Zia, A. S. (2022). Pious, populist, political masculinities in Pakistan and India. *South Asian Popular Culture, 20*(2), 181–99. https://doi.org/10.1080/14746689.2022 .2090679.

CONCLUSION

1. Shirer, W. L. (1960). *The rise and fall of the Third Reich.* Simon and Schuster.

2. Toobin, J. (2023). *Homegrown: Timothy McVeigh and the rise of right-wing extremism.* Simon and Schuster.

3. Grain, K. M., & Land, D. E. (2017). The social justice turn: Cultivating "critical hope" in an age of despair. *Michigan Journal of Community Service Learning, 23*(1).

4. Freire, P. (2014). *Pedagogy of the oppressed: 30th anniversary edition.* Bloomsbury Academic Professional. ProQuest Ebook Central. http://ebookcentral.proquest.com/lib/hioa/detail.action?docID=1745456.

5. Menasinakai, S. (2023, April 26). Karnataka will see riots if Congress wins, says Amit Shah. *Times of India.* https://timesofindia.indiatimes.com/elections/assembly-elections/karnataka/news/karnataka-will-see-riots-if-congress-wins-says-amit-shah/articleshow/99769842.cms?from=mdr.

6. Yadav, P. (2023, May 15). Decoding the Karnataka election results in 18 charts. *The Wire.* https://thewire.in/politics/decoding-the-karnataka-election-results-in-18-charts.

7. Akbar, A. K. C. Karnataka assembly elections 2023 and religious minorities.

8. Rosenfeld, B. (2020). *The autocratic middle class: How state dependency reduces the demand for democracy* (Vol. 26). Princeton University Press.

9. Brito, R., & Araujo, G. (2023, January 4). Brazil's Bolsonaro faces legal risks after losing immunity. *Reuters.* https://www.reuters.com/world/americas/brazils-bolsonaro-faces-legal-risks-after-losing-immunity-2023-01-04/.

10. Scislowska, M.& Gera, V. (2023, October 18). Poland's voters reject their right-wing government, but many challenges lie ahead. *AP News.* https://apnews.com/article/poland-election-government-tusk-c83032bf51c7017caf7dfbe2c90f1bal.

11. News Wires. (2023, August 12). French far-right leader Marine Le Pen to stand trial for embezzling EU funds. https://www.france24.com/en/france/20231208-french-prosecutores-order-le-pen-to-stand-trial-in-eu-funding-scandal.

12. Freire, P. (1995). *The pedagogy of the oppressed.* Continuum.

13. Baily, S. (2020). Neo-nationalism: A 2020 perspective. *International Educator.* Retrieved August 26, 2020, from https://www.nafsa.org/ie-magazine/2020/12/9/neo-nationalism-2020-perspective.

Index

adolescence: friends, 89; girls, 48, 50; idealism, 111; religion, 59–61
Akhand Bharath, 104
Ali, Haidar, 23
Amar Chitra Katha, 70, 137
Ayodhya, 1, 2, 64, 66, 163
Azim Premji University, 29

Babri Masjid, 1, 2, 4, 77, 163
Babur, 4
Baldwin Boys High School, 8
Baldwin Girls High School, 2, 9, 11, 50–54
Banerjee, Soumya, 67
Batra, Dinanath, 104
beef. *See* cow slaughter
Belur, 22
Bolsanaro, Jair, 159
Bombay, 8
British Raj, 8. 24
Bruhat Bengaluru Mahanagara Palike (BBMP), 31
Bhartiya Janata Party (BJP), 2, 4, 66
Brigade Road (Brigades), 7
Bumiller, Elisabeth, 72
Bush, George W., 141

cantonment, 24
Casa Piccola, 7, 28. 39–42, 163

caste, 67
Central Board of Secondary Education (CBSE), 102
Cholas, 22
Chowdiah Memorial Hall, 7
Citizenship Amendment Act (CAA), 141–146, 159
"Clean India," 148
CNN, 155
communalism, 3
Congress Party, 5, 100
Corner House, 7, 28, 163
cow slaughter, 119
COVID, 122
Cubbon Park, 28

Dabholkar, Narendra, 129–130
Dalrymple, William, 27
Deccan Plateau, 21, 23
demonetization, 141
Deshmukh, Jayant, 120
Deorala, 72
Delhi, 8, 28
Draupadi, 71
Durga (goddess), 71
Dutta, Lara, 29

education: competition, 107–108; demand, 109; extra-curricular activities, 106; textbooks, 105

Fivush, Robin, 16
Flåten, Lars Tore, 105
Frazier, Camille, 30
Freire, Paolo, 157, 162
Friedman, Thomas, 16
friendship: between classmates, 54–59

Gandhi, Indira, 1, 28, 63, 106, 158
Gandhi, Rahul, 158
Gandhi, Rajiv, 1, 63–64, 158
Gandhi, MK, 65
Godse, Nathuram, 65
Gopinath, Meenakshi, 97
Gujarat, 6, 152

Halebid, 22
Harvard University, 97
Hegde, Anant Kumar, 121
Hindutva, 61, 65–67, 99–106, 117, 125–126, 133, 141, 157–158
Hoysalas, 22

India: demographics, 98–99, 107; educational opportunities, 99–100; infrastructure, 150; linguistic diversity, 112; patriotism, 142, 147; Partition, 2, 64–65
India's First Battle of Independence. *See* Mutiny of 1857
Indian Institute of Science, 27
Indian Institute of Technology, 98
Indian Space Research Organization, 27
Infosys, 29
intellectualism, anti-, 126
Islamophobia, 121
Ismail, Mirza, Diwan, 26

Jammu and Kashmir, 147
Jawaharlal Nehru University (JNU), 132, 160
journalism, 128–129

Kalburgi, MM, 129–130, 138
Kannada, 111–112
Kanwar, Roop, 71–72
kar sevaks, 4, 79
Karnataka, 5, 21, 27, 105
Kempe Gowda, 22
Knock Out, 7
Koshy's, 163
Kumar, Kanhaiya, 133

Lady Shri Ram College for Women, 97–98, 106
Lakeview Ice Cream Parlor, 7
Lakshmi (goddess), 71
Lankesh, Gauri, 125–134
Le Pen, Marine, 159
Liberation Tigers of Tamil Eelam (LTTE), 63
linguistic diversity, 42–43
Love Jihad, 88, 122

MG Road (Mahatma Gandhi Road), 7
Macron, Emmanuel, 159
Madras, 8
male chauvinism, 92
Manusmrithi, 67
Marathas, 22
Marx, Karl, 120
Mayo, Lord, 25
Mayo Hall, 25
middle class, 35–37, 99, 159
migration, 113–116
Modi, Narendra, 6, 99, 104, 129, 148, 154, 163
Mukherjee, Prahbhati, 67
muscular nationalism, 84
Mutiny of 1857, 64
Mysore, 22–24, 26, 64

Namma Metro, 31
National Front-Left Front, 5
National Institute of Design, 29
National Law School of India, 29
National Rally, 6
National Registry of Citizens, 143

Nehru Bal Sangh, 68
Nirbhaya. *See* Pandey, Jyothi
Nehru, Jawaharlal, 111

Oklahoma City bombing, 156

Pandey, Jyothi, 83–85
Pew Research Center, 95
Premier Book Shop, 7
private space, 47–48
public space, 33–35

Q-Anon, 6, 156

Ram (god), 4, 71
Ranchi, 111
Rao, Narasimha PV, 5
Rashtriya Swayamsevak Sangh (RSS),
    65, 102, 104, 117, 133
Ravi, Disha, 11, 127, 138–140
reading, 44–46

Sadhguru, 137–138
Savarkar, Vinayak Damodar, 65
Seshadri Iyer Memorial Hall, 25
secularism, 101–102, 112–113
Sepoy Mutiny. *See* Mutiny of 1857
sex education, 90
Shah, Amit, 143, 147
Shah, Jahan, 23

Shaheen Bagh, 143, 159
Sharma, Betwa, 105
Sharma, Shankar Dayal, 5
Shirer, William, 155
Sita, 71
Sri Lanka, 63
St. Marks Cathedral, 25
Supreme Court, 2, 4, 142

Taj Mahal, 23
Tharoor, Shashi, 102
Thomson Reuters Foundation, 6, 87
Thunberg, Greta, 138
Tipu Sultan, 23–24, 105

Unity in Diversity, 64, 68, 70, 111
US Capitol riots, 155

Vasudev, Jagadish. *See* Sadhguru
vegetarianism, 100–104, 117
Vidya Bharati, 101–103
Vishwa Hindu Parishad, 4
Visveswaraya, Diwan, 25

WhatsApp, 134–138
WIPRO, 29
women: crimes against, 83; safety,
    85–90
workforce participation, 91

About the Author

Supriya Baily is an activist, a scholar, and an educator. Born in the U.S. Midwest, she spent her formative teenage years in Bangalore, where she worked as a community organizer and student leader. Returning to the United States, she received a BA in social work, an MA in international development studies, and a PhD in international education. She is currently professor of education at George Mason University in northern Virginia.

* 9 7 8 1 5 3 8 1 9 8 0 1 8 *